Adaptation
Studies

ALSO AVAILABLE FROM BLOOMSBURY

Analyzing Literature–to-Film Adaptations, Mary H. Snyder
Bloomsbury Introduction to Adaptation Studies,
edited by Yvonne Griggs
Contemporary Narrative, Fiona J. Doloughan

Adaptation Studies

New Challenges, New Directions

Edited by Jørgen Bruhn,
Anne Gjelsvik and
Eirik Frisvold Hanssen

B L O O M S B U R Y
LONDON • NEW DELHI • NEW YORK • SYDNEY

Bloomsbury Academic

An imprint of Bloomsbury Publishing Plc

50 Bedford Square	175 Fifth Avenue
London	New York
WC1B 3DP	NY 10010
UK	USA

www.bloomsbury.com

First published 2013

British Library Cataloguing-in-Publication Data
A catalogue record for this book is available from the British Library.

ISBN:	HB:	978-1-4411-9467-1
	PB:	978-1-4411-9266-0
	ePDF:	978-1-4411-0647-6
	ePub:	978-1-4411-6769-9

Library of Congress Cataloging-in-Publication Data
Adaptation studies : new challenges, new directions / edited by Jørgen Bruhn, Anne Gjelsvik, and Eirik Frisvold Hanssen.
p. cm.
Includes bibliographical references.
ISBN 978-1-4411-9266-0 (pbk.)- ISBN 978-1-4411-9467-1 (hardcover)- ISBN 978-1-4411-0647-6 (ebook)- ISBN 978-1-4411-2796-9 (ebook) 1. Literature-Adaptations-History and criticism. 2. Film adaptations-History and criticism. I. Bruhn, Jørgen. II. Gjelsvik, Anne. III. Hanssen, Eirik Frisvold.
PN171.A33A37 2013
809–dc23
2012039252

Typeset by Fakenham Prepress Solutions, Fakenham, Norfolk, NR21 8NN
Printed and bound in India

CONTENTS

NOTES ON CONTRIBUTORS

Jørgen Bruhn, PhD is Professor in Comparative Literature at Linnæus University, Sweden. Bruhn has written monographs on Marcel Proust (with Bo Degn Rasmussen) and M. M. Bakhtin, and articles on the theory of the novel, medieval literature and culture, Cervantes and Cassirer, and intermediality. Recent publications include 'Heteromediality', in Lars Elleström (ed.), *Media Borders, Intermediality and Multimodality* (Palgrave MacMillan, 2010) and a book-length study called *Lovely Violence: The Critical Romances of Chrétien de Troyes* (Cambridge Scholars Publishing, 2010). With Anne Gjelsvik and Henriette Thune, he published 'Parallel Worlds to Possible Meanings in *Let the Right One In*' in *Word & Image* (1, 2011). He is currently writing on intermedial theory and adaptation studies.

Anne Gjelsvik, Dr. Art/PhD is Professor in Film Studies at the Department of Art and Media Studies at Norwegian University of Science and Technology (NTNU). Gjelsvik has worked on popular cinema, film violence and ethics and the representation of gender in the media over a period of ten years. She has written extensively in Norwegian, her most central books being her latest publication on film and violence, *Bad and Beautiful,* and her book on film reviewing, *Eyes of Darkness: Film Reviewing, Analysis and Judgements* (*Mørkets Øyne. Filmkritikk, analyse og vurdering*) (Universitetsforlaget, 2002). She is currently working on intermediality and adaptation, as well as a book on representations of fatherhood in contemporary American cinema, and is member of the board of International Society for Intermedial Studies.

Eirik Frisvold Hanssen is Associate Professor of Film Studies at the Norwegian University of Science and Technology (NTNU) in Trondheim. He has written on colour and early cinema, adaptation and intermediality, film technology and aesthetics, fashion, visual culture, and Scandinavian television history, and published in journals such as *Film History*. Publications include *Early Discourses on Colour and Cinema: Origins, Functions, Meanings* (PhD diss., Stockholm University, 2006) and 'The Paradoxes of Textual Fidelity: Translation and Intertitles in Victor Sjöström's Silent Film Adaptation of Henrik Ibsen's *Terje Vigen*' (with Anna Sofia Rossholm, 2012).

Thomas Leitch teaches English and directs the Film Studies Program at the University of Delaware, US. His most recent books are *Film Adaptation and Its Discontents: From Gone with the Wind to the Passion of the Christ*, *A Companion to Alfred Hitchcock* (co-edited with Leland Poague) and the forthcoming *The Lessons of Adaptation*.

Kamilla Elliott is a Senior Lecturer of English Literature at Lancaster University, UK. She taught Victorian studies and interdisciplinary literature/film studies at the University of California at Berkeley from 1996–2004. During that time, she wrote articles on literature and film and published *Rethinking the Novel/Film Debate* (CUP, 2003), and has recently published her second monograph, *Portraiture and British Gothic Fiction: The Rise of Picture Identification 1764–1835* (Johns Hopkins University Press, 2012). She is currently writing a monograph on adaptation theory.

Regina Schober teaches American literature and culture at the University of Mannheim, Germany. She obtained a PhD in American Studies from the University of Hannover in 2009. Her dissertation, entitled *Unexpected Chords: Musico-Poetic Intermediality in Amy Lowell's Poetry and Poetics*, was recently published by Universitätsverlag Winter. Her research and teaching interests include, among others, American Modernism, Intermediality, Poetry, the American Grotesque and War Representation. She is currently working on her habilitation thesis on network aesthetics and virtual space.

Lars Elleström is Professor of Comparative Literature at Linnæus University, Sweden. He organizes the Forum for Intermedial Studies, Linnæus University, and chairs the board of the International Society for Intermedial Studies. Elleström has written and edited several books, including *Divine Madness: On Interpreting Literature, Music, and the Visual Arts Ironically* (Bucknell University Press, 2002) and *Media Borders, Multimodality and Intermediality* (Palgrave Macmillan, 2010). He has also published numerous articles on poetry, intermediality, gender and irony.

Jonas Ingvarsson, PhD is Associate Professor in Literary Studies at Karlstad Univeristy. His dissertation *En besynnerlig gemenskap. Teknologins gestalter i svensk prosa 1965–70* ['A Strange Community: Figures of Technology in Swedish Prose Writings 1965–70'] (2003), dealt with issues of posthumanism, cybernetics and intermediality. Among his recent publications is an anthology on the avant-garde and technology (*Media and Materiality in the Neo-Avant-Garde*, Peter Lang GmbH, 2012, (ed.) together with Jesper Olsson). Currently, he is involved in the research project 'Representations and Reconfigurations of the Digital in Swedish Literature and Art 1950–2010'.

Anna Sofia Rossholm, PhD is an Associate Professor at Linnæus University, Sweden. Her research combines a film historical interest with media theoretical perspectives and cultural theory. Her most central research discusses film versions in European cinema of the 1920s and 1930s in a modernity context. Her current research, undertaken at Sorbonne Paris III, deals with the reception of Swedish films of the 1920s and 1960s in France.

John Bryant is a Professor in English at Hofstra University, US. His principal research focus is on nineteenth-century American literature and culture, in particular the works of Herman Melville. He has specialized in textual studies and digital scholarship, paying special attention to how writers and readers revise texts – making them into 'fluid texts'. He has published several books and articles, including *Melville and Repose* (Oxford), *The Fluid Text* (Michigan), *Melville Unfolding* (Michigan) and the Longman Critical Edition of *Moby-Dick*. He is also editor of *Leviathan: A*

Journal of Melville Studies and Director of The Melville Electronic Library, an NEH-funded Scholarly Edition project.

Hajnal Király is a postdoctoral fellow at the Department of Comparative Studies, University of Lisbon, Portugal. Her actual research is on cinematic remediations of the same literary work, including films by Manuel de Oliveira. Her PhD dissertation, dealing with alternative approaches to literary adaptations, has been published in Hungarian (*Könyv és film között. A Hűségelven innen és túl – Between Book and Film – Beyond the Fidelity Discourse*, Koinonia, 2010). She has been publishing on issues of literary adaptation and intermediality in Hungarian and English, among others in *Media Borders, Intermediality and Multimodality* (Palgrave-MacMillan 2010), edited by Lars Elleström, in *Words and Images on the Screen* (Cambridge Scholars Publishing, 2008), *Film in the Post-Media Age* (Cambridge Scholars Publishing, 2012) and in the journal *Acta Sapientia. Film and Media Studies*, all edited by Ágnes Pethő.

Sara Brinch, PhD is an Associate Professor of Visual Communication at the Department of Art and Media Studies, Norwegian University of Science and Technology (NTNU). Brinch has worked on film history, documentary cinema and television, and is co-editor of several books in Norwegian. She is currently doing research within visual culture and on biopics.

1

'There and Back Again': New challenges and new directions in adaptation studies

Jørgen Bruhn, Anne Gjelsvik and Eirik Frisvold Hanssen

Many readers will be familiar with the title of this introduction. Novel readers will know it as the subtitle of J. R. R. Tolkien's first novel, *The Hobbit, There and Back Again*, from 1937. They may even know that *There and Back Again* is the title of Bilbo's diary in Tolkien's 'sequel' *The Lord of the Rings*; a diary that Bilbo gives to his nephew Frodo to continue, and Frodo then gives to his friend Samwise at the end of the story. Film viewers will know it as the title of the second part of Peter Jackson's screen adaptation of *The Hobbit* (2012), or they may remember seeing the representation of the diary in Jackson's *Lord of the Rings: Fellowship of the Ring* from 2001.

Transferring this title to the introduction of yet another book is not an original idea then. This title and its connotations indicate a circular movement that is crucial to understanding the adaptation process for several reasons. First, origin and authorship are less obvious categories than one might think. Second, not only telling, but also retelling a story, passing it on, can be considered valuable or even a gift. In addition, what we will describe as a meeting of media, such as the representation of Bilbo's book within the movie, is of particular interest to our discussion of the role, function and value of adaptation in contemporary media culture as well as within academic discourse. With this perspective, we place adaptation and adaptation studies within the broader framework of intermedial studies.

The adaptations of Tolkien's works are symptomatic of the position of the adaptation in contemporary culture. Tolkien adaptations were born from the movie industry's interest in adaptation of written material; novels have been a preferred source for stories on the silver screen since the birth of cinema. This is even more pronounced in the current economic climate, where the film industry, and Hollywood in particular, take advantage of recycling well-known material as a marketing strategy.

In a different arena and scale altogether, the number of fan-made tributes to the *Lord of the Rings* movies on YouTube is overwhelming. The internet provides tools and opportunities for sharing and retelling stories and events, true or fictional, faster and easier than ever before, including opportunities for users to create their own versions of written, aural, visual or cinematic material. For instance, a quote from the *Lord of the Rings* movie, spoken by the character Boromir – 'One does not simply walk into Mordor' – describing the difficulty involved in destroying the ring, has made it on to posters, into videos and even on to Google Maps. An internet site set up to follow these 'meme' transformations counts several thousand based on *Lord of the Rings* alone (See Thomas Leitch's article 'What Movies Want', Chapter 8 in this volume for more on meme[1]).

On the other hand, fans of Tolkien's works have been preoccupied with cinematic adaptations before and after their premieres, following the film-maker's choices and changes with Argus eyes and discussing at length the omission of central characters, the choice of actors, or the visualization of mythical creatures.[2] For the dedicated audience, fidelity to the original source is still vitally important, while at the same time fans contribute to the circular distribution of popular material and new fictions that differ considerably from the source text. The journey of this particular material – from Tolkien's typewriter to the screenwriters' solutions, to the cinematic screen, to the internet and to this introduction in an academic publication on adaptation studies – opens up the opportunity for asking many questions about what adaptations are and how they should be studied.

Our Tolkien example reflects several important themes within adaptation studies: What is an original? Should an adaptation be true to the original (the fidelity question)? What are the differences and similarities between media? What is authorship?[3] The extraordinary popularity and circulation of these particular cases illuminate the importance of adaptations within contemporary culture and in academic discourse.

This anthology brings together scholars from film, literature and intermedial studies to readdress the questions of authority and originality, re-read classical texts and investigate specific cases. The book aims to take a fresh perspective on classic topics and themes within adaptation studies, posing productive questions and using new kinds of case studies. We seek to uncover the core features of adaptation as a creative process and the core activity of adaptation studies as an academic endeavour. Consequently, we also address the current relevance of such studies: Why should anyone study products that result from transferring processes between media, either novel-to-film productions or those in a larger adaptation context?

Overview of the field

This anthology contributes to what we see as the new approaches that emerged in the very lively adaptation research over the last two decades with the perspectives of scholars such as Robert Stam, John Bryant, Linda Hutcheon, Kamilla Elliott, Tom Leitch and Christine Geraghty, among others. Our approach is a combination of theoretical reflections drawing on examples and case studies with theoretical ambitions. Our professed aim is to address this central topic with fresh perspectives, new kinds of questions and new kinds of case studies.

For the past 15–20 years, adaptation research has undergone a rich development, manifested both in a large number of articles, many annual conferences, book-length studies and even journals devoted to the field.[4] As R. Barton Palmer said, 'Arguably, the most important development during the last two decades in cultural studies has been the increasing focus on adaptation (which can now claim to be a separate field unto itself, worthy of the prominence that specialized journals would afford it)'.[5]

In this volume, Kamilla Elliott offers a somewhat provocative perspective on contemporary adaptations research. Elliott describes an atypical academic field: research dominated by scholars who do not try to get an overview of previous work and who continuously re-invent already existing terms, analytical strategies and theoretical concepts – an emerging discipline, perhaps, but without the progression, critical self-reflection and exchange of ideas that ought to characterize academic research. To decide for themselves if Elliott's portrayal is fair, readers should consider the polemical, thoroughly researched article as a guide to the wide field of adaptation research.

From a less evaluative point of view, we wish to point to a number of characteristic theoretical and analytical clusters that we find to be typical for the field. Among important aspects found in the rich harvest of material are the questions of how to use adaptation creatively in teaching, and what place adaptation studies should occupy in curricula and pedagogic practices. In addition, the relationship between screenwriting and adaptation has been discussed, and adaptation also has been studied within the broader framework of transcultural transformations and translation, as well as new media formats and technology.[6]

Five characteristic theoretical and analytical clusters are predominant in current adaptation research, and these can be seen in this volume. First is the question of fidelity, which adaptation studies universally addresses. Second is the attempt to open up the field to a broader variety of media relations beyond the usual novel-to-film relationship. A third important trend is the way that some contributors consider adaptation as a multilevel rather than a one-to-one relationship (for example, one poem interpreted into one painting). Fourth, the book probes the idea that adaptation may not be a one-way transport from source to result, but a two-way, dialogic process. Finally, some chapters examine the way that global theoretical frameworks (intermediality or genetic criticism, for example) can be used in adaptation studies.

The unavoidable question of fidelity

A central – perhaps even *the* central – question of adaptation studies has been that of fidelity, or the relationship between what has been considered an original and the more-or-less faithful rendering of that form or content into a new product. From the very outset of adaptation criticism (see Elliott's historical schematization), scholars have criticized the idea that faithfulness is the most interesting and productive instrument with which to confront adaptations; early on, critics argued that fidelity is both difficult to ascertain and problematic for normative evaluation. Accordingly, adaptation studies based on fidelity have traditionally been debunked, and most current research considers fidelity discourse as no longer viable.

Although fidelity discourse has been abandoned, the issue of similarities and differences is still very much present in contemporary research. Adaptation must necessarily incorporate some kind of comparative element – seeing one text in relation to another – and the strategic and almost universal move in the field has been to 'translate' fidelity into the more neutral, and thus useful, measure of similarity and difference on various levels of the compared texts. In part one, 'Rethinking the Core Questions', Lars Elleström offers a new approach to the question of fidelity by creating a nomenclature of adaptation, based on his larger systematization of intermediality studies and media theory.

Another way of avoiding the inherent normativity so often found in fidelity discourses (which implies, in one archetypical adaptation tradition, that literature is richer, deeper or more complex than film) is to focus once again on the medium specificity, thus rethinking, perhaps in new terms, the distinctions developed at least as early as Lessing's *Laocoon* in the eighteenth century. In the case study section, film scholar Anne Gjelsvik reactivates the medium specificity debate by rephrasing Seymour Chatman's classical study; 'What Novels Can Tell That Movies Can't Show' (Chatman 1980). Medium specificity is confronted with troublesome representations of violence in Michael Winterbottom's adaptation of Jim Thompson's *The Killer Inside Me*, and Gjelsvik is forced to rethink the objectivity of medium specificity definitions with more ethical considerations. Fidelity, then, is questioned but not forgotten in current research, where it constantly resurfaces in the form of questions of medium specificity based on non-evaluative grounds.

Widening the possible sources

Traditionally, adaptation studies focuses on novels transferred to films, 'text to cinema' or 'literature on screen', as reflected in the central book titles, such as Brian MacFarlane's *Novel To Film: An Introduction to the Theory of Adaptation* (1996), Deborah Cartmell and Imelda Whelehan's 1999 anthology, *Adaptation: From Text to Screen, Screen to Text* and Christine Geraghty's *Now a Major Motion Picture: Film Adaptations of Literature and Drama* (2008). This academic interest results in part from the film industry's preference for adapting classical literature or bestsellers, ranging from Tolkien's *Lord of the Rings*, classic novels by Charles Dickens or Jane Austen, to modern bestsellers such as the *Millennium*, *Twilight* and the *Harry Potter* series.

In part, this interest reflects a struggle for dominance between the different media (literature and film) and several academic disciplines' attempt to 'dominate' the object. Consciously or not, adaptation is often a paragone debate.[7] Thomas Leitch reformulated this conflict in the following way:

> Because "literature," unlike "cinema," is already an honorific, however, any discussion of literature on screen, as opposed to journalism or comic books or video games on screen, will begin willy-nilly with a bias in favour of literature as both a privileged field (literary texts are what movies normally adapt) and an aesthetically sanctified field (literary texts have already been approved by a jury whose verdict on their film adaptations is still out).[8]

Film adaptations of sources deemed unworthy of academic

(literary) interest is not a new phenomenon, and pulp fiction has been the source for innumerable, highly respectable adaptations, for instance by Alfred Hitchcock.[9] However, a shift in values in adaptation studies has occurred as cultural studies has redefined which content is worthy of analysis as material for adaptation. Accordingly, contemporary critical writing has taken a wider perspective on possible sources, moving from the conventional classical or heritage material to study adaptations of computer games or biographies, following the trends of contemporary cultural production.[10] For instance in *A Theory of Adaptation*, Linda Hutcheon investigates adaptation across all media, focusing on the creative and receptive process. Hutcheon includes video games and theme parks among her examples, concluding with the question, 'What is not an adaptation?' In her continuum model, the parodies of *Lord of the Rings* are regarded as adaptations. Of course, this discussion is not new: Eirik Frisvold Hanssen's essay on André Bazin (Chapter 7) examines how the French film theorist placed film adaptations within a broad cultural historical context entailing different media, different processes of adaptation and mass reproduction. Likewise, Bazin's analyses on adaptation and questions of fidelity equate literary adaptation to filmic representations of painting and theatre.

While acknowledging the multitude of the adaptation banner, many scholars coming from literature studies nevertheless continue to explore the novel-to-screen adaptation, such as Cartmell and Whelehan's notable contribution, *Screen Adaptation: Impure Cinema*. However, *Adaptation Studies: New Challenges, New Directions* includes both contributors who discuss movies based on novels and those who aim to broaden the field. For example, in her article on *Invictus*, Sara Brinch analyses the translation of biographical and photographic material into a feature film; new approaches are needed when narratives that lack the suspense and plot of literature are compared with the cinematic end product. Jonas Ingvarsson, investigating the famous Orson Welles' radio adaptation of H. G. Wells' novel *The War of the Worlds*, offers another constellation of the adaptation theory: novel to radio drama.

Networks of influence

Another detectable trend in adaptation studies is the movement away from a one-to-one relationship, that is, between *one* source (such as a novel) and *one* film. Instead, adaption is viewed within a more comprehensive understanding of the cultural and textual networks into which any textual phenomena is understood. Christine Geraghty's work is an important example of this methodology. Both in *Now a Major Motion Picture* (2008) and in her reading of Joe Wright's 2007 film *Atonement*, based on Ian McEwan's novel of the same name, she demonstrated that an adaptation necessarily relies on and cites a widespread web of influences. For example, Geraghty described how Wright represented World War II with a number of references that supported the main representation while 'quoting' non-literary visual texts.[11]

The attempt to investigate the field 'between' source and adaptation is also important for several contributors to this volume. Regina Schober proposes Bruno Latour's so-called actor-network model as a way to widen the narrow understanding of the transmedial aspect of adaptation studies. Jonas Ingvarsson, discussing Welles'/Wells' *War of the Worlds*, introduces Friedrich Kittler's media archaeological perspective to find new approaches to his material that are not limited to the novel as a source-text. Using material from the Ingmar Bergman archives, Anna Sofia Rossholm opens up new ways to discuss the creative process of artistic work; the artist's diaries are placed as a kind of highly influential and active midway station between a source (perhaps an idea or an earlier work of art) and the final result. Thomas Leitch offered a widened perspective in his influential *Film Adaptation and its Discontents* (2009); in this volume, he uses Pasolini's contemplations on the screenplay as a structure that wants to become another structure, to discuss 'the gradual changes in textual generations wrought by evolutionary processes', which is yet another way to focus on the rich field in-between a source and the adaptation. Finally, Hajnal Király broadens the narrow source-to-result understanding when she shows how aspects of nineteenth-century visual culture have a double influence, both on novelists (Flaubert and Proust) and on directors who have adapted these 'visual' novels to the screen.

Two-way understandings of adaptation

The conventional and common sense understanding of adaptation is one-directional; *adaptation* is defined as the transport of form and/or content *from* a source *to* a result, such as from novel to film or any other adaptive constellation. From a certain viewpoint, this understanding of adaptation is correct; without a source text, a result could not be imagined. However, Jørgen Bruhn poses the question: Should we not admit that the adaptive process is dialectical, and that the source text is changed in the process of adaptation as well? The idea is not new, and Elliott points out that several scholars have hinted at such a process, including Bazin, Cohen, Whelehan and Cardwell. But perhaps the strongest impetus for thinking about the source-result relationship as a dialectical one is Robert Stam's work. Stam drew his ideas not from film studies, but instead applied the ideas of Bakhtin and Kristeva on intertextuality to novel-to-film adaptations. Anna Sofia Rossholm's archival research, combined with the methodology of genetic criticism in her study, participates in this dialectical process as she moves back and forth between unpublished notebooks, printed material, verbal commentaries and the canonical films. As such, Rossholm's argument deals with the important question of the adaptive relation between screenwriting and films that, after long neglect, has surfaced in recent years as a core question in film studies, including adaptation theory. Leitch, too, moves into this underdeveloped field when he engages in a wide-ranging and almost dizzying argument involving Pasolini's arguments of the will of the screenplay, cultural memes and adaptation theory.

From a methodological perspective, Kamilla Elliott's main argument in her critical article is that adaptation studies ought to move forward with a 'dialogic' process, avoiding the atomistic details of the 'twenty-page case study article' and the abstract theoretical attempts where the specific examples are mere examples. According to Elliott, new results and creative methods in the field will come from theory developed in connection with adaptation analysis and analytical method created through theoretical reflection.

Adaptation as part of comprehensive theories on cultural processes

Recently, adaptations as a cultural phenomenon or practice have also attracted the interest of scholars who do not primarily study adaptation as such, but rather attempt to establish more comprehensive and general theories regarding cultural transfer, textuality, media specificity and intermediality.

During the 2000s, works on adaptation by scholars such as Linda Hutcheon and Thomas Leitch were influential because of the broad perspectives that they offered. Hutcheon's book *A Theory of Adaptation* (2006) proposed a general theory of adaptation as a kind of formal product, and more importantly, a creative and interpretative *process* taking place within a variety of media and cultural phenomena. This process should be examined through an established set of general and basic terms, questions and concepts that can be applied to diverse phenomena or 'media'. Hutcheon did not limit her perspective to different forms of transfer between texts, but emphasized the importance of situating adaptations within a broader framework, relating to political, economic and legal circumstances, and defining the participants contributing to the adaptations: the 'adapters', the audience and the cultural context. Although focusing on film adaptations, Leitch also broadened the variety of sources that have been made into films, posing questions that addressed more general cultural circumstances and changes.

Scholars who have examined adaptation from such a general point of view do not necessarily belong to the field of adaptation studies or film studies. For example, literary scholar Julie Sanders linked the practices of adaptation and appropriation together in what she described as 'a sub-section of the over-arching practice of intertextuality.'[12] In Chapter 3, John Bryant, coming from the field of textual editing and genetic criticism, applies his concept of the fluid text on the question of adaptation. Hutcheon, among others, has drawn on Bryant's term in her own work, arguing that a text is no fixed thing.[13] Understanding a 'work' as the sum of its versions, Bryant suggests how an adaptation can be understood as a 'version' of an originating text, taking part in the creative process that traditionally is associated primarily with the different stages taking place before a so-called 'finished work' is published. Anna Sofia Rossholm's essay is inspired by genetic criticism and notions of the fluid text as she views Ingmar Bergman's films as 'adaptations' of his pre-production notebooks. Her approach echoes Leitch's appropriation of Pasolini's claim that a screenplay is a structure that wants to be another structure (Chapter 8). Likewise, Lars Elleström, from the field of intermedia studies, examines and challenges certain definitions and practices which he locates in a number of recent theoretical works on adaptation, with regard to a more general understanding of media transformation and the modalities. In Chapter 6, Elleström explores how the term 'adaptation' relates to his own concept of 'transmediation,' how these terms overlap, and what phenomena they include and exclude. Hanssen's essay describes how Bazin in the 1940s and 1950s turned to certain cultural and aesthetic aspects of contemporary film adaptations to devise theories for the ontology of cinema as a medium.

In these examples, adaptations are understood in terms of how they function as case studies or examples that illuminate much broader questions. In Bryant's case, adaptation explores what we understand as a 'text', a 'work' and a 'version'. In Elleström's case, adaptation is used to rigorously define the concept of 'medium' and the systemic relationships between media. Finally, in Bazin's case, adaptation becomes a way to explore and understand the specificity and ontology of cinema.

If space allowed, this introduction could conduct a case study based on the five areas of interest sketched above. Such a comprehensive case study could investigate the complicated transformation of the fictional musings of an Oxford linguist and medievalist now better known as a fantasy-writer. It could describe the textual travels from Tolkien's studies of the Finnish *Kalevala* and his treaties on the history of the English language, as well as of *Beowulf*, which move into his fantasy works, among them *The Hobbit*. These texts were adapted into cinematic versions, which, following the nature of 'texts that want to be other texts' (see Leitch's contribution), continue to generate interminable discussions and parodies on the World Wide Web. But this must be the task of other writers.

The Tolkien phenomenon functions as one specific, highly exemplary part of adaptation studies that illuminates general questions about our current media-saturated culture, and pinpoints

the way images, texts, film clips and musical fragments inces-
santly cross media borders. Adaptation studies, if such a thing
can be meaningfully defined as a field or a discipline at all, is a
productive framework for analysing central and complex contemporary cultural phenomena typical of our own period.

Overview of the book

Adaptation Studies: New Challenges, New Directions establishes
a dialogue between scholars coming from adaptation studies
and intermediality studies, as well as film and literature scholars.
The contributors were asked to reconsider the basic questions
underlying adaptation studies in general, and novel-to-film studies
specifically, and to focus either on a theoretical or methodological
point of view or a case study.

The volume, accordingly, is organized into two parts: chapters
2–8 offer new approaches to adaptation studies (especially influenced by intermediality studies) and re-readings of theories of
adaptation, and chapters 9–13 that offer case studies to open up
new fields within adaptation studies (such as notebooks, screenplays, true stories and violence).

Rethinking the core questions

In the opening essay, Kamilla Elliott addresses what she considers
the excessive theoretization of adaptation studies. Her essay
calls for a deconstruction of the current one-way, hierarchical
relationship between theories and adaptations (theorizing adaptations) and recommends a reciprocal relationship that requires
theories to adapt to adaptations (adapting theories). By way
of an extensive historical survey of the field, she discusses the
divide between formal and cultural approaches to adaptations,
the repetitions of claims and the remarkable failure to accumulate
knowledge in the field. Elliott advocates a more robust engagement
with prior research as well as the need for theories to adapt to
adaptations, arguing that 'applying concepts that adaptations
themselves give rise to can help us to theorize our field.' Finally, in

line with the ambitions of this volume, she advocates for the importance of intermedial engagement among scholars from different
disciplines.

John Bryant regards adaptation studies from the viewpoint
of text genetic criticism and his own influential concept of 'the
fluid text'. He suggests, 'If adaptation is to achieve its proper
textual legitimacy, we need a broader conception of work, creative
process, and writing.' Bryant rethinks these three categories by
discussing *Moby Dick* as both a textual object that enters Edward
Said's political discussions and a text that is turned into a new
filmic text. Critics and editors – and consequently, also adaptation
studies – Bryant argues, should study the 'critical distances'
between adapted texts, keeping intact the memories of the texts
that are being adapted.

Jørgen Bruhn suggests a redirection of adaption studies, from
the one-way conveyance from novel to film to a two-way dialogic
process. Adaptation, Bruhn proposes, results in both a new filmic
version and a change in the original text. Taking Jan Troell's
cinematic adaptation of Swedish writer Vilhelm Moberg's *The
Emigrants* as an example, Bruhn stages a dialectical relationship
between novel and film, where both texts becomes precedents for
each other.

Regina Schober presents and discusses Bruno Latour's actor-
network model in adaptation studies. Schober combines classical
philosophy (Hume) and contemporary neural research to discuss
the question 'what is a connection?' She then proposes new ways to
understand the fundamental concept of 'transmediality', as found
in intermediality studies, which have direct implications for the
study of adaptations.

Lars Elleström, from the viewpoint of intermediality studies,
argues that a consistent theory of medium is necessary to understand media transformations. Through a sophisticated theoretical
discussion of media, he offers a new framework for studying media
transformations, based on the notion that all art forms and media
are interrelated, and accordingly, should be compared. At the same
time, he provides more precise definitions of what is being transferred in adaptation processes.

Eirik Frisvold Hanssen examines the recent renewed and
increasing interest in André Bazin's writings within adaptation
studies, and film studies in general. Hanssen views Bazin's writings

on adaptation and intermediality within the context of his general theory on the ontology of cinema, and argues for returning to classical film theory when attempting to consider the complex relationships between cinema and other media.

In 'What Movies Want', Tom Leitch begins with the idea that almost all texts want to be other texts. Discussing the difficult idea that texts, or movies, may 'want' anything, Leitch moves to ideas of biological evolution to reach the concept of memes, defined as 'micro-units of cultural knowledge' travelling in screenplays or movies, for instance. These meme-vehicles are 'machines like the human brain, designed for whatever purpose that also happens to have the subsidiary effect of insuring the survival and propagation of the fittest memes.' In a final, startling move, Leitch sketches a new and productive definition of agency, connecting to Latour, Serres and Yates, which may impact the way we understand the phenomenon of adaptation.

Rethinking the case study

In chapter 9, Hajnal Király addresses how novels that are particularly visual are, ironically, often considered impossible to adapt into films. Arguing the usefulness of Bolter and Grusin's concept of remediation in novel-to-film adaptation studies, Kiraly investigates the representation of, and intersection between, female characters and visual media addressed in recent adaptations of nineteenth-century novels by Flaubert and Proust.

Based on archival research, and drawing on genetic criticism methodologies, Anna Sofia Rossholm considers Ingmar Bergman's notebooks as the preparations for *Persona,* both as a source, an original and a pre-text. Rossholm considers the transition from notebook to film as an adaptation, exploring the notebook as an aesthetic form belonging to the genre of the diary, and thus the finished film as a form of diary adaptation.

In her article, 'Tracing the original', Sara Brinch investigates Clint Eastwood's film, *Invictus* (2009), based on several 'originals': a true story, a nonfiction book, photographs and a poem. What is the original source of a historical fiction film? Brinch asks, and by so doing, questions both the foregrounding of text and narrative in adaptation studies and the notion that a narrative built on a so-called true story should be considered an adaptation.

Coming from film studies, Anne Gjelsvik reframes the classical question, 'What Novels Can Tell That Movies Can't Show', by investigating an issue somewhat neglected by adaptation studies – violent representations. Historically, violent representations have been considered more challenging and provocative in cinema than in literature. Through a close reading of a violent scene in Jim Thompson's novel *The Killer Inside Me*, and Michael Winterbottom's film adaptation, Gjelsvik aims to grasp some of the differences between the two media.

Approaching the question of adaptation studies from the viewpoint of Marshall McLuhan's media theory and Friedrich Kittler's media historical framework, Jonas Ingvarsson offers a reading of Orson Welles' famous radio adaptation of H. G. Wells' novel *The War of the Worlds*. Using perspectives from media archeology, Ingvarsson reformulates the basic questions of adaptation theory while also suggesting a new reading of both novel and radio play.

Notes

1   See http://knowyourmeme.com/memes/one-does-not-simply-walk-into-mordor and http://knowyourmeme.com/mcmes/subcultures/lord-of-the-rings (accessed 2 January 2013).

2   See for instance Kirsten Pullen, 'The Lord of The Rings Online Blockbuster Fandom: Pleasure and Commerce', in Ernst Mathijs (ed.) *The Lord of the Rings. Popular Culture in Global Context* (London: Wallflower, 2006).

3   In relation to *Lord of the Rings*, we have referred to the film as a Peter Jackson movie; however, the script was collaboration among Jackson, Phillipa Boyens and Fran Walsh, with the two last as principal writers.

4   See Thomas Leitch, 'Adaptation Studies at a Crossroads', *Adaptation* 1:1 (2008), 63–77.

5   R. Barton Palmer, '*Journal of Adaptation in Film and Performance*', Numbers 1.1, 1.2 (Intellect), Richard J. Hand and Katja Krebs, (eds), *Adaptation* Vol. 2 2009, No. 1, 87.

6   Dennis Cutchins, Laurence Raw and Ray Welsh (eds), *The Pedagogy of Adaptation*. (MD: Scarecrow Press, 2010), Laurence Raw (ed.). *Translation, Adaptation and Transformation*. (New York and London: Continuum, 2012), and Thomas Leitch, 'Twelve Fallacies in Contemporary Adaptation Theory', *Criticism*, 45:2 (2003), 149–71.

7   For an updated discussion of paragone see Uta Degner and Norbert Christian Wolf (eds), *Der Neue Wettstreit der Künste Legitimation und Dominanz im Zeichen der Intermedialität*. (Göttingen: Göttinger Universitätsverlag, 2010).

8   Leitch (2008) 63.

9   See David Boyd and R. Barton Palmer (eds), *Hitchcock at the Source: The Auteur as Adapter* (Albany: SUNY Press, 2011).

10 The broadened scope of cultural studies is mirrored in the shift of name and focus of interart studies to intermediality.

11 Christine Geraghty, 'Foregrounding the Media: *Atonement* (2007) as an Adaptation', *Adaptation* 2:2 *(*2009), 91–109.

12 Julie Sanders, *Adaptation and Appropriation* (London: Routledge, 2006), 17.

13 Linda Hutcheon, *A Theory of Adaptation* (New York and London: Routledge, 2006), 170.

PART ONE

Rethinking the core questions

2

Theorizing adaptations/ adapting theories

Kamilla Elliott

Discussions of adaptation studies and humanities theories have tended to be one-sided, focused on theorizing adaptations. Given that, from the late 1970s, scholars have been advocating inter-textual exchange over one-way transfer,[1] such one-sided rhetoric warrants scrutiny. From their incipience, adaptation practices and scholarship have been castigated for their failure to conform to prevailing humanities theories. Concomitantly, their conformity to such theories has been recommended to redress the problems of both their academic study and cultural practice. The critique has persisted regardless of what the theories are, across opposing as well as similar theories. This essay seeks to redress that imbalance.

In the first half of the twentieth century, blame for troubled relations between theories and adaptations fell chiefly on adaptations as 'bad' cultural practices, castigated for violating medium specificity and formalist aesthetics. In 1910, Irving Babbitt decried adaptations as 'confusions of the arts';[2] in 1924, Béla Balázs declared adaptations inartistic;[3] in 1942, René Wellek and Austin Warren dismissed adaptation as an impossibility ('One can, of course, deny the possibility of literal metamorphosis of poetry into sculpture, painting, or music');[4] in 1957, George Bluestone assessed that film would not 'discover its central principles' until 'the current vogue of adaptation ... has run its course.'[5]

From the 1950s, blame extended from 'bad' adaptations to 'bad' adaptation scholarship for failing to conform to prevailing academic theories. As adapters of canonical literature had been criticized for violating formalist and aesthetic tenets – 'You can't make a good film from a good book'[6] – so too were scholars who failed to accept and apply such tenets to adaptation study. In the 2010s, Cahir, Welsh, Albrecht-Crane, Cutchins and others continue to argue that failure to concede medium specificity produces poor adaptation scholarship.[7]

In the late 1970s, the theoretical turn[8] brought a new set of critiques to adaptations and their scholarship, faulting adaptation studies for adhering to the very theoretical tenets that formalist and aesthetic scholars perceived to have failed. New scholars critiqued adaptation studies for maintaining elitist, modernist, aesthetic, media, disciplinary and cultural hierarchies against postmodern and left-wing democratizing forces;[9] for pursuing one-way translation models rather than dialogic, structuralist and post-structuralist modes of intertextuality;[10] for prioritizing aestheticism over political and cultural issues;[11] for setting comparative formalism, structuralism and narratology over deconstruction and situated historicism;[12] and for prioritizing textual analysis over industrial concerns.[13] Formal and aesthetic scholars responded, criticizing the theoretical turn's neglect of forms and formalist tenets; its inattention to aesthetics, artistry and practitioner processes; its lack of objectivity; its political bias; its lack of respect for tradition and accumulated knowledge; its jargon; its academic elitism; and its exclusion of other points of view.[14]

Rarely, however, have scholars considered that the failure of adaptation studies to conform to theoretical paradigms might arise from the inadequacies and limitations of the theories. Scholars have inched towards this possibility, arguing that adaptations forge critical 'commentaries' on the works they adapt,[15] and that these 'commentaries' are 'impacted upon by movements in, and readings produced by, the theoretical and intellectual arena as much as by their so-called sources.'[16] Catherine Constable has extended inter-mediality to engagements between adaptations and philosophy.[17] My essay goes further to argue that adaptations require theories to adapt to *them*. But first, I examine the more familiar discourse of 'theorizing adaptations.'

Theorizing adaptations

Surveying publications from the 1950s to the present, one finds a consensus regarding the shortcomings of adaptations scholarship:

> Personal preferences, snap judgments, isolated instances, and random impressions ... characterize most of the writing in the field.[18]
>
> The mysterious alchemy which transforms works of fiction into cinematic form is still being widely practiced without, perhaps, being sufficiently understood.[19]
>
> The overwhelming bulk of what has been written about the relationship of film and literature is open to serious question.[20]
>
> Nobody loves an adaptation.[21]
>
> In view of the nearly sixty years of writing about the adaptation of novels into film ... it is depressing to find at what a limited, tentative stage the discourse has remained.[22]
>
> The critical literature on adaptations ... has not, even now, reached a happy compromise.[23]
>
> Why has this topic, obviously central to humanities-based film education, prompted so little distinguished work?[24]
>
> ... adaptation theory has progressed very little since the 1950s.[25]

The reasons differ; the conclusions are the same. Frederic Jameson's essay, 'Adaptation as a Philosophical Problem',[26] indicates that the discourse shows no sign of abating.

In the twenty-first century, the field's failures and problems have been credited to a refusal to get fully on board with the theoretical turn. In 2010, Brett Westbrook observes that 'lack of theory about adaptation studies stands in direct contrast to the rise of theory in and of itself, at least in the academic academy, where it has become a field in its own right.'[27] Westbrook builds on a discourse of theoretical failure galvanized by Robert B. Ray in 2000. Addressing the field of literature and film studies (then synonymous with adaptation studies), Ray determines that it lacks 'a presiding poetics'. But Ray's critique is less of a *lack* of theory than a lack of the *right kind* of theory: 'the field of literature and film was not without paradigm ... it inherited the assumptions of the dominant New Criticism.' Ray finds formalist, structuralist, narratological, semiotic, aesthetic and humanist theories 'ultimately antitheoretical,' 'thoroughly discredited' and 'irrelevant.'[28] In their place, he recommends Barthsean intertextuality, Wattsean historicism, and Derridean deconstruction (44–5).

If Ray considers such approaches 'antitheoretical', Cartmell, Kaye, Whelehan, Hunter and their contributors (1996; 1999) are convinced of their theoretical clout, challenging formalism, aestheticism and humanism with postmodern cultural theories and left-wing identity politics.[29] However, even as these scholars brought the theoretical turn into adaptation studies, its belated arrival and the perception that adaptation studies was a stronghold *against* the theoretical turn has produced a polarized, often combative field. If the field continues to lack a presiding poetics, it is more because scholars cannot agree upon one rather than because one has not been propounded. In recent years, however, there has been some rapprochement. In 2007, Cartmell and Whelehan include narratological and practitioner essays in their *Cambridge Companion to Literature on Screen*, and James M. Welsh includes sociological and ideological essays in *Literature/ Film Quarterly* and edited collections.[30] Nevertheless, conflicts remain. In 2010, Cartmell and Whelehan protested against narratological and other formal approaches, describing them as 'a small body of work moving against the main tide of theory ... an attitude to adaptations that refuses to go away.'[31] Yet it is not a small body of work: in 2010–11, publications treating formal, textual and practitioner issues outnumbered those addressing sociological, political and cultural aspects.

Sarah Cardwell astutely perceives that *using* adaptations to fight theoretical battles has hampered their theorization: 'Adaptations are rarely studied for themselves – rarely is interpretation valued as much as theorizing; broader theoretical issues take precedence.'[32] Even points of agreement have been more often used to strengthen than to diminish opposition. Both sides agree that fidelity has been the bane of adaptation studies, but for entirely different reasons. Formal scholars oppose fidelity to support medium specificity and aesthetic value; cultural studies scholars protest that fidelity creates aesthetic, social and media hierarchies. Both Linda Cahir and Christine Geraghty (2008) refuse to consider fidelity to sources. Cahir does so to promote medium specificity and adaptations as 'fully new work[s] ... independent from [their] literary source[s]';[33] Geraghty does so to investigate adaptation's wider 'intertextual universe'[34] of production and consumption at the expense of the formal concerns that are the main focus of Cahir's research. Cahir's privileging of translation over adaptation, in turn, favours formal and semiotic over cultural and contextual approaches. Thus even as fidelity has become a shared scapegoat for the failures of adaptation studies, it denotes a divided field.

Methodological points of agreement between the two sides have further contributed to 'the lack of ... cumulative knowledge developing' that Ray noted in 2000.[35] Ray blames 'the endless series of twenty-page articles'[36] in journals and edited collections for hampering the development of cumulative knowledge. Cultural studies, with its postmodern suspicion of master narratives and plurality of contesting narratives, makes a virtue of the 20–page article. Scholars on both sides remain committed to local studies, setting them against larger theoretical frameworks. In 2010, Cartmell and Whelehan argued that 'every site of adaptation [presents] an entirely new set of relations which allows us to draw promiscuously on theoretical tendencies in film and literary studies';[37] in 2011, MacCabe writes similarly: 'the number of variables involved in any adaptation approach[es] infinity. There are thus no models of how to adapt in this volume. There are, however, a series of case studies.'[38] Joining the preponderance of essays and articles, many of the field's single-author monographs unfold as series of disparate essays (Bluestone 1957; Leitch 2007; Geraghty 2008; Hunter 2010). Although it is possible to theorize in smaller chunks, theories of other fields generally unfold in book-length tomes. I am not suggesting that adaptation scholars should agree on a single theory or methodology; this would be death to any field. I do, however, perceive that adaptations studies is an *especially* divided field whose polarizations have perhaps precluded new theories from developing.

More troubling still is that the two camps tend to condemn, ignore or dismiss opposing views rather than debate them. In 2002, Cardwell assessed that cultural studies scholars have not engaged adequately with formal issues of adaptation: 'the pluralist approach is a poor response to the challenges raised by McFarlane'; their arguments are 'simply asserted' rather than 'conceptually justified or theorized.'[39] Conversely, faith in medium specificity continues to be reasserted without engaging counter-arguments by Cohen, Cardwell, Elliott, Leitch, Stam and others.[40] Strangely, Albrecht-Crane and Cutchins enlist Derrida in favour of medium specificity without engaging his more substantial attack on their semiotic tenets.[41] Scholars on both sides regularly reinscribe Thomas Leitch's 'Twelve Fallacies in Adaptation Theory' without engaging his arguments against them. Formalist scholar Cahir and Marxist Jameson alike nominate film 'visual' and literature 'verbal'.[42] Cahir does so to support medium specificity; Jameson to promote Marxist dialectics.

Adaptation, which Hutcheon and others define as 'repetition with variation',[43] has produced a great deal of critical and theoretical repetition with very little variation. Joining argumentative repetition, scholars often fail to cite prior work upon which they build, exacerbating the sense of scatter and fruitless repetition. While every field has problems with citation, they are excessive in adaptation studies. Ours is an ancient as well as expanding field, crossing centuries, disciplines, media, nations and theoretical schools; thus no scholar can have read everything addressing intermedial adaptation. All the same, there have been serious short-comings in citation. The 'exigencies of publication' (to borrow Ray's term)[44] require each new publication to justify its existence in terms of originality. As a result, each new editor must claim that her/his collection introduces new paradigms, theories and approaches to adaptation studies, even if it does not. (Incidentally, claims to originality in a field that by and large rejects originals are incongruous.)

Surveying work published in 2010–11, the most common claim to innovation is that a new publication challenges prevalent fidelity mandates. And yet scholars who have read prior work know that fidelity has *always* been robustly challenged in adaptation studies: the challenge to fidelity on grounds of medium specificity lies at the heart of formalist criticism; fidelity has also been challenged on intertextual, dialogical and post-structuralist grounds from at least the late 1970s,[45] and opposed for producing cultural and aesthetic hierarchies since at least since 1996.[46] Indeed, the critique of fidelity has become so commonplace that the *critique* of this critique is also widely reiterated.[47]

A second oft-repeated claim to innovation is that a new publication is pioneering the expansion of the field beyond (canonical) literature and film to other media. But studies of adaptation among other arts and media are ancient; more recently, Cartmell's and Whelehan's assaults on media hierarchies and Hutcheon's expansion of adaptation theory to other media opened the field irrevocably and authoritatively years prior to 2010–11. Of equal concern, a tally of works addressed in publications claiming innovative attention to new media reveals that a sizeable majority continues to address canonical literature and/or films – a landslide majority if one includes the new canons of the most commonly studied works in publications and classrooms.

A third claim to innovation emphasizes two-way exchanges between media. But discourses on two-way media exchanges were common in the eighteenth century, entering literature and film studies in the late 1920s.[48] Cohen and others published significant monographs on two-way exchanges between literature and cinema in the late 1970s; Cartmell and Whelehan revitalized the discourse in 1999. It is thus not an innovation of the 2010s. While recent publications contain valuable contributions to the field, presenting established ideas as new doubly hampers theorization, as it obscures prior research and substitutes for *actual* theoretical and methodological innovation.[49]

I am by no means the first scholar to notice lapses in citation in adaptation studies, nor are such lapses new. Greg Jenkins, whose admirably comprehensive summary of the field eclipses many others, observes that '[Roy Paul] Madsen's opening comments ... echo Bluestone's almost identically, though he gives his benefactor no credit.'[50] I find that Bluestone does not credit Gilbert Seldes (1936)[51]; nor does Seldes cite Vachel Lindsay (1915) for identical ideas.[52]

Scholars who apply the theoretical turn to adaptation studies also fail to cite their predecessors. Prior to 2000, summaries of the field included work by scholars who deconstructed medium specificity, promoted intertextuality over translation models, reader response over author intent, and advocated a Marxist, historical approach to adaptations in the late 1970s and 1980s.[53] Yet neither Ray nor Stam include any of these scholars in their overviews of the field.[54] Such lapses in citation prevented them from *building* upon prior scholarship that had already answered their calls. Unfortunately, subsequent scholars have relied too much on Stam's and Ray's partial summaries of prior scholarship, producing a selective, distorted, sometimes mythological history of our field. Intriguingly, following Jenkins, critics who address individual authors and film-makers continue to provide better and more complete summaries of the field than those most often cited in adaptation studies generally.[55]

It is impossible to determine whether scholars who do not cite prior work have read it or not, have read and forgotten it or have consciously decided not to cite it.[56] Formal scholars may not cite prior work because they believe it to express self-evident truths; scholars championing the theoretical turn may not cite prior research in order to galvanize support; cultural studies scholars may be casual about citing prior work because they believe every work, fictive or critical, to be always already an adaptation or pastiche of prior works. Whatever the reasons, Table 2.1 offers an illustrative (by no means exhaustive) list of repeated claims made in adaptation studies, many without citing work they repeat, though not all. It is a table that includes me. In most instances, there are numerous additional names that could have been added. I have emphasized more influential and recent scholars.

Table 2.1: Repeated claims in adaptation studies[57]

1912 Melville declares the impossibility of complete fidelity in literature to film adaptation.[58]	So too does every scholar who has addressed the topic, e.g. Bluestone, 1957; Stam, 2000; Elliott, 2003; MacCabe, 2011.
1915 Lindsay objects to privileging literature and print over visual arts and the high-art dismissal of film adaptation.[59]	Cartmell *et al.*, 1996; Ray, 2000; Aragay, 2005.
1915 Lindsay addresses the effects of adaptation on identity politics.	Cartmell, Whelehan and contributors, 1999; Newstok and Thompson, 2010;[60] and many others.

1915 Lindsay identifies what different media can and cannot do as a result of medium specificity.	Bluestone, 1957; Chatman, 1980[61]; Cahir, 2006.
1915 Lindsay argues that you can't make a good film from a good book/play/other form.	Balázs, 1952; Bluestone, 1957; Tibbetts and Welsh, 1999;[62] Jameson, 2011.
1936 Seldes argues that an emphasis on fidelity produces bad adaptations because of formal differences.	Balázs, 1952; Bluestone, 1957; Truffaut and Burgess, cited in Beja, 1976; Boyum, 1985. McFarlane, 1996; Albrecht-Crane and Cutchins, 2010.
1949 Asheim advocates a 'How? What? Why?' approach to theorizing adaptations.[63]	Hutcheon, 2006.
1952 Bazin challenges the author/ *auteur* analogy.[64]	Elliott, 2003.
1957 Bluestone critiques the view that 'the novel is a norm and film deviates at its peril.'	Stam, 2000; and numerous others.
1963–65 Mitry rejects translation models in adaptation.[65]	Wagner, 1975;[66] Stam, 2000.
1975 Wagner posits that adaptations function as interpretations of/critical commentaries on what they adapt.	Boyum, 1985; Griffith, 1986; Sinyard, 1986;[67] Elliott, 2003.
1979 Cohen argues that literature and film undertake a two-way exchange.	Whelehan, 1999; Hunter, 2010.[68]
1979 Cohen and 1984 Orr[69] advocate intertextuality rather than one-to-one translation.	Ray, 2000; Stam, 2000; Cardwell, 2002; Leitch, 2012; and many others.

1979 Beja asks, should a film be faithful to its original source: 'Can it be? To what?', critiquing accusations of 'betrayal' as being 'needlessly or distractingly moralistic.'[70]	Boyum, 1985; Stam, 2000.
1979 Beja questions the 'you can't make a good book from a good film' maxim.	2003, Elliott.
1981 Andrew calls for a sociological turn in adaptation studies.	Naremore, 2000; Cutchins, Raw, and Welsh, 2010.
1981 Klein and Parker critique the hierarchy of literature over film in adaptation studies.[71]	Cartmell et al., 1996; Aragay, 2005.
1982 Ellis calls for attention to production and consumption in adaptation studies.[72]	Hutcheon, 2006. Geraghty, 2007.
1982 Larsson advocates contextualizing under Marxist concepts of history.[73]	Reynolds, 1993;[74] Jameson, 2011.
1985 Boyum advocates a reader response to adaptation.	Cattrysse, 1992;[75] Hutcheon, 2006.
1996 Pulping Fictions (ed. Cartmell et al.) attacks fidelity on political and cultural grounds.	Ray, 2000; Stam, 2000 Kranz and Mellerski (eds), 2008;[76] Hopton et al., 2011.
2000 Naremore calls scholars to consider the 'commercial apparatus, the audience, and the academic culture industry.'[77] (also Bazin 1948;[78] Bluestone 1957)	Murray, 2008; 2011.[79]
2002 Cardwell advocates considering adaptation as process, not just as product.	Hutcheon, 2006; Frus and Williams, 2010.[80]

While some repetition is essential to building a field, reviving buried work, reaching new audiences and expanding older points within new contexts, too much repetition, with or without citation, keeps a field from evolving, contributing to the lack of cumulative knowledge that Ray laments. A lack of cumulative knowledge inevitably hampers theorization.

Joining repetition are distortions and omissions of prior work made to support theoretical battles, agendas and advance claims to originality. More than any other critic, George Bluestone has been misrepresented in summaries of the field, which omit a great deal of his work and read implicit subtexts over and against his overt, actual claims *without citing the latter*. While Bluestone does adhere to and foreground formalist tenets, he also addresses contextual and cultural issues: the Hollywood studio system, copyright law, censorship, studio output, reviews of films, sales of books, audience responses, comments by film-makers and novelists on adaptations, the role of genre in adaptation, how psychology and phenomenology, 'political and social attitudes', 'American folklore' and cultural mythology influence adaptations, as well as 'society's shaping power' over adaptations. He identifies and critiques 'conventional myth[s] which distinguish novel from cinema.'[81] He advocates a shift 'from elucidating a fixed and unchanging reality to arresting a transient one', opposing 'familiar polarities' and challenging 'obsolete ideals and false ideologies'[82] – all attitudes and ideas that resonate with the theoretical turn. He does not advocate fidelity, as so many critics have argued erroneously, but stridently *attacks* the view that 'the novel is a norm and the film deviates at its peril.'[83] Bluestone is not alone in being subjected to partial and distorted summaries; I have found numerous other instances where prior scholarship has been misunderstood or distorted to advance a particular agenda or to make newer scholars appear more innovative than they are.

In the second half of the 2000s, new obstacles to theorizing adaptations and adaptation studies emerged. While in 2000 Ray called for adaptation studies to embrace the theoretical turn to redress its theoretical failure, in 2010 Westbrook declared the impossibility of theorizing adaptation studies *following* its embrace of the theoretical turn: 'a grand unifying theory for adaptation studies is not, in fact, possible; the sheer volume of everything involved in a discussion of film adaptation is virtually immeasurable, which means that no one single theory has the capacity to encompass every aspect of an adaptation.'[84]

The theoretical turn has not only brought new theories into adaptation studies, it has also introduced new questions, materials, topics and entities, all of which, champions of inclusivity insist, must be addressed. Adding historical, cultural, contextual, ideological, political and economic aspects of adaptation to semiotic, generic, textual and media aspects has greatly expanded the scope of the field, as have the intertextual and intermedial theories that have replaced one-to-one translation models with longer representational genealogies and wider webs of intermediality. Adding audience reception and industrial practices to artistic practices has also enlarged the field. The democratization of representation has furthermore brought discredited older media and new media into adaptation studies; changing technologies have further expanded the materials that adaptation scholars must study. And to the *impossibility* of theorizing adaptations in the wake of all of these expansions, postmodern scholars add the *undesirability* of theorizing adaptations under any master system or narrative.

Few attempts have been made to establish a theory of adaptation; no one who has done so claims that his/her theory covers every aspect of adaptation. Brian McFarlane's neo-narratological theory, informed by the Barthesean theories that Ray and Stam recommend, nevertheless troubles post-structuralist and postmodern scholars by aspiring to objectivism and by its failure to systematize the socio-cultural aspects of adaptation that are the primary concern of cultural studies: 'The fact that ... extra-cinematic influences such as the prevailing ideological climate is not readily susceptible to the quantifying possibilities referred to above does not mean that the critic of adaptation can afford to ignore them.'[85]

Linda Hutcheon's *A Theory of Adaptation* is a postmodern one, unusually and commendably aiming at formal and cultural synthesis, considering both texts and contexts, adapters and audiences, medium specificity and cultural diversity, and adaptation as product and adaptation as process. Yet in theorizing the field from a postmodern purview and opening the field beyond the usual suspects of literature, theatre and film to include 'video games, theme park rides, Web sites, graphic novels, song covers, operas, musicals, ballets, and radio and stage plays',[86] Hutcheon's theory is more pastiche than system, with unclear borders and boundaries whose fluidity some scholars welcome and others find unsatisfying. Cartmell and Whelehan conclude their assessment of Hutcheon's work: 'in the attempt to anticipate every possible permutation of the relationship between one narrative form and another we attempt a list that will never be exhaustive but is, frankly, exhausting and does not produce the holy grail of the definitive critical model which helps us further analyse the process of adaptation.'[87]

In recent years, leading adaptation scholars have turned from new theories to theoretical and critical nostalgia. After 15 years of opening up the field, in 2010, Cartmell and Whelehan 'return' to 'literature on screen', to the 'old faithfuls' of 'classic literary texts.'[88] In 2011, MacCabe returned to essays written by André Bazin in 1948 and 1952 to theorize adaptation.[89] Although Timothy Corrigan argues that 'We need to encourage the refractive spread of adaptation studies where evolutionary progress can also be a return to positions that we may have archived too quickly – from Vachel Lindsay and Béla Balázs to Bazin and Bellour and well beyond',[90] and while my own essay argues for more robust citation of and engagement with prior scholarship, returning to the past is not the only way forward, nor should we abandon all attempts at theorization because we cannot locate an all-encompassing theory or because we reject grand theory on principle, nor should we simply revert to the theories we already know, believe in and engage. While Westbrook recommends 'a plurality of theories'[91] and Cartmell and Whelehan advocate drawing 'draw promiscuously on theoretical tendencies in film and literary studies',[92] 'plurality' as we know and practice it does not go far enough in redressing the problems of theorizing adaptations, nor do existing 'theoretical tendencies'.

Adapting theories

When scholars tell the story of adaptation studies' resistance to theory, they focus on only one side of this interdisciplinary relationship: the problems that adaptations and adaptation studies present to theories and theorization. Adaptations, adaptations scholars and adaptations studies have not only failed theories;

theories have also failed them. Rather than solely adapting adaptation to theories, theories also need to adapt to adaptations.

It is a mistake to lay all the blame upon adaptations scholars for the problems of theorizing adaptations. Certainly, there are weak scholars in this field, as in any field. But Linda Hutcheon is a formidable theorist, internationally celebrated for *A Theory of Parody* (1985) and *A Poetics of Postmodernism: History, Theory, Fiction* (1987). While scholars debate her theories in these books, they don't fault her for theoretical ineptitude or suggest that these fields cannot be theorized. Similarly, Thomas Leitch's *What Stories Are: Narrative Theory and Interpretation* (1986) is as lucid an account of narrative theory as any I have read, one that was invaluable to me as I wrote my PhD thesis. Yet as we have seen, both scholars not only struggle to define adaptation, but they also recognize that their usual theoretical methodologies are inadequate for theorizing adaptations and therefore adapt those theories in order to address adaptations. Theorizing adaptations turns postmodernist Hutcheon into a quasi-structuralist and quasi-empiricist, asking 'What? Who? Why? How? Where? When?'; it turns Leitch from affirmative description (*What Stories Are*) to a discourse of fallacies,[93] negation[94] and problems (the publisher's description to his 2007 monograph indicates that it addresses adaptation as 'an array of problems').[95] These highly able and respected scholars understand that adaptations require theories and theorists to adapt to *them*.

What we in adaptation studies have learned about how stories adapt to new media and contexts suggests that theoretical stories too need to adapt to new intermedial and interdisciplinary relations and practices. Indeed, Deleuze may be ubiquitous in cinema studies today because he has challenged the one-way relationship between theory and cultural practice, in which theories are *applied* to cultural practices, with practices serving solely as proof texts for theories. As Stam notes, 'Deleuze does not "apply" philosophical concepts to the cinema; rather, he works with the concepts that cinema itself gives rise to.'[96] In a similar vein, applying the concepts that adaptations give rise to can help us to challenge our existing theoretical positions. For example, for all of our protests against fidelity mandates in adaptation studies, we often insist upon diehard fidelity to our theories, repeatedly affirming them, resisting challenges to them. We need to learn from adaptations to challenge fidelity to our preferred theories. Similarly, our protests against canonicity in adaptation studies can teach us to challenge theoretical as well as textual canonicity.

Eleanor Rosch's levels of categorization offer one way to revivify stale, inadequate and outgrown areas of both formal and contextual adaptation studies.[97] Assertions of medium specificity operating solely at Rosch's basic level of categorization, or bound anachronistically to a false verbal/visual dichotomy predicated on Lessing's theories of poetry and painting,[98] need rethinking and retheorizing. Rosch has shown how different levels of categorization can configure the relations between two entities in radically different, often opposite ways. For example, medium specificity may hold firm at the level of 'poetry' and 'painting', but these are sub-categories of 'aesthetic representations', at which level they share more similarities than differences. Similarly, at the other end of the categorical spectrum, as 'marks on paper,' they also have more in common.[99] Cultural *practices* of hybrid media, animation and digital technologies also challenge medium specificity and theories of form. Making new connections at both more macroscopic and microscopic levels of analysis can take us beyond both conventional theories of media, genres and forms, and free us from the vague, randomness of 'intertextuality' and 'intermediality.' Working at different levels of categorization can help scholars to revivify cultural topics, such as nationality, economics, politics, identity politics, industry, aesthetics and historical epochs.

In addition to revivifying both formal and cultural adaptation studies, we need to develop theories and methodologies that integrate these approaches of adaptation. Surveying publications in 2010–11, I see movements towards ecumenism in all three of the field's journals, *Literature/Film Quarterly, Adaptation* and *The Journal of Adaption in Film and Performance*. We need, however, to go further to develop methodologies for addressing adaptations that *integrate* rather than simply juxtapose formal and contextual analyses in edited collections. Integration requires both more politically inflected formalisms and more formally inflected contextual studies. Cultural studies furthermore need to expand to consider aspects of culture that may not be reducible to left-wing politics or postmodern ideologies. It is not simply our materials and subjects that need to expand: it is our theories as well.

Although Westbrook argues that 'Criticism, no matter the theory, fixes the text(s) in that moment for examination',[100] it does so only because of our current views of what theory is and should do. Here too, theories can learn from adaptations. Adaptations teach us that theories cannot predict or account for adaptations in all times and places, not only because the field is too large, but also because adaptations are always changing and adapting. Any theory of adaptation must therefore *itself* incorporate process and change. Adaptations admonish us to move continually beyond our present ideas and methodologies.

If adaptations have taught us how to cross boundaries, they can equally reveal boundaries that we have refused to cross and hierarchical binarisms we have failed to deconstruct. One under-constructed hierarchical binarism in humanities academia affecting everyone and, to my mind, seriously inhibiting the theorization of adaptations is the ancient one between soul and body, mind and matter, abstraction and concretism, philosophy and empiricism (etc.), which deems the former superior to and more valuable than the latter. The binarism, which elevates the abstract, the conceptual and the theoretical, while subjugating the concrete, the material and the practical, seeps into every area of scholarship. We tend to equate the best scholarship with either the most abstract philosophical scholarship or with the most evangelical, political polemics. We therefore mine adaptations to prove abstract points or to locate cultural ideologies. We reward student essays for philo-sophical reflection and downgrade them for descriptive summaries. We value their abstract thinking and discourage comparing and contrasting as a means of generating ideas.

This has been a particular problem for adaptation studies, which foregrounds adaptations as concrete cultural forms, paying attention to their construction and consumption, and incites comparisons and contrasts between them. In 'Materializing Adaptation Theory: The Adaptation Industry',[101] Simone Murray argues that adaptation foregrounds practice and resists abstraction. MacCabe attests: 'The fact is that people are still interested in how and why film-makers adapt books and what they did to adapt them. So these issues and questions are not going to go away'.[102]

In their material persistence and cultural prominence, adapta-tions challenge the excesses and errors of theories as well as the limitations of theories for adaptation studies. For example, adaptation defies the Barthesean death of the author with resolutely undead screened writers and contests Foucault's claim that the author function 'impedes the free circulation, the free manipulation, the free composition, decomposition, and recomposition of fiction'[103] by proliferating and redistributing meaning, including 'the meanings of philosophical theories of authorship.'[104]

Beyond the ancient, undeconstructed binarism of mind and matter, the theoretical turn has created new, unacknowledged hierarchical binarisms between left- and right-wing politics, patriarchy and feminism, capitalism and Marxism and more. These binarisms operate under the same rhetoric of good and evil, right and wrong, superior and inferior, etc. as the binarisms they worked to deconstruct (Christians/non-Christians, whites/non-whites, men/women, straight/gay, etc.). All too often in academia, scholars who infinitely nuance and meticulously differentiate their own theories, ideologies and favoured groups produce contemptuous, unilateral, reductive dismissals of minority theories (formalism), ideologies (humanism) and social groups (Americans, right-wingers, etc.). Adaptations rebuke these tendencies. In our field, we attend with interest to how earlier works feed into later works; we embrace the multi-facetedness of adaptations to the point of being overwhelmed by inclusivity; surely there is also room for older theories, as Corrigan argues, and for theories, ideas and methodologies that we may ourselves oppose in our field. The exemplary inclusivity of adaptations, and of calls within adaptation studies for greater inclusivity, can teach the humanities to be more inclusive of minority voices within academia, even when they are majority voices in society. It is hypocritical to promote democratic intertextuality and intermediality among adaptations but not among theories. It is incongruous to protest the marginalization and exclusion of minority voices in society, if we marginalize and exclude minority voices in academia. Jefferson Hunter writes poignantly from the margins of adaptation studies: 'There is a backlog of works awaiting formalist appreciation.'[105] Making room for excluded voices and debating them rather than dismissing them as outmoded or antitheoretical will help us to retheorize the field inclusively.

Responding to critiques of the theoretical turn, Griselda Pollock suggests that one way to revivify theory is

by transdisciplinary encounters with and through concepts.

Concepts themselves arose inside specific theoretical projects. They now move out of—travel from—their own originating site to become tools for thinking within the larger domain of cultural analysis, a domain that seeks to create a space of encounter between the many practices that constitute the arts and humanities.[106]

Adaptation studies, already well versed in travelling narratives, seems ideally poised to inform this endeavour. In place of postmodern pastiche and post-structuralist randomness, Pollock, inspired by Mieke Bal's work on 'travelling concepts',[107] recommends tracing conceptual threads across disciplines. This offers a middle way between totalizing grand theory and random local case studies drawing 'promiscuously' on random theories. It also suggests a way to bridge the formal/cultural divide of adaptation studies, as we allow concepts to travel between sides.

Finally, one of the main reasons that theories fail adaptation studies is that most stem from single disciplines and are therefore inadequate to address intermedial operations. For all the claims of semiotics and narratology to encompass all arts, media, representations and significations, they derive from linguistics and literary studies and they cannot account adequately for non-linguistic aspects of representation.[108] Moreover, semiotic theories are at odds with adaptation. Chapter 5 of *Rethinking the Novel/Film Debate* lists some of the convoluted, contorted ways in which scholars, fearful of challenging the structuralist dogma that form does not separate from content and the post-structuralist tenet that content does not exist at all, have tried to get around the failure of semiotic theories to account for adaptation.[109] The recent return to post-formalist, pre-Metzian semiotics undertaken by McCabe, Corrigan and Hanssen in this volume is helping us to understand what went wrong with semiotic theory in accounting for adaptations and to develop new semiotic models for analysing adaptations.

My way of probing these problems in *Rethinking the Novel/Film Debate* was to turn to other disciplines for help, asking whether cognitive theory could redress the failures of semiotics, as well as theories of medium specificity, to account for adaptations. While philosophically inclined scholars balked at my interdisciplinary foray into cognitive science, I am convinced that further research in this area, a discipline proposed as a domain of consilience between the sciences and humanities,[110] could offer consilience between formal and cultural divides within our field, as well as between disciplines and media. Nicklas Pascal is currently researching in this area; I look forward to his findings.

Consilience between the humanities and sciences or between subjective and objective theories, however, doesn't go far enough in redressing theoretical lack within adaptation studies. It inscribes middle grounds rather than thoroughgoing interdisciplinary inclusivity; it favours empiricism over deductive epistemologies and does not privilege the ideologies that are the raison d'être for political scholars. Neither does theoretical pluralism as we currently apply it go far enough to redress our theoretical problems. A truly interdisciplinary theory of adaptation would go beyond the usual theoretical disciplinary suspects to include *every* discipline. Martin Mull coined a widely reiterated phrase: 'Writing about music is like dancing about architecture.'[111] It implies the impossibility and ludicrousness of explicating a non-verbal art with a verbal art by analogy to a more impossible, more ludicrous interdisciplinary relation in which one non-verbal art becomes 'about' another one. But under a fully interdisciplinary theory of adaptation, every movement between forms or media can be an act of theorization 'about' intermedial relations. Applying concepts and methodologies developed in one or few disciplines to other disciplines has colonizing effects. As postcolonial scholars attend to how colonized subjects talk and write back to their colonizers (e.g. Spivak 1985[112]), so too, adaptations need to talk, write, film, dance, sculpt, game, compose, costume, photograph and computer program (etc.) back to the theories that have colonized them.

I have for many years now required my undergraduate students to theorize about adaptations through interdisciplinary practice. In addition to writing the usual essays and exams, they undertake a project whose only requirement is that it engages at least two media. They must then write a critical analysis of that engagement. My students have gone beyond translation models that find an equivalent in one form for an expression in another and beyond random, unintentional and unconscious intertextuality to make media be *about* other media. They *have* danced about architecture, drawn about music, played rugby matches about theatre, gamed about films, computer programmed about graphic novels, baked layer cakes about book chapters, produced chemical explosions about character metamorphoses, made tactile sculptures about reader responses and made music about philosophy. All of these produced concepts about intermedial relations unavailable through the usual disciplines applied to media (history, rhetoric, philosophy, religion, politics) or through the thesis-argument-conclusion structure of academic essays. Beyond the conceptual insights and theoretical constructs that such aesthetic and intermedial engagements create, they challenge the vice-grip of abstraction, empiricism, didacticism and moralizing in the humanities with aesthetic concretism and interdisciplinary play. Their ability to surprise supersedes the value of theory to predict, as their surprises produce innovation rather than repetition without variation.

Notes

1   Seymour Chatman, *Story and Discourse: Narrative Structure in Fiction and Film* (Ithaca: Cornell University Press, 1978); Keith Cohen, *Film and Fiction: The Dynamics of Exchange* (New Haven: Yale University Press, 1979).

2   Irving Babbitt, *The New Laocoön: An Essay on the Confusion of the Arts* (Boston: Houghton Mifflin, 1910), 205.

3   Béla Balázs, *Visible Man*, in *Béla Balázs: Early Film Theory:* Visible Man *and* The Spirit of Film, (ed. and trans.) Erica Carter and Rodney Livingstone (Oxford and New York: Berghahn Books, 2010), 23–5.

4   René Wellek and Austin Warren, *Theory of Literature* (New York: Harcourt, 1942), 126.

5   George Bluestone, *Novels into Film* (Berkeley: University of California Press, 1957), 216.

6   Balázs (2010), 19.

7   Linda Costanzo Cahir, *Literature into Film: Theory and Practical Approaches* (Jefferson, NC: McFarland, 2006), 8; James M. Welsh, 'Introduction: Issues of Screen Adaptation: What Is Truth?' in *The Literature/Film Reader*, (eds) James M. Welsh and Peter Lev (Lanham, MD: Scarecrow Press, 2007), xiii–xxviii; Christa Albrecht-Crane and Dennis R. Cutchins, 'Introduction: New Beginnings for Adaptation Studies,' in *Adaptation Studies: New Approaches*, (eds) Christa Albrecht-Crane and Dennis Cutchins (Cranberry, NJ: Associated University Press, 2010), 11–22.

8   'The theoretical turn' in the humanities refers to the latter twentieth-century turn in higher academia from prevailing humanist, formalist, aesthetic scholarship focused on high-art, canonical texts towards Marxist, post-structuralist, and postmodern studies of popular culture and from traditional historical, existential, and Freudian analyses of canonical texts to New Historical, phenomenological, and Lacanian psychoanalytic examinations of all manner of texts.

9   Deborah Cartmell *et al.*, (eds), *Pulping Fictions: Consuming Culture Across the Literature/Media Divide* (London: Pluto Press, 1996).

10 Robert Stam, 'Beyond Fidelity: The Dialogics of Adaptation,' in *Film Adaptation*, (ed.) James Naremore (New Brunswick, NJ: Rutgers University Press, 2000), 54–76; Robert B. Ray, 'The Field of "Literature and Film",' in *Film Adaptation*, (ed.) James Naremore (New Brunswick, NJ: Rutgers University Press, 2000), 38–53; Thomas Leitch, 'Twelve Fallacies in Contemporary Adaptation Theory,' *Criticism* 45.2 (Spring 2003): 149–71.

11 Imelda Whelehan, 'Adaptations: The Contemporary Dilemmas,' in *Adaptations: From Text to Screen, Screen to Text*, (eds) Deborah Cartmell and Imelda Whelehan (New York: Routledge, 1999), 3–19.

12 Ray (2000).

13 Simone Murray, 'Materializing Adaptation Theory: The Adaptation Industry," *Literature/Film Quarterly* 36.1 (2008): 4–20.

14 Welsh, 2007; Colin MacCabe, 'Introduction. Bazinian Adaptation: *The Butcher Boy* as Example,' in *True to the Spirit: Film Adaptation and the Question of Fidelity*, (ed.) Colin MacCabe *et al.* (Oxford: Oxford University Press, 2011), 3–25.

15 Geoffrey Wagner, *The Novel and the Cinema* (Rutherford, NJ: Farleigh Dickinson University Press, 1975); Dudley Andrew, 'The Well-Worn Muse: Adaptation in Film History and Theory,' in *Narrative Strategies: Original Essays in Film and Prose Fiction*, (eds) Syndy M. Conger and Janet R. Welsh (Macomb: Western Illinois University Press, 1980), 9–17.

16 Julie Sanders, *Adaptation and Appropriation* (London: Routledge, 2006), 13.

17 Catherine Constable, *Adapting Philosophy: Jean Baudrillard and the Matrix Trilogy* (Manchester: Manchester University Press, 2009).

18 Lester Asheim, *From Book to Film: A Comparative Analysis of the Content of Selected Novels and the Motion Pictures Based upon Them* (Chicago: University of Chicago Press, 1949), 289.

19 Bluestone (1957), 215.

20 Louis D. Giannetti, *Godard and Others: Essays on Film Form* (Madison, NJ: Fairleigh Dickinson University Press, 1975), 89.

21 Joy Gould Boyum, *Double Exposure: Fiction into Film* (New York: Plume, 1985), 15.

22 Brian McFarlane, *Novel to Film: An Introduction to the Theory of Adaptation* (Oxford: Clarendon Press, 1996), 1.

23 Whelehan (1999), 4.

24 Ray (2000), 38.

25 Albrecht-Crane and Cutchins, 2010, 11.

26 Frederic Jameson, 'Afterword: Adaptation as a Philosophical Problem.' In *True to the Spirit: Film Adaptation and the Question of Fidelity*, (ed.) Colin MacCabe *et al.* (Oxford: Oxford University Press, 2011), 215–33.

27 Brett Westbrook, 'Being Adaptation: The Resistance to Theory,' in *Adaptation Studies: New Approaches*, (eds) Christa Albrecht-Crane and Dennis R. Cutchins (Cranberry, NJ: Associated University Press, 2010), 25.

28 Ray (2000), 44–6. In spite of Ray's protest, these modes of analysis continue to have a substantial presence in *Literature/ Film Quarterly* (founded by James M. Welsh and Tom Erskine in 1973), monographs (e.g. Cahir, *Literature into Film*), edited collections (e.g. Lars Elleström *Media Borders, Multimodality and Intermediality* (Basingstoke: Palgrave Macmillan, 2010); Albrecht-Crane and Cutchins, *Adaptation Studies*; Dennis R. Cutchins, Laurence Raw, and James M. Welsh, *Redefining Adaptation Studies* (Lanham, MD: Scarecrow Press, 2010); MacCabe *et al.*, *True to the Spirit*), and teaching guides (John M. Desmond and Peter J. Hawkes, *Adaptation: Studying Film and Literature* (New York: McGraw-Hill, 2006); Welsh and Lev, *The Literature/Film Reader*; Dennis R. Cutchins *et al.*, *The Pedagogy of Adaptation* (Lanham, MD: Scarecrow Press, 2010).

29 Robert Stam was also highly influential in bringing the theoretical turn to bear on adaptation studies in his monographs, edited collections, and teaching guides (Stam 2000; Robert Stam and Alessandra Raengo, (eds), *A Companion to Literature and Film* (London: Blackwell, 2005); Robert Stam and Alessandra Raengo, (eds), *Literature and Film: A Guide to the Theory and Practice of Film Adaptation* (London: Blackwell, 2004)). *Adaptation*, founded by Deborah Cartmell, Imelda Whelehan, and Ian Hunter in 2008, joins *The Journal of Adaptation in Film and Performance*, founded by Robert Hand and Katja Krebs in 2008, various monographs

(Sanders, *Adaptation and Appropriation*; Christina Geraghty, *Now a Major Motion Picture: Film Adaptations of Literature and Drama* (Lanham, MD: Rowman and Littlefield, 2008)), co-authored books (Cartmell and Whelehan, *Screen Adaptation*), and numerous essay collections edited by Cartmell *et al.* (*Pulping Fictions, Adaptations: From Text to Screen, Screen to Text; The Cambridge Companion to Literature on Screen* (Cambridge: Cambridge University Press, 2007); *The Blackwell Companion to Literature, Film, and Adaptation* (Oxford: Blackwell, 2012)) and by other scholars (Mireia Aragay, *Books in Motion: Adaptation, Intertextuality, Authorship* (Amsterdam: Rodopi, 2005); Rachel Carroll, *Adaptation in Contemporary Culture: Textual Infidelities* (London: Continuum, 2009); Tricia Hopton *et al.*, *Pockets of Change: Adaptations and Cultural Transitions* (Plymouth: Lexington Books, 2011)) in developing the theoretical turn in adaptation studies.

30 Cartmell and Whelehan (eds) 2007; Welsh (ed.) 2007.

31 Cartmell and Whelehan (2010), 11.

32 Sarah Cardwell, *Adaptation Revisited: Television and the Classic Novel* (Manchester: Manchester University Press, 2002), 69.

33 Cahir (2006), 14.

34 Geraghty (2008), 3.

35 Ray (2000), 44.

36 Ray (2000), 47.

37 Cartmell and Whelehan (2010), 22.

38 MacCabe (2011), 8.

39 Cardwell (2002), 72.

40 Cohen 1979; Cardwell 2002; Kamilla Elliott, *Rethinking the Novel/Film Debate* (Cambridge: Cambridge University Press, 2003); Leitch, 2003; Robert Stam, 'Introduction: The Theory and Practice of Adaptation,' in *Literature and Film: A Guide to the Theory and Practice of Film Adaptation*, (eds) Robert Stam and Alessandra Raengo (London: Blackwell, 2004), 1–52.

41 Albrecht-Crane and Cutchins (2010), 17–18.

42 Cahir (2006), 175; Jameson (2011), 226.

43 Linda Hutcheon, *A Theory of Adaptation* (New York and London: Routledge, 2006), 4.

44 Ray (2000), 44–5.

45 See, for example, Cohen (1979).

46 Cartmell *et al.*, (1996).

47 See, for example, MacCabe (2011).

48 See Jeffrey Egan Welch, *Literature and Film: An Annotated Bibliography, 1909–1977* (New York: Garland, 1981).

49 At the risk of seeming hypocritical by not citing the scholars who do this in a segment on the failure to cite prior work, not wanting to discourage new scholars, I leave readers to survey recent work themselves to locate these tendencies.

50 Greg Jenkins, *Stanley Kubrick and the Art of Adaptation: Three Novels, Three Films* (Jefferson, NC: McFarland, 1997), 17.

51 Gilbert Seldes, *The Movies Come from America*. New York: Arno Press Reprint, 1978 [1936].

52 *Bluestone, 1957, Seldes 1936*; Vachel Lindsay, *The Art of the Moving Picture* (New York: Macmillan, 1915).

53 Cohen, Orr, Larsson, Boyum – see Table 1.

54 Ray (2000); Stam (2004).

55 See, for example, Paul J. Niemeyer, *Seeing Hardy: Film and Television Adaptations of the Fiction of Thomas Hardy* (Jefferson, NC: McFarland, 2003); Mary Donaldson-Evans, *Madame Bovary at the Movies: Adaptation, Ideology, Context* (Amsterdam: Rodopi, 2009).

56 While some such slippage is inevitable, I have been troubled to discover that established, celebrated scholars cite the less significant points of newer scholars, while claiming their major points as their own.

57 Where authors have been cited already, consult their references above.

58 Lewis Melville, 'Vanity Fair: Special Review by the Eminent Thackeray Biographer,' *Bioscope* 14.279 (15 February 1912): 415–17.

59 Lindsay (1915).

60 Scott L. Newstok and Ayanna Thompson, (eds) *Weyward Macbeth: Intersections of Race and Performance* (New York: Palgrave Macmillan, 2010).

61 Seymour Chatman, *Story and Discourse: Narrative Structure in Fiction and Film* (Ithaca: Cornell University Press, 1978).

62 John C. Tibbetts and James M. Welsh., *Novels Into Film: The Encyclopedia of Movies Adapted from Books* (New York: Checkmark Books, 1999).

63 Lester Asheim, *From Book to Film: A Comparative Analysis of the*

Content of Selected Novels and the Motion Pictures Based upon Them (Chicago: University of Chicago Press, 1949).

64 André Bazin, 'In Defense of Mixed Cinema,' in *What Is Cinema?*, trans. Hugh Gray (Berkeley: University of California Press, 1967 [1952]), 1.53–75.

65 Jean Mitry, *The Aesthetics and Psychology of the Cinema*, trans. Christopher King (Bloomington: Indiana University Press, 1997 [1963–5]).

66 Geoffrey Wagner, *The Novel and the Cinema* (Rutherford, NJ: Farleigh Dickinson University Press, 1975).

67 Neil Sinyard, *Filming Literature: The Art of Screen Adaptation* (New York: St. Martin's Press, 1986).

68 Jefferson Hunter, *English Filming, English Writing* (Bloomington: Indiana University Press, 2010).

69 Christopher Orr, 'The Discourse on Adaptation,' *Wide Angle* 6.2 1984: 72–6.

70 Morris Beja, *Film and Literature* (New York: Longman, 1976), 80–1.

71 Michael Klein and Gillian Parker, 'Introduction,' *The English Novel and the Movies* (New York: Frederick Ungar, 1981), 1–13.

72 John Ellis, 'The Literary Adaptation,' *Screen* 23 (1982): 3–5.

73 Donald F. Larsson, 'Novel into Film: Some Preliminary Reconsiderations,' in *Transformations in Literature and Film*, (ed.) Leon Golden (Tallahassee: University Press of Florida, 1982), 69–83.

74 Peter Reynolds, *Novel Images: Literature in Performance* (New York: Routledge, 1993).

75 Patrick Cattrysse, 'Film (Adaptation) as Translation: Some Methodological Proposals,' *Target: International Journal of Translation Studies* 4.1 (1992): 53–70.

76 David L. Kranz and Nancy Mellerski, (eds), *In/fidelity: Essays on Film Adaptation* (Newcastle: Cambridge Scholars, 2008).

77 James Naremore, 'Introduction,' *Film Adaptation*, (ed.) James Naremore (New Brunswick. NJ: Rutgers University Press, 2000), 10.

78 André Bazin, 'Adaptation, or the Cinema as Digest,' in *Film Adaptation*, (ed.) James Naremore (New Brunswick, NJ: Rutgers University Press, 2000), 19–27. Original essay date 1948.

79 Simone Murray, *The Adaptation Industry: The Cultural Economy of Contemporary Literary Adaptation* (London: Routledge, 2011).

80 Phyllis Frus and Christy Williams, (eds), *Beyond Adaptation: Essays*

on Radical Transformations of Original Works (Jefferson, NC: McFarland, 2010).

81 Bluestone (1957), 42–6.

82 Bluestone (1957), 12, 10.

83 Bluestone (1957), 5.

84 Westbrook (2010), 42.

85 McFarlane, *Novel to Film*, 210. A year later, James Griffith's *Adaptations as Imitations* (Newark: University of Delaware Press, 1997) offered a less systematic 'inductive,' neo-classical theory of adaptations. It has been less widely read and discussed than McFarlane's narratological theory.

86 Hutcheon (2006), xiv.

87 Deborah Cartmell and Imelda Whelehan, *Screen Adaptation: Impure Cinema* (New York: Palgrave Macmillan, 2010), 21.

88 Cartmell and Whelehan (2010), 22.

89 MacCabe, 2011. Indeed, Bazin now holds the position in adaptation studies that Deleuze holds in cinemas studies; he is everywhere. Introduced to taxonomies of adaptation by Andrew (1980), he is reprinted in Corrigan (1999) and Naremore (2000), cited by Aragay (2005), Stam (2006), Tomasulo (2008), Carroll (2009), Constandinides (2010), DeBona (2010), and present in Cartmell's and Whelehan's 2010 subtitle, *Impure Cinema*, to name only some of his legion appearances.

90 Corrigan (2010).

91 Westbrook (2010), 43.

92 Cartmell and Whelehan (2010), 22.

93 Leitch (2003).

94 Thomas Leitch, 'What *Isn't* an Adaptation?' in *The Blackwell Companion to Literature, Film, and Adaptation.* (ed.) Deborah Cartmell, (Oxford: Blackwell 2012)

95 Leitch (2007).

96 Stam 'Introduction,' 10.

97 Eleanor Rosch, 'Principles of Categorization,' in *Cognition and Categorization*, (eds), Eleanor Rosch and Barbara B. Lloyd (Hillsdale, NJ: Lawrence Erlbaum, 1978), 27–48.

98 Elliott (2003), 11–16.

99 See Elliott (2003), 29.

100 Westbrook (2010), 43.

101 Murray (2008), 8.

102 MacCabe (2011), 5.

103 Michel Foucault, 'What Is an Author?' in *Modern Criticism and Theory: A Reader*, David Lodge and Nigel Wood (eds) (Edinburgh: Pearson Education, 1988), 292. Original essay date 1988.

104 Kamilla Elliott, 'Screened Writers', in *The Blackwell Companion to Literature, Film, and Adaptation*. (ed.) Deborah Cartmell (Blackwell 2012)

105 Hunter (2010), 3.

106 Griselda Pollock 'Editor's Preface: New Encounters,' in *Conceptual Odysseys: Passages to Cultural Analysis*, (ed.) Griselda Pollock (New York: Palgrave, 2007), xv.

107 Mieke Bal, 'Working with Concepts,' in *Conceptual Odysseys: Passages to Cultural Analysis*, (ed.) Griselda Pollock (New York: Palgrave, 2007), 1–10.

108 Elliott (2003), 27–8.

109 Elliott (2003), chapter 5.

110 Edward O. Wilson, *Consilience: The Unity of Knowledge* (New York: Knopf, 1998).

111 Gary Speranza, review of *Sam & Dave*, *Time Barrier Express* (September–October 1979): n.p.

112 Gyatri Spivak, 'Can the Subaltern Speak? Speculations on Widow-Sacrifice,' *Wedge* 1.7/8 (1985): 120–30.

3

Textual identity and adaptive revision: Editing adaptation as a fluid text

John Bryant

Until recently, our profession has taken adaptation to be sub-literary, at best merely tangential to the project of interpretation.[1] Adaptation is creativity's stepchild, always vying for validation, never catching up to its originating source. But this view depends upon an exclusionary and inadequate notion of the written 'work' and the writing process in general. The assumption for geneticists who focus solely on the originating writers is that writing is confined strictly to the texts associated with the creation of the originating *work*. But if adaptation is to achieve its proper textual legitimacy, we need a broader conception of geneticism in which the notion of *work* embraces all versions of a text, including sources and adaptations, and the *creative process* is extended to include all forms of revision, both authorial and cultural.

In the fluid-text approach I propose here, a *work* is the sum of its versions; *creativity* extends beyond the solitary writer, and *writing* is a cultural event transcending media. That is, if we see the writing process as progressing beyond the originating author's work, stretching back in time to sources that precede the work and forward from the moment of publication across genres and media; and if we see creativity as both an individual and social process involving moments of solitary inspiration but also collaboration with readers; then we can conceive of a 'version' of geneticism at its fullest, one that embraces the social text in its broadest material incarnations, and in particular texts in revision, or what I call the *fluid text*.[2] A fluid text is any work that exists in multiple versions in which the primary cause of those versions is some form of revision. Revisions may be performed by originating writers, by their editors and publishers, or by readers and audiences, who reshape the originating work to reflect their own desires for the text, themselves, their culture.

This third category, which I have elsewhere tentatively called 'cultural revision', is the proper arena of *adaptation*.[3] As revising readers, adaptors of the originating version of a work are collaborators in the making of the *work* in its totality. Like translators, they transform a text for new or different audiences, and address new conditions and problems in a culture. Herman Melville is surely the author of *Moby-Dick* (1851), but adaptors generate new versions of the text and thereby re-author the work, giving it new meaning in new contexts, and in some degree drawing out in sharper delineations the originating author's original intentions. My focus here is to explore the ways in which the study of versions and of adaptation and what I call 'adaptive revision' intersect textually, critically, ethically and editorially.

I would like to begin by making a few important distinctions. The ideas and terms involved can be laid out in the following argument:

- Adaptation is an **announced retelling** of an originating text.

- Announced adaptations are distinct from but related to **adaptive revision**, in which an originating writer or adaptor appropriates a borrowed text and, by 'quoting' it, essentially revises it and therefore adapts it, though in an intertextual and necessarily partial rather than comprehensive way.

- Both announced adaptation and adaptive revision are **versions** of the originating or borrowed text.

- The meaning of any adaptation is essentially a measuring of the **critical distances between and among adaptive versions.**

- Interpretation is the analysis of the **strategies of revision** perceived in the making of these textual distances.

- While versions are necessarily interconnected, they possess distinct **textual identities.** The *ethics* of adaptation is knowing and acknowledging **the boundaries of textual identity.**

- Editing adaptation and adaptive revision is best achieved through **digital** and **fluid text** approaches.

I have bulleted these definitions knowing that in the space allotted I cannot argue for them fully. Even so, by putting them on the table, I want to gesture toward the scope and depth of adaptation, and not only the validity, but also the necessity of adaptation studies in the analysis of texts, writing and culture. My principal example is *Moby-Dick* – or rather, I should say, the cultural phenomenon or adapted works associated with this book – as it relates to the matter of creation, interpretation and 'adaptive revision'.

It goes without saying that *adaptation* is an act of interpretation.[4] But to suggest that the adaptor is in some way extending a work or collaborating with the originating author might seem a stretch, especially if we hold authorial intentions to be sacrosanct. We like to place a wall between originating work and its adaptation when it comes to defining textually the *work*. I would like to breach that wall, but not tear it down. The breaching begins when we contemplate the symbiosis of writing and reading. Publishing writers write for readers, and they write in order to be read. Indeed, a text does not truly exist until a reader – even if that reader is 'only' an editor – converts the written words into the mental thoughts those words convey. The act of reading also involves a reader response, which is as sacrosanct as the writer's intentions during isolated acts of composition. Moreover, willful readers notoriously ignore authorial intentions and read or interpret as they wish. Our (mis)reading is an inalienable right. Indeed, we critics make our living by it. Given the very nature of reading and writing, we are hard pressed to insist upon an insurmountable wall dividing originating and adaptive texts.

But adaptation takes us into a specialized arena in which reading and interpretation are themselves embodied in a revision of the originating text. Adaptors are 'revising readers' who enact their interpretations, not through criticism, but by altering the material text itself through quotation, allusion and plagiarism, in what might be called 'partial adaptation' or 'adaptive revision', and in larger more comprehensive projects through announced adaptation. Adaptation is both a transgression of the originating work and a liberation. And like any form of liberation, the adaptor's sense of empowerment can infuriate or delight.

Until fairly recently, adaptation has been taken as a form of textual corruption, and, in fact, a principal impetus for much of modern scholarly editing has been to preserve the textual identity of a given originating work, and that originating work only. Post-authorial versions of a work are typically left out of a scholarly edition for the obvious reason that such adaptations are generally not performed, sanctioned or even witnessed by the originating writer; they have a different textual identity altogether. Different, of course, but not unrelated; and, in fact, the existence of the adaptations of a work helps to establish the post-publication and posthumous reception or 'life' of a work as it continues to be consumed well after the moment of its inception. The delight that a culture takes in revising works by Shakespeare or Melville, let's say, speaks directly to that culture's own evolving identity. Readers show their love of a work by changing it, remaking it, retelling it, adapting it. Indeed, a readership's obsessive revisions of a work insures that work's continued life and, ironically, inspires scholars to study, teach and edit those revered originating works. It would seem only natural, then, for scholarly editions to include rather than exclude adaptation as part of its analysis of the text of the *work*, broadly conceived.

Nevertheless, the exclusion of adaptation from editorial projects seems justified for the sake of establishing and preserving the distinct boundaries of an originating work's textual identity. At the heart of such preservationist editorial projects – and let me be clear that all editing is inherently preservationist whether the editorial object is an originating or adaptive text – is the anxiety that readers and the culture will forget the original text, its wording and the biographical condition of its genesis. Adaptation is taken, then, not so much as a corruption but as the threat of amnesia, a forgetting of the original. However, and interestingly enough, the act of adaptation necessarily requires some awareness of or relation to origination, and that link alone should justify the inclusion of the editing of adaptations and adaptive revision in what might be called the 'normative' scholarly editions of 'great works'. But to expand scholarly editing in this way suggests a shift of focus. Rather than retrieving and preserving the author's 'intended text' of a work as a textual object, fluid text editing attempts to trace the phenomenon of textual evolution by focusing on the text as a dynamic process that charts the changing textual identities of originating version, authorial revisions and adaptive revisions.

As we know, adaptations have been too often judged by the yardstick of fidelity to their originals and too readily disposed as pale imitations or wretched bowdlerizations, driven by mass marketing. But the causes of imitation, censorship and markets are themselves worthy of study, and adaptation gives us direct access to these aesthetic and social phenomena. This critical focus is enough to warrant new, largely digital approaches to the editing of original and adaptive texts in tandem. But adaptation need not be exclusively derivative; it has its own genius and reason for being. Furthermore, we can see originating authors engaged themselves in isolated acts of adaptation. Particularly compelling is the degree to which a focus on particular announced adaptations as discrete but interconnected projects encourages us also to recognize and validate the adaptive nature of intertextual behaviours operating within originating works.[5] I see this kind of 'adaptive revision' happening, for instance, in Melville's contemplation of Shakespeare and in Edward Said's problematic (mis)reading of *Moby-Dick*. And these phenomena, in turn, urge us even more toward a fluid text approach to the editing of adaptation.

Moby-Dick and adaptive revision

As a reader of Shakespeare, Melville sensed not only Shakespeare's greatness but also Shakespeare's inability fully to enact his intentions, or what Melville interpreted Shakespeare's intentions to be. In an 1849 letter to his editor Evert Duyckinck, Melville wishes that Shakespeare 'had lived later, & promenaded in Broadway.'

He argues that in his own Elizabethan day, Shakespeare was forced to wear a 'muzzle ... on [his soul].' 'I hold it a verity,' he wrote, "that even Shakespeare, was not a frank man to the uttermost. And, indeed, who, in this intolerant Universe is, or can be?' But, he concludes, 'the Declaration of Independence makes a difference.'[6] That is, in democratic America and free from courtly censors, Shakespeare would have written more freely, more directly, more dangerously.

A year later, in his review of Hawthorne, Melville claimed that American writers were poised to match, even out-do 'Shakespeare and other masters of the great Art of Telling the Truth.' 'Shakespeares,' he insisted, 'are this day being born on the banks of the Ohio.'[7] Elsewhere, I argue that in over-dramatizing Ahab, Melville was attempting to out-Shakespeare Shakespeare and purge himself of bardolatry.[8] But here, let me add that Melville was also paying homage to Shakespeare by revising, extending – in fact fulfilling – Shakespeare. Melville was acting out the rights of expression denied to Shakespeare but granted, by the American Revolution and the Declaration of Independence, to Melville.

In *Moby-Dick*, Melville was removing the Elizabethan muzzle that Shakespeare had to wear, so that Ahab could speak truths that Shakespeare only thought but dared not speak. Thus, Hamlet is frozen by the question of Being and Nothingness. For Hamlet 'the dread of something after death, / The undiscovered country from whose bourn / No traveller returns, puzzles the will' (*Hamlet* 3.1.77–9). But for Ahab in a thunderstorm at sea, defiance is our 'right worship', and he makes no question of his will to be: 'In the midst of the personified impersonal, a personality stands here... . [T]he queenly personality lives in me, and feels her royal rights.'[9] Defiant Ahab is not 'puzzled'; he does not hide his superior intellect from the queenly Elizabeth; he becomes Elizabeth, with all her rights of imperial self-expression.

Surely, fatherless Ahab is, in part, Melville's rewriting of the father-vexed Hamlet, but this kind of rewriting both is and is not adaptation. Let's explore how Melville's version of Shakespeare may and may not be an adaptation to help grasp the limits of adaptation as a critical and creative phenomenon.

We can pretty much dismiss the idea that in writing *Moby-Dick*, Melville was attempting an adaptation, or 'announced retelling' of Shakespeare. While the text echoes Hamlet, Lear and Macbeth, the novel does not retell those tales, and its borrowings from Shakespeare are no more prominent than the novel's reliance on the Bible or Milton. *Moby-Dick* mixes homage, echo, allusion, quotation, paraphrase and even plagiarism in a kind of inter-textual weaving that is evident in any highly imbricated modern work. But no one would argue that these layerings constitute an 'announced adaptation'. Even so, Melville's text enacts the liberating function of what I mean by 'adaptive revision'. Ahab's defiant soliloquy set in a tempest takes certain liberties of thought not allowed by Elizabeth in Hamlet's less determined soliloquy. Whereas Shakespeare takes death as sleep and dream and then as a puzzlement of the will, Melville figures human consciousness – the fact of its very existence – as a defiance of death. In a sense, Melville's adaptive revision enables Shakespeare to engage more fully in the 'great Art of Telling the Truth.'

Although not an announced adaptation, Melville's version of Shakespeare embedded in *Moby-Dick* supplies us with an epitome of adaptation in general. Melville adopted Shakespeare's voice for Ahab, and like an adaptor, he blended that performed voice with his own voice thereby giving Shakespeare a new presence. An informed, transatlantic reader cannot fail to 'hear' Shakespeare in *Moby-Dick* as it is inflected and transformed through Melville's voice. And yet, Melville's adaptive revision of Shakespeare is an implicit critique of Shakespeare, which, as we have seen, holds the Elizabethan stage in light of American democracy, and both eras in the light of what Ishmael calls the 'ungraspable phantom of life.' To be or not to be? You bet that's the question, but for Melville channelling and revising Shakespeare, that question is not a question but an assertion of will: an emphatic I AM struggling to survive in a republic, at sea, and in confrontation with nothingness and 'the naught beyond.' Melville's adaptive revision frees Shakespeare to speak what previously was unspoken or even unspeakable.

I would like to seize upon this liberationist potential as a springboard to a fluid-text approach to adaptation. What I am calling Melville's adaptive revision of Shakespeare is also Melville's version of Shakespeare, not at all a retelling of Hamlet but a re-writing and a mingling of two 'textual identities', Melville and Shakespeare. Shortly, I want to explore how others have rewritten Melville as well so that, going forward in the broader creative collaborative process, today's adaptors have incorporated Melville's textual identity into their own, perhaps with a congruent agenda of freeing Melville to engage 'the great Art of Telling the Truth.' But for the moment, let's continue to inspect the larger theoretical field of textual fluidity, including its textual, critical, editorial and ethical dimensions.

Adaptation and ethics

Textually speaking, and as noted before, a written *work* (as textual object) is the sum of its versions. It is the collocation of texts derived from various activities: the borrowing from sources, revisions found in manuscript, in the tinkerings in proofs, in the expurgations of subsequent editions, and the like. The announced retellings of adaptation (and translation as well) are interpretive creations, which, as readers' revisions, are homologous versions that find shelter under the ever-lifting umbrella of the further *workings* associated with an originating text. From a fluid-text perspective, adaptation extends the textual field of creativity and hence interpretation.

Critically speaking, the focus of fluid text analysis cannot be on single versions, but rather on how to measure the critical distances between versions and on what is the meaning inherent in that distancing. But the frequently heard question of whether an adaptation is 'true to its original' or whether it preserves the integrity of the original misconstrues the problem of distance. The anxiety that adaptation cheapens the original stems from a kind of 'textual narcissism' in which we not only assume that the goal of adaptation is to reproduce the original 'faithfully', but also presume that it never can be. In fact, adaptation has the entirely different agenda of revising the original, for whatever social or aesthetic end, through a re-performance or re-writing of it, in order to reposition the originating text in a new cultural context.

This textual narcissism I speak of is itself a fantasy of retrospection that is, interestingly enough, contingent upon the very existence of adaptation. Consider how the nature of an 'original' changes in retrospect once it has become adapted. When *Moby-Dick* first appeared, no reader would have thought at the time to remark how close the novel comes to the 'original' of itself; such a comment would be logically absurd. Similarly, the anxiety over the fidelity of an original is absurd because it is a phantom that exists not in the original but only after the original has been adapted. Only when we read *Moby-Dick* in the context of subsequent versions of it do we begin to worry about being faithful to the original. But this worry is a false concern because the original version of *Moby-Dick* has not been altered by the revisionary adaptations of it; its newly achieved status as 'the original' remains intact. Put differently, the integrity of the original exists only in the concrete and material particulars – the words on the first edition page or its variants in subsequent authorized editions – that constitute the textual identity of the originating version. A fluid text approach detaches itself from the retrospective anxieties that derive from a false sense of originality and respects the textual identities of both adaptation and original, but does so primarily to sharpen the focus on the differences between the identities and how one textual identity may be seen to evolve into the other.

In this regard, ethics follows aesthetics. Adaptation is not only inevitable; it is a form of retelling that is so inherently irresistible to human beings that it is an inalienable right. It is a remix; it is a mash-up. In this regard, adaptation may be seen as an epitome of multicultural democracy with its inescapable anxieties over the evolution of one's ethnicity, the threat of assimilation, the forging of a new identity and the retention or forgetting of past identities. Texts evolve through adaptation just as people adapt and evolve between and within cultures. We cannot know how textual identities evolve – or, in the case of adaptive revision, how they are mixed – until we can identify those identities. Editing is the process by which we gather, define, sort, search, sequentialize and narrativize textual identities, just as we might lay out our ancestors in a genealogical 'family tree' and tell the story of how these separate identities grew, merged and evolved.

How, then, might we edit adaptation? The challenge here, as with editing any fluid text, is to maximize access to all versions for all people, to clarify the boundaries between textual identities so that the mixing of versions can be perceived, and to facilitate the reader's navigation from version to version. Editing is a critical enactment of ethics, for its goal is to make us as aware of the boundaries that define textual identities as we are of the boundaries of our own evolving identity.

Just as Melville rewrote Shakespeare, so have we rewritten Melville. And just as the distances we find in Melville's revising of Shakespeare have meaning, so, too, are contemporary rewritings of *Moby-Dick* a reflection of our need to adapt Melville's vision into ours, with, of course, critical and perhaps unintended consequences. To explore these complexities, I draw upon an intriguing textual episode related in my essay titled 'Rewriting *Moby-Dick*', a part of which I quote below, altering it slightly from its original in order to adapt it in this volume for those focused on adaptation studies.[10]

Rewriting *Moby-Dick*

Less than a week after the attacks of 9/11, critic Edward Said condemned the 'senseless destruction' based on the misguided 'religious and political abstractions and reductive myths' of terrorists.[11] He appealed for more 'sense' and less 'claptrap' in exposing 'the roots of terror in injustice' so that 'terrorists [may be] isolated, deterred or put out of business.' But, Said argued, the media's conversion of Osama bin Laden into a cartoon villain falsely prioritizes the agents of destruction over the imperialism that incites them.

Said then made the following comparison: 'collective passions are being funneled into a drive for war that uncannily resembles Captain Ahab in pursuit of Moby Dick.' The prophetic implication was that the Bush administration had become derailed by its benighted anger over this affront to its 'imperial power'.

In a subsequent interview, Said clarified his reference to Melville. Ahab, he explained, will pursue Moby Dick 'to the ends of the Earth'; his mission is 'suicidal'.[12] Bush, he continued, has a similarly 'apocalyptic' vision: he has made bin Laden into 'a symbol of all that's evil', and like Moby Dick, he will be falsely viewed as something 'mythological', and the justification for retaliatory violence that will make us as demonic as our false image of bin Laden. To crystallize his argument, Said describes Ahab's death: 'In the final scene of the novel, Captain Ahab is being borne out to sea, wrapped around the white whale with the rope of his own harpoon and going obviously to his death. It was a scene of almost suicidal finality.' The powerful image underscores Said's point that America's obsession to kill a terrorist rather than understand terrorism is America's undoing: like Ahab we are tangled to a beast of our own creation.

But in fact, the 'final scene' Said recounts is not in *Moby-Dick*. In Melville's version, Ahab's departure is far less dramatic. Ahab harpoons Moby Dick, and as the white whale races off, the line attached to him whizzes out of the tub in Ahab's whaleboat. A kink in the line creates a flying loop that seizes Ahab by the neck, garottes him and zips him into the sea. He simply disappears: swiftly, silently, anticlimactically. Ahab's demise occurs so quickly that readers can miss it. Given Melville's effort to stage Ahab as if he were Hamlet, Macbeth or Lear, we expect more sound and fury; but in Melville's version of *Moby-Dick*, Ahab is gone before we know it.

In the originating novel, Ahab is killed not by a whale but a whale line, and Melville prepares us for this fact in earlier chapters that explain the physical and metaphorical 'lines' that shape the conditions of whaling and the fates of whaling men. Consider the meaning of rope. In 'The Line' (Ch. 61), Ishmael explains its destructive properties. If not properly coiled in its tub, the whale line can snatch you and take you down. Moreover, Melville weaves strands of oriental imagery into his descriptions of whale lines. The prophetic Parsee, Fedallah, declares that only hemp can destroy Ahab; only hemp, and hemp alone, the fabric of whale lines, which in 'The Line', Ishmael calls 'a dusky, dark fellow, a sort of Indian.' Furthermore, in Ahab's demise, the line takes Ahab out 'voicelessly as Turkish mutes bowstring their victim.' Thus, in Melville's death scene, Ahab is not entangled by lines on the symbolic whale, as Said relates it. Instead, he is strangled by a symbolic, orientalized line linked to Fedallah, the orientalized emblem of Ahab's fate.

Of course, rope is integral to Said's rewriting of Ahab's demise: Said sees Ahab 'wrapped around the white whale with the rope of his own harpoon', so that the impression of Ahab's (and America's) fatal obsession with the terroristic whale is associated with a rope of his own undoing, much like the ironic death by hemp that Fedallah prophesies for Ahab. But Said adaptively revises this image of entanglement not from Melville's novel but from the powerful conclusion of John Huston's 1956 film version. In this announced adaptation, Ahab, played by Gregory Peck, harpoons Moby Dick, falls into the sea and climbs on to the back of the whale, which is wrapped in whale lines. The whale submerges with Ahab stabbing away, and when it surfaces, the drowned Ahab is tangled in the harpoon lines as if crucified. The rocking of the cinematic whale imparts movement to Ahab's lifeless arm, which beckons the crew to their cinematic annihilation.

This rendition of Ahab's death is powerful cinema, but it was not entirely invented for the film. It comes from another scene in *Moby-Dick*. In adapting Melville's novel, screenwriter Ray Bradbury had triumphantly reported to Huston that he had given the 'heave' to Fedallah, cutting him entirely from the film. And his decision to eradicate Fedallah and the dense imbrication of orientalist allusion that he represents, constitutes by itself a politically significant revision strategy. A version of *Moby-Dick* without Fedallah poses a significant critical distance between novel and film. As for the revision of Ahab's death scene, Bradbury claims, 'That's my addition; that's not Melville. I eliminated Fedallah and allowed Moby Dick to come into direct contact with Ahab.'[13] But, in fact, Bradbury's version of Ahab's demise – the version Said recalls – is not the 'addition' he claims it is. Bradbury cribbed it from Melville. Having given Fedallah the 'heave', Bradbury nevertheless assigned to Ahab a version of the death scene that Melville had given to Fedallah.

In 'The Chase – Second Day' (Ch. 134), the Parsee is reported missing at sea. However, on the third day, the dead Fedallah returns: 'Lashed round and round to the fish's back; pinioned in the turns upon turns in which, during the past night, the whale had reeled the involutions of the lines around him, the half torn body of the Parsee was seen; ... his distended eyes turned full upon old Ahab.'[14]. In rewriting Melville's *Moby-Dick* for the Huston film, Bradbury puts Gregory Peck as Ahab in Fedallah's place and transforms Fedallah's 'distended eyes' staring at Ahab 'into Ahab's lifeless beckoning of the crew.' In the film, the crew respond to the beckoning 'dead arm' and 'pursue the white whale to their doom.' Bradbury's revision also transforms Melville's ineffectual crew stationed on the *Pequod*, who go down with the ship when Moby Dick strikes it, into a rage-enabled crew dispersed in whaleboats destroyed by the whale's repeated pummelings. It is a scene of heroic loyalty, resistance and martyrdom in the face of merciless 'intelligent malignity'.[15]

Bradbury's rewriting of Ahab's death consists of three

'distancings': the elimination of Fedallah, the transference of Fedallah's entanglement in whale lines to Ahab and the transformation of Fedallah's prophetic stare into Ahab's martyred beckoning arm. These strategic revisions of Fedallah have suggestive affinities with Said's linking of Ahab's demise to the terrorist attacks and his own predictions for post-9/11 America. Of course, Said's rewriting of *Moby-Dick* is an adaptive revision, not an announced retelling of the novel, and it might be taken as an honest confusion of a great critic who has otherwise cogently nailed his flag to Melville's mast-head. But in remembering Bradbury's film as Melville's novel, Said has also mixed two versions of *Moby-Dick*, and rendered that conflation of textual identities in print.

For the purposes of transforming a complicated novel into a memorable film, Bradbury's rewriting of *Moby-Dick* is, from the perspective of concision if not politics, remarkably effective. Said's adaptive revision of the film for his own political statement, however, is more complicated. His revision process has two critical consequences: by quoting Bradbury, Said not only validates the textual identity of Bradbury's version but also, through his adaptive revision, makes an application of the adaptation that, by virtue of its being in print, constitutes its own sub-version. And, secondly, by extending the whale-line symbolism to present-day politics, he discloses a cultural necessity in the dynamic of rewriting of *Moby-Dick*. To clarify this dynamic, let's consider Melville's own critique of orientalism.

In *Moby-Dick*, politics and water are wedded. In earlier works, Melville had drawn upon his years at sea as an occasion to critique imperialism, evangelism, American politics, naval authoritarianism, slavery and immigration. However, in writing *Moby-Dick*, he would travel waters he had never actually sailed. Instead of turning west into the familiar Pacific, the *Pequod* turns east into the Indian Ocean, China Sea and waters 'off Japan.' Melville was writing beyond personal experience and depicted the 'Orient' exclusively through written sources, or what Said calls the 'representative figures, or tropes' of 'Orientalist discourse.'[16] In some instances, Melville's rhetoric betrays a Westerner's dependency upon what Said calls the 'clap trap' mysticism of orientalism in its various modalities: Islamic, Persian, Hindu, Chinese and Philippine. But Melville was able to work beyond what Said calls the 'vacillation between the familiar and the alien'[17] that is typical of Western stereotypes. With Fedallah and Queequeg, Melville attempts to familiarize the alien East, in order to imagine a more diverse West. His use of Fedallah amounts to a controlled deconstruction of the culture's pernicious orientalism.

Although dark-skinned Fedallah commands a lighter-skinned crew of 'Manillas, a race notorious for a certain diabolism of subtlety',[18] he is himself a 'Parsee', belonging to an Indian sect of Zoroastrians descended from Persia, yet he has an Arabic name. He wears a turban and yet a Chinese jacket. In effect, Fedallah is a cosmopolitan concatenation of oriental tags: a stereotype and yet a parody of stereotyping. But Melville's more effective deconstruction of orientalism is in Fedallah's role as Ahab's prophetic other self in deconstructing outmoded notions of fate.

Part of Melville's daring in writing *Moby-Dick* was to detach the notion of 'fate' from the gods, linking it instead to ontology. His stated position is to dismiss 'predictions from without' and locate our fate in 'the innermost necessities of our being'.[19] Fate is not supernatural; nor is it 'character'; it is located in an argument regarding consciousness itself reminiscent of Hamlet: To be is to deny hierarchies beyond the self: to be is to defy. But to defy is to die and not be. As an emblem for the fate of being, Fedallah is both familiar and alien. Rather than being the 'clap trap' of orientalism, Fedallah is the Orient's revenge. He redefines human necessity and denial, and serves, too, as an ironic critique of Western stereotyping.

According to Dorothee Finkelstein, Fedallah's name recalls the 'Fedai' or avenging angels, 'a secret order of Islamic mystics pledged to commit murder in the service of Allah.'[20] For centuries and in recent decades, *fedayeen* has been a word in the Islamic world ascribed to terrorists and terrorist organizations. The Fedai were also associated with the eleventh-century 'Assassins', who acted under the influence of hashish, which is derived from hemp, which is the fabric of rope, which is the symbol of Ahab's fate. For Finkelstein, Fedallah is a killer 'sent to "assassinate" Ahab, the heretic, who will be killed by the secret weapon which makes assassination possible – hashish, or hemp – i.e. intoxication beyond the reach of reason'.[21]

Finkelstein's etymology binds Fedallah to the Orient, mysticism, terror, rope and 'fate'. Ahab's hyper-awareness of the inexplicable fact of consciousness and his defiance of God's indifference amounts to the 'fate' of his ontological arrogance, which prevents him from correctly interpreting Fedallah's prophetic signs. In failing to comprehend Fedallah's riddles as riddles, he exposes the limits of his self-knowledge. And to extend Ahab's fateful ontology politically, Ahab's misreading of Fedallah's prophecies is tantamount to a misreading of the orient. A captain of industry, Ahab cleaves to his 'assassin' Fedallah, careless of the Parsee's complicity in the mutual self-destruction inherent in his ontological and imperialist venture. Ahab and Fedallah – like Christian, Muslim and Jew – have mingled identities; but they die separately, each caught up in Western whale lines made of Eastern hemp.

Given Melville's critique, Bradbury's deletion of Fedallah and yet his transference of Fedallah's death on to Ahab are aesthetic revisions with political ramifications. For anyone measuring the distance between novel and film, the absence of Fedallah constitutes an uncanny presence. In transforming Fedallah's death stare at Ahab into Ahab's crucified pose and beckoning of the crew, Bradbury replaces Fedallah's oriental gaze with Ahab's Christian martyrdom, thus effectively westernizing Melville's critique of orientalism. Bradbury's *Moby Dick* concludes with a scene of futile but heroic resistance to the white whale, an indestructible symbol of all that needs to be destroyed. Released in 1956, in the decade after the revelations of Hitler's genocide and at the height of the Cold War, the film may deny Melville's warning against an Ahabian imperialism that neglects the East, but with Ahab now a martyr in the fight against evil, and with his crew in blind allegiance to mad authority, it is an apt, post-McCarthy warning against the absurdity of demonization, extremism and that blind heroism that leaves the surviving Ishmael (and America) yet 'another orphan'.[22]

But to return to Said's rewriting of *Moby-Dick* and the problem of textual identity: Most would argue that Said has not revised Melville; he has simply paraphrased the ending of Bradbury's *Moby Dick* and misattributed it to Melville's *Moby-Dick*. At worst, Said has made an honest mistake. But let's consider the distancing, inevitability and consequences of that mistake. Paraphrase is a form of adaptive revision because the paraphraser creates a new text out of a source text, and that new text is a materially revised version of the original. Since no act of textual transformation is without interpretation, a paraphrastic version is all the more significant as a form of revision or intra-lingual translation. When properly cited, the identity of a paraphrase is distinguishable from its source. But

Said's unexplained mixing of versions – Bradbury and Melville – ambiguates textual identities. Presumably, the confusion derives from the inevitable slippage between the false memory of a text and its readily inspected material text. Memory (false or true) trumps textuality, and plays fast and loose with our desire to make texts in our own image. Said's apparent memory lapse, then, is emblematic of our own cultural amnesia: we know the text we think we know or want to know, and we forget the variant textual identities of the umbrella work and the differences and distances it covers. Thus, by confusing the boundaries between originating text, announced adaptation and the text of his own paraphrastic adaptive revision, Said's mixing of textual identities perpetuates, despite his own critique of orientalism, Bradbury's erasure of Melville's similar critique of orientalism.

Said's rewriting of *Moby-Dick* is a meaningful textual event. It is an adaptive revision of Melville's text and Bradbury's text into a separable but linked textual identity. But to make Said's version interpretable, we must edit the event, so that its mixture of textual identities can be disambiguated. Thus, in returning to a fluid text approach to adaptation, let me conclude with a final focus on what constitutes a version or adaptation, and on the interdependency of editing and interpretation.

Adaptation as distance and rhetoric

Earlier, I observed that announced adaptation and adaptive revision are versions. Versions are not by themselves sacrosanct; that is, they are, like the versions that come before them and after, subject to revision. Just as Melville revises Shakespeare during his moment in history, and Bradbury revises *Moby-Dick* for his moment, so, too, does Said remix Melville and Bradbury, creating a revision suited to his. But for a text to exist as an identifiable version of something, it must have boundaries that define its textual identity *vis à vis* the textual identities of other versions. Editors of scholarly editions clarify the walls that distinguish one text from another, but, as I have argued from the beginning, a distinctive feature of cultural evolution is that these textual walls are permeable and often breached through adaptation. The critical question, then, is what meanings can we make in assessing the relation of adaptive and originating text? And the editorial problem is how to make these versions accessible; how might the editor clarify the boundaries of related textual identities and provide methods of navigating those versions? But editing itself is a critical act because identifying a version means performing the interpretive act of measuring the distance between versions to confirm that the two are indeed versions to begin with. How, then, do the editor and critic measure the meaningful distance between versions?

If written works can be known by their rhetorical strategies, then versions, like any written work, can be similarly defined, with the added understanding that the act of revision, which generates the version, is itself a rhetorical strategy. We know a version, then, not only by its revisions, but also by its revision strategy. A revision strategy may be defined as a set of textual changes designed to have a rhetorical effect that is meaningfully distinct, or distant, from its original. Indeed, I would say that if a revised text reveals to us no revision strategy distinct from its original's rhetorical strategy, it is probably not a version in its own right, but rather the product of a kind of tactical tinkering. Put another way, for a version to have its own textual identity, its revision strategy must create a theorizable distance from its predecessor.

For instance, Bradbury's removal of Fedallah and reassignment of his death to Ahab is an erasure designed primarily, no doubt, for no other tactical reason than to cut the film to a manageable length, but as an erasure of the Orient, the removal of Fedallah also appears strategic to readers; it now has interpretive consequences: the substitution of Fedallah's orientalism with Ahab's Christian martyrdom re-makes the film's conclusion into an argument against cold war fanaticism. Needless to say, the loss of Fedallah is a missed opportunity to critique orientalism in a twentieth-century context, just as Melville had critiqued it in his own century. Instead, the film's rhetorical revision strategy is to privilege cold war anxieties over Middle East tensions, which in 1956 were no less evident in the Third World than in 1851, and which by 2001 would prove disastrous globally.

Said's privileging of Bradbury's adaptation in order to crystallize the relation of America and terrorism reveals another, more ironic rhetorical strategy. In his adaptive revision of Bradbury's announced adaptation, Said redirects reactionary Western anger against terrorists on to the causes of terrorism. Said's version of *Moby-Dick* re-focuses attention on the Orient but not as a conscious critique of Bradbury's erasure. By attributing the film's death scene to Melville, Said mixes versions and reveals a rhetorical path not taken: by stressing Ahab's anger as conveyed through Bradbury, Said forgets Fedallah's prophesy of Ahab's demise and Fedallah's far deeper warning of the East's revenge upon the West. These three textual identities – Melville's novel, Bradbury's screenplay, Said's remix – are versions of a work called *Moby-Dick*. Each grew from a textual identity that precedes it; each is vitally connected to the other; each involves adaptive revisions; and each is definable by its distinct revision strategy.

While I do not have space here to propose detailed protocols for the editing of adaptation, I would be remiss in not underscoring the critical function of fluid text editing. If Said's appropriation of Melville tells us anything, it is that our ability to forget textual identities is itself meaningful. Our role as editors and interpreters of adaptation is to prevent amnesia, or at least provide ways to account for it. The critical and ethical function of editing is to preserve not just the past, but also our textual links to the past.

With today's swiftly advancing digital technology, textual editing is now poised to bring readers in contact with all versions of a written work. In the Melville Electronic Library (MEL), an online critical archive of Melville's writing and texts associated with it, users will be able to witness the array of versions associated with Melville's works. With a tool called TextLab, presently under development at Hofstra University, they will be able to mark-up revision sites on manuscript leaves, transcribe the revision texts on those leaves, generate revision sequences that show the steps Melville took in revising his text, and then compose revision narratives that explain the sequence of steps. TextLab will also allow you to generate a full diplomatic transcription of each leaf, a base version of the text that maps all revision sites, sequences and narratives; and a user-friendly 'reading text' of the work in manuscript. Visitors to MEL will also have access to TextLab and can work interactively with scholars to track revisions and develop alternative revision sequences and narratives. With another tool called Melville ReMix being developed at MIT, users can create links between sources, Melville texts and adaptations. For instance, they might bring into one digital workspace texts from Shakespeare

or from plagiarized whaling sources together with their corresponding adaptive revisions in *Moby-Dick*. Or they could bring
together four variant texts: Melville's original of Ahab's death
scene, Bradbury's film script, Huston's filming of that script and
Said's quotation of it. Such editorial tools as TextLab and Melville
ReMix empower readers to visualize, narrativize and critically
reproduce the otherwise invisible energy fields that constitute the
cultural revisions embedded in adaptation. And by participating in
these interpretive and editorial acts, readers will engage in a new
kind of critical thinking that asks them to read texts as they evolve,
and to see their own identities and their culture's identity as a form
of evolution as well.

Textual editors like to retell a little allegory, which I here freely
adapt for a conclusion on adaptation. One day a ship set sail, and
in its long journey, it would stop in one port after another to refit
its riggings. After many years at sea, the crew had replaced each
rope, plank and rib of the ship. It had replaced the rotted deck, and
put up new sails, masts and spars. The crew as well had changed;
the sailors had died or run off and been replaced by new seamen;
the first and second mates had died. The skipper was replaced as
well. Even the name of the ship and its figurehead were changed.
In fact, the owners had sold it to another shipping firm. So after its
many years at sea, and when the ship finally returned to port, not
a sliver of the original ship had survived. So, I put it to you: What
is this ship?

As an announced retelling of an earlier work, an adaptation
cannot exist without its tether to its originating source. When
audiences lose their hold on this tether, the adaptation becomes
at best a retelling only, like a fairy tale whose Ur-text cannot be
found. And if readers were to forget as well the original story
it retells, the adaptation would become perhaps an originating
textual identity of its own, a text without a link to a defining past
or originating source.

What, then, is this ship? A version or adaptation, moored in
some way to the narrative of its origination? Or is it a vessel
untethered, without a link to its former selves? Only memory keeps
the ship tethered to its textual past. And critics and editors are the
keepers of that memory.

Notes

1   In *A Theory of Adaptation* (Oxford: Routledge, 2006), Linda Hutcheon offers a thoroughly substantiated alternative, arguing for the critical relevance of adaptation, calling it 'repetition without replication' (xvi, 7).

2   John Bryant, *The Fluid Text: Editing Revision for Book and Screen* (Ann Arbor: U of Michigan P, 2002). For further extensions on the critical applications of fluid text analysis and editing, see my 'Versions of *Moby-Dick*: Plagiarism, Censorship, and Some Notes toward an Ethics of the Fluid Text,' *Variants* 4 (2005): 1–27; and 'Witness and Access: The Uses of the Fluid Text,' *Textual Cultures* 2.1 (Spring 2007): 16–42.

3   This essay is an extension of the notion of 'cultural revision' introduced but not fully developed in *The Fluid Text* (62, 108–10). In *A Theory of Adaptation*, Hutcheon draws a parallel between adaption and fluid texts in general (Hutcheon 95) and acknowledges her particular interest in adaptation as a form of 'cultural revision' (170–1). One focus here is to build on our independent but similar thinking on 'oscillation'—a word we both use in different contexts regarding revision and the reading of originating and adaptive texts—as a way of addressing the need for and challenge of editing adaptation.

4   As Hutcheon succinctly puts it, 'adaptors are first interpreters and then creators' (18).

5   Like many who study adaptation, Hutcheon concludes that 'In the workings of the imagination, adaptation is the norm, not the exception' (177), and she is, therefore, inclined to include a wide-range of works under the rubric of adaptation. However, she draws the line at fragmentary as opposed to 'extended engagements,' such as literary allusion, echoes, musical sampling, and plagiarism (9, 170). My argument, though, is that these borrowings are one writer's rewriting or version of another writer and as a form of 'adaptive revision' can be included as adaptation.

6   Herman Melville, *Correspondence*, (ed.) Lynn C. Horth (Evanston and Chicago: Northwestern University Press and The Newberry Library, 1993), 120.

7   Herman Melville, *The Piazza Tales, and Other Prose Pieces, 1839–1860*, Harrison Hayford, Alma MacDougall, and G. Thomas Tanselle (eds) (Evanston and Chicago: Northwestern University Press and The Newberry Library, 1987), 244, 245.

8   John Bryant, '*Moby-Dick* as Revolution,' in *The Cambridge Companion to Herman Melville*, (ed.) Robert S. Levine (New York: Cambridge University Press, 1998), 65–90. Rpt. in Harold Bloom (ed.), *Moby-Dick* (Chelsea House, 2007).

9   Herman Melville, *Moby-Dick* (New York: Longman, 2006), Ch. 119.

10   John Bryant, 'Rewriting *Moby-Dick*: Politics, Textual Identity, and the Revision Narrative.' *PMLA* 125.4 (2010): 1043–60. In revising part of the Said section of the 2010 essay for inclusion in this section of my 2012 essay on adaptation, I freely acknowledge the irony of this 'adaptive revision' designed to adapt an earlier text so that it will speak more directly to the problem of adaptation. I have added text and terminology not present in the originating text, and I am happy for the opportunity to do so because the revision process has given me new words by which to explain myself more clearly.

11   Edward Said, 'There Are Many Islams,' *London Observer* (16 September 2001).

12   David Barsamian, 'Edward Said Interview,' *The Progressive*. The Progressive Magazine. November 2001. Web. 12 October 2008.

13   Andersen, Kurt. 'He Rises' (interview with Ray Bradbury). *American Icons: Moby-Dick*. Studio 360, Public Radio International. n.d. Web. 12 October 2008.

14   Melville (2006), 496.

15   Melville (2006), 175.

16   Edward Said, *Orientalism*. 25th Anniversary edn. (1978; New York: Vintage, 2003), 71–72.

17   Said, 72.

18   Melville (2006), 202.

19   Melville (2006), 160.

20   Dorothee Metlitsky Finkelstein, *Melville's Orienda* (New Haven, CT: Yale University Press, 1961), 230.

21   Finkelstein, 234.

22   Melville (2006), 500.

4

Dialogizing adaptation studies: From one-way transport to a dialogic two-way process

Jørgen Bruhn

Introduction

Argentinian writer Jorge Luis Borges was a crucial predecessor of contemporary understandings of literature, text and writing. Borges considered literary history an open, fluid structure: a kind of mobile, changing in structure and scope every time a sufficiently important new work enters the literary scene. After the publication of James Joyce's *Ulysses*, the meaning of Homer's *Odyssey* changed, if ever so slightly, and its position in literary history has been altered. This somewhat counterintuitive understanding of history – new texts changing older literary history – was perhaps a result of Borges' speculative ideas about time and repetition, or it may have been powered by more familiar philosophical thoughts from, for instance, hermeneutics and phenomenology. From the hermeneutic philosopher Gadamer's point of view, we cannot establish an objective version of literary history, we are instead forced to establish a reception history of a given work in relation to our own understanding of it, as well as the contexts surrounding the work.

In other words: Borges and Gadamer suggest that a one-way route between an originary text and its successors is as naïve and impossible as Søren Kierkegaard's pseudonymous Constantin Constantius, who dreams of repeating the trip he once made to Berlin: repetition is an illusion.[1] Any rewriting or adaptation of a text is always influencing the original work and even the most 'loyal' or repetitive adaptation imaginable is bound to be unsuccessful in terms of copying the original. Or, to quote adaptation scholar Thomas Leitch: 'whatever their faults, the source texts will always be better at being themselves.'[2]

In this chapter I wish to show that such an idea concerning the dialogic, interdependent interrelation between texts, and its successors, may prove useful when we consider another area of cultural analysis, namely the studies of the transformation from literature into film that I consider a part of the wider field of adaptation studies.

Adaptation studies

The study of adaptation from novel to film, from Bluestone's 1957 classic *Novels into Film* and up until today, has been transformed in recent years. Compared to earlier decades, a great number of (what used to be the) fundamental ideas concerning medium specificity and the evaluative question of fidelity towards the literary source now seem to have been more or less overcome.[3]

After decades of adaptation studies being a relatively secluded field, devoid of any attractive aura, several studies – articles, books, conferences and even journals – manifest this higher interest towards the subject from the academic community. I believe that a change in adaption studies might come from discussions of methodology and theory rather than from investigating more and more widespread examples. The aim of such theoretical discourse should probably not be to establish one Grand Theory; the systematic and theoretical discussions should instead try to answer questions related to both *methodological* debates and *cultural and historical* discussions. The basic systematic and theoretical questions that need to be asked over and over again include: how do adaptations from novel to film resemble comparable media-transformations between other media? What is being transferred from one medium to another? The *cultural and historical* investigations may include questions like: what is the place of novel-to-film adaptations in contemporary society, and how does this position differ from earlier historical constellations? In what ways have ideas of fidelity or originality changed historically? And what does the phenomenon of novel-to-film adaptations do to the idea of literature as the more or less foundational element in Western culture?

Unfortunately, much of the current boom in adaptation studies lies beyond both the 'methodological' debates and the 'cultural and historical' questions; most studies conduct (often very valuable) case studies, which are still the predominant form of novel to film studies.[4] The problem with case studies is, of course, that they tend to produce an atomistic and often non-generalizable form of knowledge, a 'schlechte Unendlichkeit', in the words of Hegel, a 'bad' infinity of isolated insights. There are, of course, exceptions to this rule: Robert Stam's idea of reading literature through film and thus avoiding case study criticism is a fruitful reaction to the problems of adaptation studies; Thomas Leitch's attempt to read adaptations more thematically avoids the strict from-one-novel-to-one-film approach, too; Kamilla Elliott's *Rethinking the Novel/Film debate* rearranges and works through basic questions underlying the entire literature-film debate, partly by discussing older material posing familiar questions again; and both Linda Hutcheon and Lars Elleström stress the fact that novel to film adaptation studies must necessarily be understood as part of a larger 'transmedial' (Chapter 6, this volume) or 'adaptation'(Hutcheon's *A Theory of Adaptation*) field of research.[5] In my own contribution below, I will suggest a discussion of the methodology of adaptation, that is, the questions concerning the micro-relation of the two texts of novel to film adaptation, but I believe that the ideas related to the novel-to-film adaptations may be generalized to the adaption field as a whole. A short case study is provided in order to exemplify my methodological points.

Establishing a new relation between source and result in adaptation studies

There is a crucial insight to be developed concerning what I would like to call the dialogic relation between the media engaged in adaptation. With dialogic, I refer to a dimension of the adaptation process that is probably well known and familiar to students (and practitioners) of adaptation, but it is nevertheless an aspect that is seldom actively investigated, and consequently it is not considered a central element in adaptation research. I shall argue that whenever a source text – say, a novel – is turned into another medium – say, a film – two things happen simultaneously. The most obvious part, and the one that has been studied the most intensely in adaptation research, is the way that novelistic plot, main characters, settings and thematic content in the source text is transferred into a new medium. It is the selection of parts of the source text for the voyage from one medium to another that makes it possible to make some kind of adaptation analysis that must necessarily, and I stress this, take as its starting point the vexed question of similarities and differences (but without investing these questions with normative and/or hierarchical evaluations). In other words, I think it is impossible to conceive of any analysis of adaption without some kind of comparative move establishing what is similar and what is different in the two (or more) texts involved.

I want to focus on the fact that when a scriptwriter or a director has turned the lifted or loaned parts of a source text into a new, aesthetic text, the original text has been changed. The obvious objection to this claim would be that nothing is changed in the source text after it has been turned into film, and this is, in one sense, true: the text – the amount of words in the novel, for instance – will of course be identical after the adaptation. The parts used in the film version have not been removed from the text, and no pictures consisting of print or pixels are being inserted in the novel that was not there in the first place. The fact that literature is an allographic medium (following Nelson Goodman's definition) is one reason for this; there simply is no place to go and 'steal' from the original; the only possible manoeuvre is to copy (parts) of an earlier text.

The change I am advocating here is not easy to establish within conventional analytical frameworks, so let me briefly mention the two basic ways in which it is normally agreed upon that source texts may change in the adaptation process.

- *Editorial/authorial changes in the paratext* (following G. Genette's terminology): the well-known changes in cover, blurbs and other strategies often subsumed under the disclaimer 'Now a major motion picture'.

- *Changes in readers' reception*: this is a very large category including 'popular' readers acknowledging new aspects to an otherwise well-known text after an adaptation; expert/professional readers' discussions of adaptations as 'interpretations' of a work; changes in hierarchical position according to canon-formation or age-differentiation (a children's book being transformed into a grown up text, for instance).

These elements constitute what I think is an undervalued aspect of the adaptation process, and in order to include this in our understanding of adaptation, I suggest that adaptation studies should avoid an exaggerated goal-orientedness (focusing on the end result) and instead try to describe, analyse and interpret the inherent meaning in *the process of adapting*. Adaptation (be it from novel to film or between other media) ought to be regarded as a two-way process instead of a form of one-way transport. And we should therefore not take for granted the idea that adaptation studies is 'the systematic study of films based on literary sources.'[6] Instead we should study *both* the source and result of the adaptation as two texts, infinitely changing positions, taking turns being sources for each other in the ongoing work of the reception in the adaptational process. This is what I call *dialogizing adaptation studies*, and perhaps I could define my own target for novel to film adaptation studies with the following formula: *Novel to film adaptation studies is the systematic study of the process of novels being turned into film, focusing on both the change of the content and form from novel to film and the changes being inferred on the originating text.*

There are several problems with conducting such research, the main one probably being that an analysis of the dialogic process tends to mix two normally distinct parts of the communication process: the process of production and the process of reception. The production dimension is related to questions of which parts are chosen, what is changed and what remains the same, as compared to the original, concerning both form and content. And the dimension of reception is normally related to how abstract or specific readers or spectators react to and change the cultural texts presented to them.

Dialogizing adaptation studies

Naturally, I am not the first to notice this processual aspect of adaptation. To mention a few examples, Morris Beja claimed that 'what a film takes from a book matters; but so does what it brings to a book'[7]; Keith Cohen's *Film and Fiction: The Dynamics of Exchange* (1979) is an early and productive discussion of the generic interchanges between novel and film, in a dynamic relationship.[8] These authors remind us that *in the film* it is possible to change the content or form of a given text, but this is really just another way of defining adaptation as the transport of form or content from the area of one media specific setting to another. And neither Beja nor Cohen quite reflect my point, because even if these remarks are more productive than a conventional comparison of novel versus film, they do not question the fact that the film is the conclusive 'result' of the adaptation; consequently, more radical measures must be taken in order to free adaptation studies from the grip of one-way analyses. When it comes to my suggestion to acknowledge a dialogic trait in our analysis of and encounter with adaptations, I have, in more recent adaptation studies, found work that prefigure my ideas.

As mentioned already, I consider Robert Stam's work on adaptation to be an important contribution to the field. Stam has, together with Raengo, edited two anthologies (accompanying his own *Literature Through Film*, see below) and, in 'Beyond Fidelity. The Dialogics of Adaptation' and 'Introduction: The Theory and Practice of Adaptation', Stam develops an intertextual model of adaptation studies.[9]

In *Literature Through Film*, Stam engages in a reading of the history of the novel in the light of a number of important adaptations from novel to film. In order to do so, he construes a relatively simple division in the history of the European novel with a Cervantic, metafictive, fantastic line vis à vis a more realistic, mimetic line, starting with Defoe's *Robinson Crusoe*. The division resembles both Erich Auerbach's influential dichotomy in *Mimesis* and M. M. Bakhtin's ideas about two stylistic lines of the European novel in *Discourse in the Novel*, but Stam's innovative gesture is formed by the way he manages to read the history of the novel in the light of the history of cinema – but also how he manages to read the history of cinema as deeply related to the history of the novel. A core concept in his book is the inspiring but rather elusive idea of 'protocinematic' style, employed in discussions of Flaubert's *Madame Bovary* and the Flaubert adaptations of Vincent Minneli, Claude Chabrol and Ketan Mehta. The most important achievement of the idea of protocinematic style is not the concept's ability to clarify problematic aspects of adaptation studies, neither is it to function as an analytical tool. Instead, the force of the concept lies in its ability to enable the cultural critic to do an inspiring back and forth movement, from the stylistic, narrative and symbolic aspects of Flaubert's work and back to the films that made these traits visible – and then back again to the novel.

Cultural intertextuality or dialogic intertextuality, exemplified in the idea of protocinematic style, is Stam's preferred term for his method. I think it is fair to say that whereas the first wave of modern adaptation studies (starting with Bluestone) was very interested in medium specific discussions of adaptation, another wave, from around 1980, perhaps inaugurated with Dudley Andrew's essay on adaption (and in the work of Keith Cohen), focused on, in the words of Andrew, a 'sociological turn' of adaption studies.[10] Stam and other writers are about, I believe, to open up yet another dimension, namely an 'intertextual turn' of adaptation studies; a turn widening the idea of a one-to-one relation in adaptations (see, for instance, Christine Geraghty's notable article on *Atonement*[11]) which could be developed into an even more radicalized idea of a dialogic adaptation analysis strategy.

Together with my colleagues Anne Gjelsvik and Henriette Thune, and before we had really delved into the richness and complexities of adaptation theory, I made an outline of how to read a novel in the light of the film, using the Swedish vampire novel *Let the Right One In* as an example. In this sketch text, we described our methodology as follows:

> When claiming that the adaptive process works "both ways,"
> we mean that not only are aspects of the novel transmitted,
> of course, into the film. Even the novel changes, it alters
> appearance and may be interpreted in new ways, in light of the
> adaptation. It is exactly this back and forth movement, common
> to any adaptation, which allows us to talk, for instance, about
> a common motif for novel and film. Consequently, our example
> shows that it might be fruitful to consider adaptation as an
> on-going and incessant process. Adaptation is a negotiation that
> takes place across the preliminary borders of the two (or more)
> works included in the process. Traits of the adapting text infer
> upon the adapted text and the other way around in a process
> that may be termed chiasmic or, perhaps more relevantly,
> *dialogic* in Bakhtin's understanding of the word.[12]

The common inspiration behind both Stam's and my own and my colleagues' work is the theories of M. M. Bakhtin, for instance in *Problems of Dostoevsky's Poetics*, where he mentions the possibility of 'dialogical relationships' existing among not only words and texts, but also 'between intelligible phenomena of unlike types, if those phenomena are expressed in some sort of *symbolic* material. For example, dialogical relationships are also possible between images of various art forms.'[13] Consequently, basing our definition on Bakhtin, we defined adaptation 'as a dialogic process of negotiation between transmedial similarities and media specific differences.'[14]

This definition of adaptation analysis, based on a Bakhtinian framework has affinities with the work of Kamilla Elliott, even if she never refers to Bakhtinian intertextuality. Elliott's important *Rethinking the Novel/Film Debate* discusses the interrelationship between source and result in a highly illuminating way. Elliot finds her sources of inspiration partly in isolated texts of adaptation studies, in cognitive science and in the mind-bending *Alice in Wonderland*. Elliott shows that mixedness is the condition of any medial configuration, and thus her work indicates that differences between the texts of a novel-to-film-adaptation are always already partaking in each other's media-aspects. This helps me to analyse and interpret adaptation as a two-way process, and my aim is to try to specify what has been brilliantly suggested in Elliott's more theoretical and abstract terms.

Moberg and Troell – exemplifying a dialogical adaptation analysis

I wish to relate the theoretical argumentation above to a specific adaptation example, namely the Swedish author Wilhelm Moberg's novel-cycle *The Emigrants*, written from 1948–58, and which was turned into a film version by the Swedish director Jan Troell in 1971 and 1972.

I shall focus my discussion of the novel and film on the first five minutes of it only, 'corresponding' to the first pages of the novel; I'll be making relatively formal comparisons between film and novel, and only later on shall I return to a contextualization of the works. There seems to be a double intention lying behind Troell's entire adaptation: seen from one perspective, Troell follows the pretext as close as possible, thus creating a large degree of similarity between the source text and the adaptation, but he also produces significant differences between novel and film, sometimes forcing the loyal representation to an extreme point, sometimes following other artistic strategies. The specific relation between difference and likeness from novel to film and from film to novel is what I am looking for here.

The first minutes of Troell's version of Moberg's novel might be called a very long 'establishing shot', or perhaps an 'establishing scene', and Troell has chosen to begin his retelling with what seems to be an almost provocatively 'literary' opening. The title sequence, *'Utvandrarne'/The Emigrants*, is followed by six title cards, the first one being an exact quotation of the first words of the novel, the other five cards shortening and concentrating Moberg's original text. The very use of title cards may be a reference to the cards of the silent period of early film, but it is probably more fruitful to interpret them as a sign that Troell enters the tradition of literary film adaptations where such a gesture is a more or less conventionalized sign, from the book pages being turned in David Lean's classical opening of *Great Expectations* (1946), via the writing sequence opening Volker Schlöndorff's *Un Amour de Swann* (1984), to the parody of the book pages being used as toilet paper in *Shrek* (Adamson and Jenson 2001). The cards quote the main points of the information being related on the first pages of Moberg's novel, which is a short but historically exact demographic description of a small society in southern Sweden in the 1840s. The sixth and final card states laconically: 'This was the way it was in all other counties.' By synecdoche, part for whole, the text by way of a single county claims to describe all of Sweden at the time.

A typical Swedish spectator in 1971 would have no difficulty recognizing the verbal quotations as the introduction to Moberg's canonized and widely read novel, so at first sight it looks as if the (mostly negative) Swedish film critics were right 40 years ago: this opening seems indeed to signal the extremely loyal adaptation that critics found problematic. But when we take a closer look, the loyalty of Troell turns out to function as a discussion of fidelity, a discussion that is particularly manifest in the opening scene. Interestingly, Troell never represents the source in terms of a book; the book as such is absent; only quotes, represented on title cards, from the book remain. Furthermore, or as a result of this, Troell avoids representing his adaptation process as a book (original) that is transformed into a film (copy or result); instead he represents the diegetic world of the film simultaneously with the words of the book. The differences between literary 'original' and cinematic 'result' in Troell's opening is not only produced by Troell's adaptational strategy, it is also a very simple result of the medium differences between novel and film: to quote longer textual fragments than these title cards would slow down the speed of the film intolerably. So the first and obvious medial difference in the opening regards the quantity of text: whereas the novel spends six full pages making the 'establishing shot', the film represents six cards, taking less than two minutes.

To understand this quantitative difference it is crucial to note the basic representational difference, regarding the enunciative positions of the novel and the film respectively. In the book, these introductory six pages aim to show Moberg's intention to distinguish an extra-fictive reality from the 'fiction' in the main body of the novel. So where the novel creates a more or less clear boundary, distinguishing between facts and fiction (a difference accentuated in the English translation of the novel where this introduction is signed with the initials 'V. M.'), the film refers to the verbal description, that is to a semiotic modality outside the conventional range of post-silent cinema – in order to indicate the extradiegetic, non-fictional level outside fiction.

Therefore, the difference must of course also be related to the different semiotic registers being used, regarding the representation of the symbolic signs forming letters and words: the words in the book are represented as black letters on white pages, whereas the film's text is lettered with white signs on a black ground. The background of the letters becomes crucial: the text is not projected or copied on to the neutral black or white on which the symbolic sign (letters) appears, instead the background is filled with an iconic likeness of the moving pictures.

The cinematic representation of verbal language differs from a literary one, of course, because of a more fundamental difference: producing meaning in literature relies to a great extent on the symbolic sign function, whereas film can produce a much broader range of signs, bringing together symbolic, iconic and indexical signs relating in complicated ways to film's use of sound, music, verbal speech and written words, moving images and cinema's active engagement with the senses (mostly, but not exclusively, hearing and seeing) in what Robert Stam calls a 'multitrack' medium.[15] In other words: the same semiotic process – letters forming words – plays different roles in novel and film due to medial differences.

The visual representation of written language on the background of moving images co-operates with another 'track' of the clip, namely sound. The constant noise of the wind (and perhaps rain) is interrupted only by a metallic sound that signals stone being worked upon with an iron tool, and at the end of the clip, church bells form a sound bridge to the next scene where the words of a preacher form yet another aural background, now as a kind of accompaniment for the working man. Even though the editing creates a continuity to the different settings of the scene, the soundtrack actually produces an estranging effect: the spectator simultaneously registers the beating of the stone in the field, the church bells *and* the voice of the priest; this tripartite soundscape is – from a realistic point of view – heard only from an impossible place, beyond the realistic space of the film itself. It is impossible to imagine a position in the diegetic space of the film where it would be possible to listen to church bells, the noise of the farmer's work and the voice of the preacher all at once.

The 'impossible' soundtrack accompanying the represented letters and the moving pictures refers to nature as well as human and cultural work, whereas the sound of the preacher's words relates directly to the content of the text plates (including the criticism of the clergy of the period). The preacher is stressing the fact that opposing the worldly powers equals opposing the divine order of things. Here, a less 'literary' (and more accepted cinematic) way of representing words in film takes over for the rest of the film, namely spoken words uttered by individuals instead of words represented in an extradiegetic dimension.[16]

Both in the film's particular soundscape and specific words (in relation to the sum total of words), the film adaptation thus makes significant choices that must be described as far from, but at the same time very close to, the novelistic text. Visually, Troell has elegantly placed the stones of Småland in southern Sweden in the centre of the introduction. In this particular scene, he has chosen to follow (parts of the) literary text scrupulously when representing Moberg's own words while also adding a relatively independent plotline to Moberg's text. In the seven cuts (following the sequence with the title cards) the presence of the stones seems to grow in a threatening exponential curve; they go from being merely represented in sound corresponding to a single stone to dominating the visual representation entirely. The stoniness increasingly grows and finally turns into a massive stone wall, the man working the stone is buried or at least overcome by the stones, and at the same time the verbal cards represent the demographic and sociological facts of Ljuder county in Småland, the soundtrack represents the working with stones. This process of overwhelming stoniness (of the images, the title cards and the sound) is produced as a complicated effect of several 'tracks' in the film, but in the novel a comparable meaning is achieved through the linguistic representation of exact demographic and geographical facts that amount to the same negligible free space for an ordinary (that is: poor) farmer in nineteenth-century Sweden.

Central features of the novel's opening – the details of the historical background, the specific numbers and demographic facts – can only with difficulty enter the film. Only the informed spectator (that is, the one familiar with the literary source) will be able to notice the very detailed information in Troell's version, where sound, images and verbal text produce a staggering introduction. For this reader, the impression of the growing 'stoniness' of the film, and the supporting but non-realistic sound-bridge, is highly suggestive, but it only makes sense when the novelistic source is known. When we analyse them together, as a processual or dialogic reading, instead of searching for a novelistic source and a cinematic result, the film and novelistic fragment comment on each other, and I would argue that the two texts enrich each other: the two versions point to interpretations of each other that would have been hard to reach with the knowledge of one and not the other. Such a reading involves what Stam would call the protocinematic parts of the novel as well as what I will call the 'protonovelistic' traits of the film, and these two parts engage in a complicated relation.

And this is, of course, the other side of the coin: the cinematic version casts a new light on Moberg's novel, in which the spectator, by way of Troell's interpretation, detects the underlying 'stone motif' of the first volume as early as in the first pages. In the novel, the 'stoniness' is thematized in the introductory pages, which are held in a relatively accurate and conventional tone. After the 'historical' and non-fictional introduction, one of the very first events in the fictive plot is the scene where Karl-Oskar's father is being caught under a huge stone while working in the fields, making him an invalid, and this scene symbolically expresses the harshness of life, the interminable battle against the stone – and functions as the indirect trigger of the immigration of Karl-Oskar and his family from Sweden to America.

This is an example of the two-way process of adaptation. In two minutes, Troell is able to clearly state the stoniness theme that takes up a considerable amount of pages in Moberg's novel; the film shows us that the non-fictive introduction in Moberg is actually an ideological critique of a post-feudal and pre-welfare society in Sweden in the second half of the nineteenth century. The fact-burdened text is, and this becomes clear only in the light of the film-adaptation, an attempt to create the emotional and also phenomenological (the spectator 'senses', bodily, the overwhelming stoniness) background for the immigrants trying to escape the barren 'stoniness' of Swedish agricultural work.

Consequently, and to sum up my remarks, the introduction of the film shows, not surprisingly, that the film is as complex and as sophisticated as the novel. My analysis of the film also shows, again unsurprisingly, that the film and the novel achieve different effects, but my main point is to suggest that going back and forth in a continuous reading of the novel in light of the film and the film as interpreted by the novel can lead to fruitful insights. This enables me to sum up this part of the analysis by stressing that the almost exaggerated loyalty of the film, much criticized by the critics, is really an adaptational and creative liberty, which may be brought to the fore by the dialogical reading I am proposing here.

In order to draw some general conclusions from my theoretical framework and my analytical example, I will discuss three dimensions opened up by the discussion above: a) a methodological dimension; b) insights into the two texts themselves; and c) the necessity of contextualizing the analysis.

Generalizing: Methodology

The back-and-forth movement demonstrated above may yield methodological insights: We discern the media constellations from each other, and find crucial likenesses as well as important differences when we discuss, to quote Seymour Chatman's important essay, 'What Novels Can Do That Films Can't (and Vice Versa)' (1980). That is: we recognize, in each specific case, that media are different, and very much alike at the same time.[17] As has often been noted, each specific adaptation – indeed any intermedial encounter – poses fundamental questions of representation, it questions the possibility of a meta-fictive dimension and discusses ideas of medium essentialism.

According to Thomas Leitch, the aim of adaptation studies is not (only) to study the passage from novel to film, but also to create a higher level of consciousness about the fact that what we do in the literature and the film departments are in many ways comparable. Therefore, he argues, adaptation studies needs to be considered part of another enterprise:

> 'Adaptation study will emerge from its ghetto not when cinema studies accepts the institutional claims that would make cinema a poor relation of literature or succeeds in refashioning analysts

of adaptation into loyal citizens of cinema studies, but in some larger synthesis that might well be called Textual Studies—a discipline incorporating adaptation study, cinema studies in general, and literary studies, now housed in departments of English, and much of cultural studies as well.'[18]

As mentioned above, the common trait of Stam's and Leitch's work is the idea of 'dialogism' as a guiding principle behind adaptation/textual studies, which for both scholars largely amounts to an extended concept of intertextuality.[19]

I agree with Leitch's proposal, but I will nevertheless argue that he does not go all the way in his attempt to dialogize adaptation studies. Both an extended intertextual field of study and, of course, a de-hierarchization of the different cultural studies is important. Nevertheless, the most efficient way to achieve these goals is to de-hierarchize the relation between the primary and the secondary text, the source and the result, in order to make both texts results of each other. Or, to use a somewhat paradoxical statement, make both texts secondary to each other.

Generalizing the analytical results: Troell's verbo-visual cinema and Moberg's phenomenological dimension

The inter-illumination of the media leads to new insights concerning the specific texts: when we are familiar with the novelistic source, we get a deeper understanding of the possible dimensions of the film, but by engaging with Troell's cinematic version of (in our case: the first pages of) Moberg's novel, we are also able to reread Moberg in the light of Troell and thus sense and almost physically perceive, so to speak, a version of Moberg's enumeration of facts. When performing such a cross-reading, I believe we approach very deep artistic dimensions in the works of both Moberg and Troell; in Moberg's realist novel, a number of painterly and, in particular, photographic references occur in key situations, suggesting a longing, on Moberg's part, to transgress the boundaries of his verbo-textual universe. In Troell's case, a similar longing towards a transgression, or to put

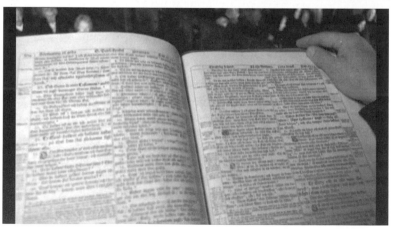

it differently, an extended inter-illumination of literature and film, occurs directly after the scene discussed. The three frame grabs reproduced on the previous page may illustrate my point.

In a two second visual montage, Troell creates an artistic image lying in-between – or perhaps beyond – literature and cinema. This powerful montage is, in a certain sense, the epiphanic formal conclusion of the adaptational meta-level of the film: here, the words of the novel that had become stone in the film become words once again; the almost mystical transformation from words to matter is turned upside down and the film may begin.

Generalizing: Contextualization

The short analysis of the isolated sequence leading to the metafilmic statement should, however, be complemented with a wider contextualization of the texts, and once again the negative critical reception in Sweden is important.[20] Interestingly, the film received no awards or nominations in Sweden, whereas it was very well received in the US, where it gained several Oscar nominations. For instance, the leading Swedish film magazine at the time, *Chaplin*, chose to give neither the first nor the second part a critical review, and instead constructed a (written) roundtable discussion which did not go gently on Troell's Moberg-adaptation. The criticism that met the film in Sweden (as opposed to the much more benevolent reception abroad) provides us with an interesting insight into a critical mentality focused on medium specificity (a film ought not to be too 'literal', i.e. bookish) that has now, 40 years after the adaptation, largely been left behind in theoretical criticism and theory.

The difference between the Swedish reception, as compared to that in the US, may be understood along two lines. Whereas the source of the adaption was (very) well known in Sweden (half of Sweden read it, claimed Moberg himself![21]), and the film was produced for a mass audience, as the most expensive film in Swedish film history, the source text was largely unknown in the US, and there the film was circulated in the art cinema circuit. The question of fidelity or infidelity was thus beyond the interest of the US viewers. Another important reason behind the sceptical contemporary reception has to do with a reception dichotomy between

realism and modernism, a schism that may be discussed as part of
Moberg's novel as well as Troell's film. Suffice to say that Moberg's
novel apparently enters the tradition of realist literary representations, but is adapted by Troell as a work with a modernist,
non-continuity feel to it. To take an example: the cinematic
non-continuity of Troell was described negatively by several critics
as non-homogenous and episodic.[22] What the critics considered a
flaw, but that we today may consider an attractive stylistic feature
in certain parts of Troell's film (disclosing Troell's interest in the
nouvelle vague), could be analysed in terms of the contexts of the
two works originally: Moberg strongly favours a realistic style that
he is forced to abandon in crucial moments of his cycle of novels,
whereas Troell, of a more modernist inclination, is more or less
forced to approach his subject with a more realist cinematic style
than he would normally employ. Thus the original reception of the
film paradoxically points to the deep, and deeply fruitful, dialectical
relation between the modernist film and the realist novel.

Troell is loyal to the literary source and he is quite radical in his
visual and aural choices, thereby creating a modernist version of
a conventionally realist novel. Moberg's reconciliatory melancholy
is met by Troell's modernist vision, creating medial interfaces and
medial fractures. The film is an investigation, and even documentation, of the fractures, but also the possible meetings and dialogues
between novel and film as media, and the particular novel and the
particular film. Both function, I would say, as a source to and a
result of each other.

Notes

1   See Søren Kierkegaard, *Gjentagelsen/The Repetition*, ca. 1835. In
     this context I have chosen not to enter the rich post-structuralist or
     Deleuzian discussion on repetition.

2   Thomas Leitch, 'Twelve Fallacies in Contemporary Adaptation
     Theory,' *Criticism* 45.2 (Spring 2003): 149–71, 160.

3   For a useful historical overview, see Mireaia Aragay's introduction
     in Aragay (ed.), *Books in Motion. Adaptation, Intertextuality,
     Authorship* (Amsterdam and New York: Rodopi, 2005). See also James
     M. Welsh's discussion of the history of adaptation studies in 'How
     Should We Teach It? How Could We teach It?' in Dennis R. Cutchins *et*

al. (eds), *The Pedagogy of Adaptation* (Lanham, MD: Scarecrow Press, 2010) and the provocative essay by David L. Kranz, 'Trying Harder: Probability, Objectivity, and Rationality in Adaptation Studies' in James M. Welsh and Peter Lev (eds), *The Literature/Film Reader: Issues of Adaptation* (Lanham, Maryland: The Scarecrow Press, 2007). Recently, an anthology was dedicated to the question of fidelity, though with very mixed results, see *True to the Spirit. Film Adaptation and the Question of Fidelity*, (ed.) by MacCabe, Murray and Warner (Oxford: Oxford University Press, 2011).

4   For a discussion of this phenomenon, see Kamilla Elliott's article in this volume.

5   Kamilla Elliott, *Rethinking the Novel/Film Debate* (Cambridge: Cambridge University Press 2003. Linda Hutcheon, *A Theory of Adaptation*. (New York and London: Routledge, 2006), 170.

6   Thomas Leitch, *Film Adaptations and its Discontents. From Gone With the Wind to The Passion of Christ* (Baltimore: Johns Hopkins University Press, 2007), 1. Leitch is, though, one of the proponents of a less autonomous novel-to-film adaption theory in most of his writings.

7   Morris Beja, *Film and Literature: An Introduction* (New York: Longman 1979), 88.

8   Keith Cohen's *Film and Fiction: The Dynamics of Exchange* (New Haven: Yale University Press, 1979).

9   For a discussion of Stam's model of intermediality, see Pedro Javier Pardo Garcia, 'Frankenstein's Postmodern Progeny' in Aragay 2005, 239–40. The larger argument of Stam, namely that the film form influences the novelistic development is prefigured in Cohen 1979.

10 See Dudley Andrew, 'Adaptation' in Timothy Corrigan (ed.), *Film and Literature. An Introduction and Reader* (Abingdon and New York: Routledge, 2012), 70.

11 Christine Geraghty, 'Foregrounding the Media: *Atonement* (2007) as an Adaptation' in *Adaptation*, Vol 2, issue 2, 91–109.

12 See Jørgen Bruhn, Anne Gjelsvik, Henriette Thune, 'Parallel Worlds of Possible Meetings in *Let the Right One in*' in *Word & Image* 1, 2011, 9.

13 See M. M. Bakhtin, *Problems of Dostoevsky's Poetics* (University of Minnesota Press: Minneapolis and London 1984), 184–5.

14 See Bruhn, Gjelsvik, Thune (2011), 12.

15 Robert Stam, 'Introduction: The Theory and Practice of Adaptation,' in *Literature and Film: A Guide to the Theory and Practice of Film Adaptation*, (ed.) Robert Stam and Alessandra Raengo (Malden,

MA: Blackwell, 2005), 17. Stam seems to consider literature a single-track medium which I find problematic; see the discussion of this idea in Lars Elleström's contribution in this volume.

16 In the final part of the novel, the adventures of Daniel on the Golden Track to California is narrated in a similar way, which is marked in the adaptation by way of different camera-lenses and a markedly differentiating musical score.

17 This basic idea can be developed in terms of several different scientific traditions: it is a basic component of what I wish to call a theory of heteromediality (see Jørgen Bruhn, 'Heteromediality' in Lars Elleström (ed.), *Media Borders, Multimodality and Intermediality* (Baskingstoke: Palgrave Macmillan, 2010)), and it is also the founding premise in Lars Elleström's attempt to combine intermediality and multimodality research (see Lars Elleström, 'The Modalities of Media: A Model for Understanding Intermedial Relations.' in Lars Elleström (ed.), *Media Borders, Multimodality and Intermediality* (Basingstoke: Palgrave Macmillan, 2010).

18 Leitch 2003, 168.

19 Here discussed by Leitch: 'The question adaptation study has most persistently asked—in what ways does and should an intertext resemble its precursor text in another medium?—could more usefully be configured in dialogic terms: How and why does any one particular precursor text or set of texts come to be privileged above all others in the analysis of a given intertext? What gives some intertexts but not others the aura of texts? More generally, in what ways are precursor texts rewritten, as they always are whenever they are read? Such questions, though not subsuming dialogism to adaptation, would extend both dialogism and adaptation study in vitally important ways.' Leitch 2003, 168.

20 The contexts of the adaptation has been discussed and documented in Erland och Ulla-Britta Lagerroth, *Perspektiv på Utvandrarromanen: dokument och studier* (Rabén & Sjögren: Stockholm, 1971) and retold by the producer and scriptwriter of the film Bengt Forslund, in *Wilhelm Moberg, filmen och televisionen* (Carlsson Bokförlag: Stockholm, 1998). Extracts from the critical reception may be found at the homepage of the Swedish Film Institute (SFI), http://www.sfi.se/sv/svensk-filmdatabas/Item/?itemid= 4865&type=MOVIE&iv=Comments (accessed 5 August 2012).

21 Quoted in Forslund, 118. The full quotation is interesting in itself: 'I am convinced that this novel cannot escape the destiny of being turned into film at some point, partly because of its suitability for film, partly because *half of the Swedish people have read the books*.'

22 For the critical reception, see the SFI homepage mentioned above.

5

Adaptation as connection – Transmediality reconsidered

Regina Schober

Adaptations can be understood as processes in which connections are established between two different modes of representation. These connections can be explicit or implicit, total or partial, and can be formed by different agents – the author or creator of a specific medial expression, the recipient or the medium itself – by implicitly or partially drawing on and adapting elements of another medium. As soon as we speak of a media transformation, we have already established such a connection, assuming or, in constructivist terms, creating an inherent relationship between two medial expressions, whether the adaptation is 'intended' or a more covert appropriation of transmedial or modal constituents. Adaptation processes always entail a creative and interpretative act of (re)combination, since as soon as an adaptation has been created, it is automatically emancipated and disconnected from its source medium. Consequently, I argue against an essentialist notion of adaptation as adaptation *per se*, while at the same time assume that adaptations cannot be viewed *only* as adaptations. Linda Hutcheon rightly points out that adaptations can potentially be treated both as original texts in their own right and *as adaptations*. In considering what she calls an 'adaptation's double-nature', she argues that to label something as 'adaptation' is already an interpretative choice made by the observer.[1] In order for an adaptation to be identified as such, and to acquire its status as an adaptation, there must be an active process of forming specific connections to a reference medium either on the production or the reception side. Accordingly, issues such as faithfulness, difference and modes of translation must be discussed within the level of this particular connection. Neither adaptation nor source text alone can answer such questions, but only in relation to each other or, more importantly, to their reception or production process.

For example, the film *No Country for Old Men*, directed by the Coen Brothers,[2] makes an explicit reference to Cormac McCarthy's novel of the same title[3] and thereby links the two media and their respective cultural discourses. Yet, while remaining relatively faithful to the novel in plot development, tone and character constellation, the film is (and has to be) highly selective in forming these connections. The medial change alone (introduction of audio-visual elements, cinematographic decisions, performative necessities and so on) requires a significant divergence from the source medium. Despite its unmistakable connections with the literary source, the film bears just as many, or even more, references to other films, genres and cultural or aesthetic contexts. Audiences recognize the film as an adaptation of a novel only if they have received this information prior to watching the film, for example, through its accompanying paratexts on film posters or reviews. Without making such an explicit connection, the film will simply remain a film, an artwork in itself. To the viewer to whom this piece of information remains unknown, the film will make just as much sense being detached from its source as it does in reference to it.

These connections between two (supposedly) related media products are not necessarily or essentially given and could be imagined otherwise. The fact that such connections are highly context dependent makes them more or less selective, arbitrary and highly specific, determining the quality not only of the intermedial relationship between source medium and adaptation, but also of the individual media at their particular moment of convergence. In the following, I will argue for a revaluation of adaptation as a set of contingent connections. In applying post-structuralist notions of intertextuality as well as recent network studies to the process of intermedial transformation, I suggest that adaptations are embedded in complex intermedial, cultural and perceptional configurations shaped by dynamic and reciprocal interactions. Such a view of adaptations as dynamic connections challenges the notion of transmediality, which presumes the existence of shared attributes between different media.[4] Instead, I suggest that media are always bound to their specific aesthetic, cultural and production contexts. Thus, this paper seeks to answer the following questions: Assuming that media borders do exist, how can we rethink not only the notion of boundaries in terms of their 'dynamic and creative potential,'[5] but also the process of interaction between such media borders? How can we describe the creative and dynamic flows that occur in between such boundaries? And how do they, in turn, shape medial boundaries and our conceptions thereof? How does the notion of 'medium' have to be reconsidered in terms of a more ephemeral, contingent and dynamic arrangement? Finally, what are the implications for regarding media adaptations in terms of such creative and interdependent interconnections and how valuable is such a view for critical analysis?

The problem of transmediality

Considering adaptation as a process of forming *connections*, I propose a view of intermediality that emphasizes the dynamic, reciprocal and relational nature of media adaptations as opposed to traditional approaches built on the presupposition of clear-cut medial borders and unidirectional cause and effect relationships. Recent adaptation studies have abandoned such essentialist and simplistic notions of adaptation, most overtly in deconstructing the normative implications of a fidelity discourse prevalent in the discussion of book-to-film adaptation. Thomas Leitch, in listing questions that have arisen from recent publications in the field of adaptation studies challenging some of its common assumptions, registers a number of interesting additional contestations to this field, for example, by opening it up to other media than film and novels, by emphasizing the importance of historical and cultural context and by questioning the existence of clearly assignable source-adaptation relations.[6] The latter, in fact, is one of the most interesting problems in adaptation studies, since it challenges the supposition that adaptation is a process that occurs between two media – the source medium and the adaptation medium. However, adaptation must be regarded as a much more complex assemblage of cross-influences rather than a seemingly unidirectional procedure between two media. My thesis is based not only on Thomas Leitch's supposition that, in the process of adaptation, media 'demonstrably draw on other sources than their putative source texts',[7] but also on the claims of Christa-Albrecht Crane and Dennis Cutchins that adaptation studies should adopt 'a poststructuralist lens' based on 'a richer notion of intertextuality', thereby acknowledging that 'all [...] adaptations are intertextual by definition, multivocal by necessity, and adaptive by their nature.'[8] Accordingly, adaptation must be regarded as a process that entails a much larger range of influences, implications and repercussions than suggested through an exclusive focus on adapted work and adaptation. Christine Geraghty rightfully suggests that studying an adaptation 'involves both textual and contextual analysis',[9] taking into account other texts than source text and adaptation, and thus giving credit to its intertextual embeddedness. Therefore, to discuss adaptations means to acknowledge their complex textual environment, their cultural implications and their multi-layered processes of signification. In particular, I argue that such a notion of adaptation as a reciprocal and dynamic network of connections could offer an alternative to the concept of transmediality because this view focuses on the fundamentally unstable nature of intermedial links rather than on a presumed existence of common features.

Irina Rajewsky defines transmediality as 'media unspecific phenomena that can be employed in various media', suggesting that media share certain fundamental elements such as rhythm, sound, temporality and so on.[10] Assuming such a notion of transmediality – if only as a discursive bridge that breaches medial boundaries – is essential to understand on which grounds adaptation processes take place, how different media relate to each other and to compare different media at all. Without understanding what media (potentially) have in common, it is impossible to recognize medial differences and thus to define the distinctive quality of media in the first place.

The notion of transmediality is valid and necessary for creating the prerequisites to make statements on medial quality, difference and borders. Yet, it is based on the assumption that we can actually differentiate among media and their modal constituents. But what if there are no such things as 'media unspecific phenomena'? What if every mediated phenomenon is automatically bound to its mediality, its cultural context and its perceptional circumstances? If it is true that implicit and explicit connections are not only inherent but indispensable prerequisites in media adaptations, we may have to abandon, or at least modify, such a notion of transmediality that assumes a universal ontological realm independent of, and thereby disconnected from, its medial expression. In a more recent publication, Rajewsky alludes to this predicament in the wider context of problematizing current debates on intermediality. Distinguishing between 'medium' as a generic term and 'medial configuration' as a concrete medial expression, Rajewsky emphasizes how delineations of seemingly distinct media are not only abstractions and theoretical constructs, but also 'always dependent on the historical and discursive contexts and the observing subject or system.'[11] This general problem of theoretical abstraction, however valid for all attempts of classification and generalization, becomes all the more relevant for the concept of transmediality, which, I argue, cannot adequately describe relations between individual medial configurations, but, in a more general sense, function only as a heuristic system of reference in terms of constructed notions of media.

A crucial question in this context concerns medial boundaries. Rajewsky rightly suggests:

> We ask ourselves what exactly we mean when we talk about "individual media", medial specificities, or of crossing media borders ... . Drawing borders of this kind clearly cannot be a matter of "fixed" and "stable" borders between "fixed" and "stable" entities, but if not this, what then?[12]

Her answer to this question consists largely of the argument that medial boundaries become increasingly blurred and, as a result, are constructed in consideration of concrete intermedial configurations. Rajewsky places particular emphasis on the fact that such medial boundaries are always based on historical and cultural conventions deeply shaped by discursive contexts.[13] According to Rajewsky, the 'idea' of a medium underlies intermedial relations rather than an assumed notion of naturally given distinctions, whether talking about intermedial transpositions, media combinations or intermedial references. In stressing the discursive constructedness of media distinctions, Rajewsky does not abandon the notion of medial boundaries altogether but, on the contrary, reinforces it. She clarifies that a differentiation between different media is necessary to understand intermediality and medial border crossings; however, only in considering 'specific medially bound *frames*',[14] or

> it is only due to our constructing borders in the first place that we are able to become aware of ways of transcending or subverting those very boundaries or of ways of highlighting their presence, of probing them, or even of dissolving them entirely. At the same time, it is precisely these acts of transcending, subverting, probing, or highlighting which draw attention to the conventionality and (relative) constructedness of these boundaries.[15]

It is important to note that medial boundaries are flexible and dynamic not only in relation to their discursive constructedness, but also in terms of their constant historical and aesthetic transformation as well as their interaction with other media. Lars Elleström's model of media and modalities, which addresses the fundamental challenge of medial complexity, proves helpful in this regard. Since media themselves are a complex assemblage of materiality, perception and semiotics, Elleström argues, their interaction can be understood only in relation to each other under certain circumstances and in explicit reference to the specific perspective taken.[16] Elleström's model of modalities, according to which media can be described, compared and distinguished in terms of their material, sensorial, spatiotemporal and semiotic modality, makes it possible to specify intermedial relations by abstracting from the notion of media specificity, and thereby liberating the intermedial discourse from hierarchical assertions and ideological implications often attached to such notions as adaptation, ekphrasis or multimedia. However, most importantly, Elleström's model suggests that intermedial transfer becomes a question of critical perspective if media are composed of particular modalities. Hence, the model implies that such defining elements of media are under constant cross-influence and interdependency.

In the case of adaptation, these cross-influences materialize within the connection established on a modal level. Both Rajewsky's and Elleström's considerations open up opportunities for reconsidering intermedial relations and, most importantly in this context, for regarding adaptations as relative, dynamic and interactive rather than unidirectional, fixed and hierarchical processes.

An example of intermedial transposition in modernist poetry illustrates the implications of Rajewsky's and Elleström's models. Consider Amy Lowell's poetic adaptation of Igor Stravinsky's *Three Pieces for String Quartet* (1912),[17] entitled, in close association with the music, 'Stravinsky's Three Pieces "Grotesques", for String Quartet' (1914).[18] In her attempt to 'reproduce the effect of the music in another medium',[19] Lowell created an experimental poem that, on the level of sound, rhythm and structure, imitates the energetic and mechanical gestus of Stravinsky's experimental music. The medial change occurs in an associative process that puts great weight on the music's sonic material and its creative potential for enhancing poetic language. In translating the highly idiosyncratic rhythmic motif of two eighth notes followed by a quarter note into the onomatopoeic 'Tong-ti-bump' (7), for example, Lowell emphasizes the anapest rhythm of this motif – two unaccented stresses followed by an accented stress. Following Elleström's model of modality, one could argue that the transformation process from music to poetry occurs on several modal levels: First, the material modality of sound waves is translated into printed words on a flat surface which, in turn, may be (re)transformed into material sound waves in poetic performance. Then, on the level of sensorial modality, the auditory data received in the musical motif is appropriated for visual and, to a certain extent, cognitive perception. Again, this transformation process applies only to written texts. In a spoken performance, which Lowell would most likely have preferred to a silent reading of her poetry,[20] the two media are relatively close in their sensorial modality. The same applies to the spatiotemporal modality. Both music and poetry display a 'fixed sequentiality'[21] as a result of their linear process of performance and perception, although the latter may create a retrospect impression of spatial depth, a phenomenon Elleström describes as 'virtual space'.[22] So far, poetry and music seem to be closely related on the grounds of modality, at least in a performed enactment. So, why not call rhythm a transmedial element which, on a modal level, is transposed from one medium into the other? Obviously, a general notion of rhythm is not media specific, but, as an abstraction, may figure in various media and thus can freely float between different medial configurations.

Although such a view may be enticing, this abstraction bears certain fundamental problems. In this example, the source medium is explicitly incorporated as an intertextual reference, not only through the poem's title, but also in concrete semantic allusions to a previously existing programme accompanying the pieces. Therefore, Lowell's poem translates not only a piece of music into the poetic medium, but also – and this is important – an *idea* of this musical configuration, as Rajewsky suggests. The poetic text constructs its own concept of the musical medium in order to have the capacity to represent it within its own medial material – words printed on a page – thereby distinguishing itself from the source medium. This medial distinction, as Rajewsky argues, is necessary 'for the production and inner functioning and the reception of a given medial configuration.'[23] Quite clearly, the poetic adaptation is a representation of the idea of musical rhythm rather than a transposition of musical rhythm within the poetic medium. Rhythm, as an abstract transmedial phenomenon, could be defined as a linear pattern of stressed and unstressed elements. But what does 'stressed' and 'unstressed' mean in music? Does it imply the same as in poetry (or in other media such as film, the visual arts or dance)?

In considering the translation of the musical motif in this example, we encounter one of the fundamental and widely discussed challenges in comparing poetic rhythm to musical rhythm. While English prosody is based on accentual syllabic rhythm, musical rhythm is based first and foremost on note length. So, strictly speaking, the rhythm of this musical motif does not indicate a distribution of stress per se, but only a distribution of note value. Although Stravinsky's motif does not have an explicit accent on the quarter note, the note is to be played by a down-bow, and thus to be slightly accented. Accordingly, the verbal representation more or less corresponds to the sound impression. Therefore, one could argue that the problem lies within the distinction between performed and noted text rather than within source medium and adaptation, since the musical performance served as the basis for Lowell's translation, not the written score. Yet, even if we were to consider only the performed version of the poem, the concept of rhythm would not be completely analogous. In terms of its material modality, the rhythm of the musical motif is produced by the strings' playing pizzicato, which creates a specific reverberation effect that intricately shapes the rhythmic quality of this motif in perceived pauses, quality of attack and textural coherence. In the musical medium, concepts like 'stressed' and 'unstressed' have very specific implications that are distinct from the quality of the human voice rendering the motif in a poetic reading. This difference in material modality also causes slight divergences in relation to the spatiotemporal modality of musical and poetic rhythm, since effects of reverberation, in particular, influence the way in which temporal sequences are perceived spatially. On closer examination, the sensorial modality of rhythm cannot be attributed to a single cause, but is affected by a reciprocal interaction of material and spatiotemporal modality.

The multiple impact of interrelated factors on such a seemingly universal feature as rhythm is further complicated when considering the media's historical and cultural constructedness. Lowell's poem is both a formal adaptation of Stravinsky's music and also a medial conceptualization shaped by cultural discourses and ideological implications. The music's first movement, from which the motivic example is taken, is a folkloristic peasant dance inspired by Stravinsky's Ukrainian background and his experiments with modernist tone color. This culturally and aesthetically embedded 'text' is transformed into an Imagist poem that reflects Lowell's aesthetics of a distinctly American primitivism. Thus, the poem reinterprets Stravinsky's cultural ideology, adapting it to an American context. This relates to what Elleström calls 'qualifying aspects' of media, in terms of specific medial context and aesthetic and communicative aspects of operation.[24] On this level, the aspect of rhythm, as employed in Stravinsky's and Lowell's examples, differs most notably. For Stravinsky, rhythmic complexity as an expressive feature is a defining aesthetic idiosyncrasy of his compositional style, embodying a strong rootedness in national folk music and his background as a ballet composer; but for Lowell, rhythm has a much stronger ideological function. Her poetic style is not markedly rhythmic, compared with modernist poets such as Gertrude Stein, for instance. Instead, to a large extent, the material modality of rhythm is inscribed into the primitivist semantics of her poems, resulting in a vivid description of colours, movement and energy.

Evidently, seemingly universal elements such as rhythm are much less stable in the process of intermedial adaptation than the term 'transmedial' might suggest. In this regard, Elleström's model accounts for the fact that each medium is already dependent on and attached to material, perceptional, cultural and historical circumstances. Rhythm cannot be the same in music and poetry, but is highly media specific, and therefore bound to its material quality as well as to its aesthetic and cultural context. In other words, what counts as rhythm in Stravinsky's music can be 'translated' only into something that is comparable to musical rhythm in Lowell's poems and – this is crucial – has to be recognized as such. The same applies to sound or, most obviously, to cultural themes such as primitivism. There can be no 'true' transmediality, if we assume that every medium operates within a closely knit set of connections between interdependent variables. Instead, media transformations can only highlight the differences between media through focusing on the ever-changing processes of forming contacts. In so doing, such transformations constantly oscillate between challenging and establishing medial boundaries.

Media can be conceived as more or less ephemeral realms separated by even less tangible borders that are under constant influence of recipients' perception, cultural discourse, circumstances of production and performance, all of which constantly modify their specific qualities and implications. Therefore, I suggest that media be discussed not as independent and self-contained entities, but rather as highly interconnected nodes in a larger network of medial, cultural and receptional actors. Correspondingly, intermedial relations are considered as transient connections that are latently existent. To form a significant relation, medial connections must be activated both by the system of reference and the research perspective taken. Only when an inherently 'passive' connection is actively invoked is this relationship created, which consequently can contribute to creating meaning, but in a more complex and ambiguous way than often assumed.

Adaptation as connection

Connections unify previously separate entities. According to its dictionary definition, a connection can range from a simple 'joining together', to 'consecutiveness, continuity, or coherence of ideas', to more hermeneutic or even deterministic notions, such as 'context' and 'the condition of being related to something else by a bond of interdependence, causality, logical sequence.'[25] Indeed, connections have long been associated with causal, and therefore, predetermined and essential relations. However, David Hume warns against assuming the existence of any 'necessary connection' between two seemingly causal events, since our experience of causal relations 'is the whole that appears to the outward senses. The mind feels no sentiment or inward impression from this succession of objects: Consequently, there is not, in any single, particular instance of cause and effect, anything which can suggest the idea of power or necessary connexion.'[26] Hume makes an important epistemological distinction between connections and causal relations, even if his observations remain within the level of perception. He argues that just because something is perceived as being causally related, does not mean on an ontological level that it is necessarily connected. For him, connections are not essentially 'necessary', but induced by' the operations of our own mind.'[27] Still, Hume does not claim that connections are always and fundamentally contingent, but if there are underlying causal relations between the effects we perceive and underlying laws, these flows of energy are too complex and transient for the human mind to grasp:

> The scenes of the universe are continually shifting, and one object follows another in an uninterrupted succession; but the power of force, which actuates the whole machine, is entirely concealed from us, and never discovers itself in any of the sensible qualities of body. We know that, in fact, heat is a constant attendant of flame; but what is the connexion between them, we have no room so much as to conjecture or imagine. It is impossible, therefore, that the idea of power can be derived from the contemplation of bodies, in single instances of their operation; because no bodies ever discover any power, which can be the original of this idea.[28]

Hume's skepticism towards a 'necessary connection', grounded on the supposition that the complexity of cause and effect relationships inhibits a unidirectional understanding of connections, has been radicalized in post-structuralism. In deconstructing the significative relation between signifiers and signifieds, and thereby emphasizing their dependency from both performance and intertextual referentiality, post-structuralists query the assumption of inherent causalities and also postulate the view that the act of forming connections itself is foregrounded as being significant. There is no fixed meaning, no immanent connection between language and reality, between 'appearance' and 'essence', because meaning is always shaped by contaminated language. In contrast to Hume, who still acknowledges the existence of a prelinguistic or preconceptual form of causality, post-structuralists dismiss such an idea of primary meaning, emphasizing the level of discourse in the creation of meaning. Along these lines, only discourses that are in the process of constant (re)formation can be traced, since they are bound to an intertextual interdependence. Connections are considered a matter of (constant) linguistic inscription and creation rather than a representation of pre-existing relations. On such a linguistic level, however, connections play a decisive role. In their intertextual webs of cross-references and interdependences, texts form a complex web of interconnections. Therefore, Julie Sanders rightfully calls adaptation 'a subsection of the over-arching practice of intertextuality.'[29] Along these lines, meaning is understood to lie not exclusively within a single text but, following Mikhail Bakhtin's notions of heteroglossia and chronotope, in contextual relations, and more specifically, in intertextual interactions, cross-dependencies and interrelations.[30]

Adaptation and the network model

The notion of intertextuality as interconnected assemblage of cross-references is effectively expressed by Gilles Deleuze's and Félix Guattari's image of the rhizome. This nonlinear, horizontal and deterritorialized formation presupposes a structure in which multiple 'lines of segmentarity and stratification' form an 'acentered, nonhierarchical, nonsignifying system ... defined solely

by a circulation of states.'[31] As a continuation of the rhizome, the
network metaphor can be understood as a manifestation of the
post-structuralist notion of intertextuality. The network metaphor
succeeds in describing the relations between individual entities in
terms of complex interconnections, and in grasping some of the
fundamental dynamics specific to complex configurations. Both
natural sciences and cultural studies have shown a growing interest
in the network as an explanatory model, as social, economic and
cultural trends accompanying processes of globalization and virtu-
alization in recent decades have increasingly been described as
'network society',[32] 'connected age'[33] or 'moment of complexity'.[34]

Networks consist of a complex set of links between individual
nodes. Unlike more hierarchical forms of organization, networks
are decentralized, interactive, dynamic and spontaneous. In a
network, individual nodes, which are defined only through their
relationship to one another, are less important than the whole.
In a network, an individual identity is not stable within itself,
but something that results from reciprocal interaction with other
entities, which is therefore in constant flow, depending on the
orientation and intensity of its connections. Accordingly, nodes
often are described less as independent entities than as intersections
of links, themselves in constant transformation.

The network is a prevalent metaphor in computer sciences,
where the image of the network illustrates data flows, especially in
the highly interconnected virtual space of the internet, as well as in
neuroscientific research. Connectionist approaches have been used
in cognitive science to model brain activity as neural networks,
assuming that the brain is similar to a computer network. The brain
is composed of different nodes (neurons or group of neurons) and
links (synapses). Neurons or units of neurons have a certain degree
of activation determined by the weight of their connection to other
units. These neurons are interlinked by synapses, which enable
active nodes to excite or inhibit less active nodes. One of the basic
propositions of connectionism is that neurons themselves are significant only in connection with each other, since neural networks are
dynamic systems in which neurons constantly interact with each
other. Connections are weakened or strengthened according to
the intensity or 'weight' attributed to them as determined by the
degree of activity of certain neurons.[35] Connectionist models have
been applied successfully to cognitive psychology, particularly to

theories of learning. What makes neural networks such a popular metaphor in other research fields is its creative implication. 'A key motivation for such [network] models', John Daugman asserts, 'is the notion of *synergy*, that the whole is significantly greater than the sum of its parts, so that remarkably intelligent behavior might emerge from surprisingly elementary subunits if they are collectively configured properly, and with sufficiently rich interconnections.'[36] The extensive explanatory implications of neural networks make them a metaphor for all sorts of complex relationships and adaptable systems of exchange, ranging from business models to artificial intelligence.

Such models of connections and interconnected networks also present interesting prospects for intermedial research, in particular for adaptation studies, because they allow for specifying the implications of calling something an adaptation. Hume's critique of the 'necessary connection' suggests that intermedial relations, like any presumed relationships, are first and foremost a matter of perception. Knowing (or assuming) that a certain text is an adaptation of a source text does not necessarily reflect a presumed ontological connection, but, as Linda Hutcheon's postulation of 'adaptation *as adaptation*' suggests, only gives account of our (mediated) sensory impression and our critical perspective.[37] Post-structuralist theories of intertextuality advocate a similar argument, if from a somewhat different perspective: The fact that we discern a certain intertextual relationship is less an act of interpretation than a necessary result of the inherent interconnectedness between texts. This observation evokes a fundamental question: What function do critics or recipients have in the process of establishing connections and thus meaning? Do intertextual (or intermedial) connections formed by interrelated texts exist prior to our perception or are they created in the process of making such observations? According to the connectionist model, it is a combination of both. Since neurons, the 'nodes' of neural networks, are activated primarily through their interaction with other neurons, the number and quality of synapses is significant for their activity. Deliberate external stimulation or the dynamics of the interconnected web itself (through its emergent properties) can trigger such activation. Therefore, the connectionist model argues for a combination of directed activation and a reliance on interconnections. Applying the connectionist model to the studies of media adaptation is not unproblematic, since its conclusions are drawn within the context of neuroscientific data and may be too specific to be used in an interdisciplinary transfer. However, a metaphorical use of this model within the case of media transformation may be helpful in describing the dynamics of complex systems that involve similar processes. Accordingly, it could be inferred that, in a complex set of intermedial relations, connections are both inherently present, depending on the intensity of interrelations, *and* triggered by external (perceptional) stimuli. Accordingly, an adaptation is an adaptation not (only) because we call it an adaptation. But calling something an adaptation strengthens or creates the ties between the two medial configurations, thus confirming the connection as such, while exciting or inhibiting other connections through its interdependent dynamics.

The process of connecting cannot be understood without considering the notion of creation. As David Gauntlett has effectively shown regarding a culture increasingly influenced by the collective culture of Web 2.0, 'making is connecting', because every act of creativity not only requires the association of two (or more) previously separate things, but also always involves human interaction within and with the social and cultural environment, to a certain degree.[38] Gauntlett's thesis is largely politically motivated, as he suggests that a society that values and fosters creativity promotes social connectivity and encourages personal self-fulfilment and happiness.[39] So, while Gauntlett's argument is mainly geared towards the social implications of a participatory culture based on interconnected creativity, from a slightly different perspective, his motto also can be applied to the field of intermediality. If 'making is connecting', any supposedly 'new' medial configuration connects to already existing 'pretexts'. Clearly, adaptations as well as all kinds of media creation follow the basic tenets of intertextuality: Any 'text' is always embedded within a large network of other texts. However, in the case of media transformation, this observation needs to be extended in one crucial aspect: This network of interconnections is constructed not only of other verbal or nonverbal 'texts' or media, but also, to the same extent, of recipients, production contexts and sociocultural and aesthetic factors. Presuming that intermediality, especially media transformation, is a transformation of semiotic systems and also always a process of cultural and social transformation, the relationship between different media and their respective translations can be described in analogy to social relations as network, which Bruno Latour's Actor-Network Theory suggests. In *Reassembling the Social*, Latour explicates the basic tenets of this theory and its application for understanding social relations and process. Most notably, the social is described as 'a type of momentary association which is characterized by the way it gathers together into new shapes.'[40] Accordingly, social phenomena and constellations are understood as transient assemblages of ephemeral connections rather than as fixed entities. Latour's emphasis that the social is 'an association between entities' gives credit to the fact that, in this view of the social as network, the entities themselves are not coherent unities, but rather only comprehensible in their momentary relations, analogous to connectionist models of cognition. Following this network logic, effects cannot be clearly allocated to particular causes because action occurs in the collaboration and interaction of different agents. This makes the emergence of both effects and events highly complex and almost impossible to trace, or only partly.

What is more, Latour rightly claims that these agents are not necessarily human agents, but can very well be conceived of as objects:

> *Anything* that does modify a state of affairs by making a difference is an actor ... ANT [Actor-Network-Theory] is not the empty claim that objects do things 'instead' of human actors: It simply says that no science of the social can even begin if the question of who and what participates in the action is not first of all thoroughly explored, even though it might mean letting elements in which, for lack of a better term, we would call *non-humans*.[41]

With such an inclusion of non-human actors into the network of social interaction, media can be considered agents in a complex network of production and signification just as well as human creators, recipients or cultural institutions. Or, to argue the other way around: In media adaptation, media creators, recipients, social institutions and technological circumstances are just as involved in the process of signification as media themselves. Media, in fact, are perhaps closest to what Latour calls 'mediators', which, due to their complexity, 'transform, translate, distort, and modify the meaning or the elements they are supposed to carry',[42] as opposed to 'intermediaries,' which simply carry meaning without transforming it. Therefore, media have two functions within the assemblage of the social, being at once conveyers of social 'meaning' as well as actors generating and reflecting this meaning. To complicate matters even further, media as actors not only represent the process of flow between entities, and thus constitute part of the intermedial network, but also are themselves what Latour calls 'large network[s] of attachment making [these actors] act.'[43] In radical continuation of the post-structuralist notion of intertextuality, intermediality can thus be understood as a dynamic and highly complex network in which media are in constant reciprocal interaction, not only with each other, but also with their recipients, various social and cultural forces and, most importantly for our purposes, within the intricate network of remediations.[44]

Adaptation as remediation in David Fincher's *The Social Network*

An interesting example of such a remediation is David Fincher's film *The Social Network* (2010),[45] an adaptation of Ben Mezrich's non-fiction book *The Accidental Billionaires: Sex, Money, Betratal and the Founding of Facebook* (2009).[46] The film's narrative picks up on the book's main theme of the strivings and intrigues within an elite college community, and, most notably, a damaged relationship between two friends, the co-founders of the social networking site Facebook. Not surprisingly, the film has been widely received as a quasi-documentary about the real company's founding, disregarding Mezrich's book as source medium. Accordingly, public debates following the film's release predominantly focused on the film's fidelity towards the founding myth of the social networking site itself rather than the literary text on which it is based. Intriguingly, the film's audience, not the film-makers, made the claim that the film was 'based on a true story'. As Thomas Leitch has shown in his discussion of films supposedly based on real events, such truth claims are 'always strategic or generic rather than historical or existential.'[47] In other words, such a connection between film and reality (as source text) is arbitrary and constructed for a particular reason. In this case, the audience made a generic connection between film and a supposed reality, not only because the film represents a real-life phenomenon – the online platform Facebook, which most viewers are familiar with (and members of) – but also because the book claims to be a non-fictional report of 'the real story'. So, even for those viewers who are aware of the book, the quality of the book-film relationship as 'truthful' suggests that the film must be depicting 'reality', and that a filmic adaptation of a non-fiction book must be a 'truthful' documentary. This connection becomes a necessary one since one entity in the chain of adaptations is reality, and this one link outweighs the other fictional links. The 'reality node' is such a powerful one that all further connections are inevitably related to and measured against it.

Hence, to understand and discuss the film as an adaptation, it is vital to consider its relationship with other cultural and aesthetic 'actors', in this case its intricate entanglement with realist expectations. The film's medial and generic status becomes apparent in considering the transformation process from source text to adaptation, but equally important, through a thorough analysis of all cultural, institutional and aesthetic factors at play in production and creation. Each of these actors – whether Mezrich's book, the company Facebook, the audience (who are Facebook users to a large extent), David Fincher, Mark Zuckerberg or the virtual community that constitutes this social networking site – contributes to the signification of the film and to the intricate interconnections among them.

What is the common thread that runs through these discourses of interdependence and interaction? Is there an element which, despite the constant transformation and negotiation of meaning, remains stable throughout the process of adaptation? Obviously, the traditional notion of transmediality is problematic when considering the logic of interconnected networks of reciprocation. If, at all (and this may sound paradoxical), the only media unspecific element in this complex configuration of remediation is the film's theme itself – the idea of interconnectedness. This core theme is present in the content and on a formal level both for the social networking site Facebook and for the film *The Social Network*. In addition to the paratextual and programmatic title of the film, the idea of being connected in the sense of being virtually present, also is reflected on an aesthetic level (through a frequent and dynamic use of quick cuts, highly emotive non-diegetic music and motivic references to notions of participation, self-expression and reconfiguration). However, the theme is even more obvious in relation to the entire process of adaptation. The film not only adapts a literary text that refers to a company and a form of social community, but the film becomes embedded in, and is constantly 'rewritten' by, various actors. An important group of recipients is the Facebook community itself. One user has described this constant and highly self-reflexive rewriting process on the Facebook fan page of *The Social Network* as: 'A page ... about the movie ... about the website ... that the page is on ... it seems like a cycle ...'.[48] The process of film-book adaptation is only one relationship in this complex texture of cross-references and interconnections. Which connection becomes activated, and thus meaningful, depends on the perspective that producers or recipients take or enable through their specific sociocultural configuration as they inflict their own meaning on to the medium.

Conclusion

In proposing a view on media transformation as connection, I have repeated claims that have been made in similar ways, namely that media transformations should be regarded as complex sociocultural configurations. First, as James Heffernan has shown regarding ekphrasis, an adaptation does not only represent or 'speak about' a work of art 'but also *to* and *for* them.'[49] Second, and perhaps even more significant, these media are already inherently connected to a specific aesthetic, cultural and production context that concerns matters of style, themes, form, ideology and an assumed 'intention'. They already form a closely knit web of 'influences' or, as Latour puts it, 'a type of momentary associations'. Third, as recipients, we identify media adaptations or transformations as such, thereby establishing a connection and, in turn, entering a reciprocal relationship with not only the single media, but also – and this is crucial – their connected identity. If we imagine intermedial relations as networks consisting of various actors, the already

complex dynamics of media production, reception and contextualization become even more complicated in the specific case of
adaptation because not only are the actors themselves interconnected, but also their respective interrelations. Most notably, the
notion of transmediality as 'common denominator' connecting
different media is challenged, since such intermedial relations are
under constant transformation, re-conceptualization, and thus
become relatively unstable.

No matter how valid this model may be as a theoretical
approach, one needs to consider critically its practical implications
for the studies of media adaptation. Even if a perspective on social
or intermedial relationships as a complex network may claim to be
more exhaustive and, therefore, closer to cultural 'reality', it seems,
in fact, impossible to trace such complex configurations compre-
hensively. Moreover, how important or relevant is it to understand
the 'whole picture' in order to reach plausible conclusions about
adaptation? Is not academic criticism always caught in logocen-
tristic and pragmatic constraints and, therefore, necessarily bound
to simplify complex reality? How can we discuss something that
seems almost too complex to speak about? For Latour, the solution
does not lie in ignoring what he calls such 'sources of uncertainty',
but in slowly unraveling them:

> We first have to learn how to deploy controversies ... then we
> have to be able to follow how the actors themselves stabilize
> those uncertainties ... and finally, we want to see how the assem-
> blages thus gathered can renew our sense of being in the same
> collective.[50]

To understand complex interconnections, Latour argues, we
have to engage in a thorough process of observing actors and
the incongruities of their behaviour and interactions. Latour
seems to suggest that it is, in fact, possible to make valid and
exhaustive statements about such intricate social relations as
dynamic assemblages. Even if this optimistic view is contestable,
an awareness of intermedial complexity alone can certainly be
productive for thinking about intermedial relations, even if it
unavoidably leads to a certain amount of modelling and, thus,
to a simplified reduction. The network metaphor, of course, is a
model that reduces an assumed level of complexity to a visually

graspable structure that unavoidably creates hierarchies. However, in considering intermedial relations as connections, I claim not so much to put forward a cohesive model to explain intermedial relations, but rather to propose a shift in perspective.

Connections are always versions of possible relations that we, as critics, can construct to gain an understanding of certain phenomena, assuming that these relations might be noteworthy. Connections can give identity individual elements. However, in identifying connections, we may neglect other connections that are potentially present. As Linda Hutcheon rightly asserts, audiences recognize adaptations as 'directly openly connected to recognizable other works, and that connection is part of their formal identity, but also of what we might call their hermeneutic identity.' She adds that the act of identifying an adaptation as such automatically deserts 'all the other intertextual parallels to the work the audience might make that are due to similar artistic and social conventions, rather than specific works.'[51] Accordingly, an intermedial reading of Lowell's poem or David Fincher's film as adaptation may have ignored certain other relations, intertextual or even intratextual, thus emphasizing the adaptation link as particularly significant. As the poetic example has shown, the same process takes place on the side of media production: There may be certain intermedial connections, such as sound, rhythm or cultural context, while other intra- or intermedial connections have been neglected. Therefore, instead of considering media transformations as processes that lead to more or less closed media products with clearly fixed medial boundaries, I opt for a view of media transformation in which the transformation itself, the act of creating connections, is the focus. Media transformations, I argue, are best grasped in terms of constant, reciprocal processes of interaction, conscious or unconscious, made by human or non-human agents. Within a network of potentially activated links, media continuously refer and relate to each other. The network model can help us to reconsider all sorts of intermedial relations. The important question in describing a particular case of adaptation seems to be not only how different media reinterpret each other, but also what happens within this process of connecting – whose action, under which circumstances, makes a connection significant, and how the complex dynamics of medial change can be described as they occur within this continuous processes of remediation, reconfiguration and recontextualization.

To regard adaptations as intricate webs of connections may help us to illuminate the multiple contextual entanglements of adaptations and to reflect on the potential and limitations of critical adaptation studies.

Notes

1   Linda Hutcheon, *A Theory of Adaptation* (New York: Routledge, 2006), 6.

2   Ethan and Joel Coen, dir. *No Country for Old Men* (2007).

3   Cormac McCarthy, *No Country for Old Men* (New York: Vintage Books, 2005).

4   Transmediality is not understood as a synonym for media transformation, but as shared features among different media, as defined by Irina O. Rajewsky in *Intermedialität* (Tübingen: Francke, 2002).

5   Irina O. Rajewsky, 'Border Talks: The Problematic Status of Media Borders in the Current Debate about Intermediality', in *Media Borders, Multimodality and Intermediality*, Lars Elleström, (ed.) (Basingstoke: Palgrave Macmillan, 2010), 65.

6   Thomas Leitch, 'Review Article. Adaptation Studies at a Crossroads', *Adaptation* 1:1 (2008), 65–8.

7   Ibid., 67.

8   Christa Albrecht-Crane and Dennis Ray Cutchins, 'Introduction: New Beginnings for Adaptation Studies', *Adaptation Studies: New Approaches,* Christa Albrecht-Crane and Dennis Ray Cutchins, (eds) (Cranbury: Rosemont, 2010), 19.

9   Christine Geraghty, *Now A Major Motion Picture: Film Adaptations of Literature and Drama* (Lanham: Rowman & Littlefield, 2008), 4.

10   Rajewsky (2002).

11   Rajewsky (2010), 53–4.

12   Ibid., 54.

13   Ibid., 60–1.

14   Ibid., 60–1.

15   Ibid., 64.

16   Lars Elleström, 'The Modalities of Media: A Model for Understanding Intermedial Relations', *Media Borders, Multimodality and Intermediality*, op.cit, 15.

17 Igor Stravinsky, *Trois Pièces pour Quatuor à Cordes* (New York: Edition Russe le Musique, printed by arr. Boosey & Hawkes, 1922).

18 Amy Lowell, 'Stravinsky's Three Pieces "Grotesques", for String Quartet', *The Complete Poetical Works of Amy Lowell* (Boston: Houghton Mifflin Company, 1955), 148–9. For a more detailed discussion of this poem, see Regina Schober, 'Amy Lowell's Peasant Dance: Transcribing Primitivism in "Stravinsky's Three Pieces 'Grotesques', for String Quartet"', *Amerikastudien* 53:2 (2008), and Regina Schober, 'Translating Sounds: Intermedial Exchanges in Amy Lowell's 'Stravinsky's Three Pieces "Grotesques", for String Quartet', in *Media Borders, Multimodality and Intermediality*, op.cit, 163–74.

19 Amy Lowell, 'Some Musical Analogies in Modern Poetry', *The Musical Quarterly* 6:1 (1920), 148.

20 For Lowell's performative aesthetics see Amy Lowell, 'Poetry as a Spoken Art', in *Poetry and Poets: Essays* (New York: Biblo and Tannen, 1971), 10–23.

21 Elleström, 19.

22 Ibid., 20.

23 Rajewsky (2010), 61.

24 Elleström, 24–5.

25 'Connection', *Oxford English Dictionary*, http://www.oed.com/view/Entry/39356 [accessed 29 June 2011].

26 David Hume, *An Enquiry Concerning Human Understanding* (Oxford: Oxford University Press, 1999), 136.

27 Ibid., 137.

28 Ibid., 136–7.

29 Julie Sanders, *Adaptation and Appropriation* (London: Routledge, 2006), 17.

30 For Mikhail M. Bakhtin's concepts of 'chronotope' and 'heteroglossia' see his essays 'Forms of Time and of the Chronotope in the Novel', and 'Discourse in the Novel' in *The Dialogic Imagination: Four Essays*, Michael Holquist, (ed.) (Austin: University of Texas Press, 1981).

31 Gilles Deleuze and Félix Guattari, *A Thousand Plateaus. Capitalism and Schizophrenia*, transl. Brian Massumi (London and New York: Continuum, 2010 [1980]), 23.

32 Manuel Castells, *The Rise of the Network Society*, 2nd (ed.), with a new pref., The Information Age: Economy, Society and Culture; vol. 1 (Chichester: Wiley-Blackwell, 2010).

33 Duncan J. Watts, *Six Degrees: The Science of a Connected Age*, 1st edn (New York: W. W. Norton, 2003).

34 Mark C. Taylor, *The Moment of Complexity: Emerging Network Culture* (Chicago: University of Chicago Press, 2001).

35 Cynthia MacDonald, 'Introduction: Classicism vs. Connectionism', *Connectionism: Debates on Psychological Explanation*, Cynthia MacDonald and Graham MacDonald, (eds) (Oxford: Blackwell, 1995), 9.

36 John G. Daugman, 'Brain Metaphor and Brain Theory', *Philosophy and the Neurosciences: A Reader*, William Bechtel, (ed.) (Malden: Blackwell Publishing, 2001), 29.

37 Linda Hutcheon, *A Theory of Adaptation* (New York: Routledge, 2006), 6.

38 David Gauntlett, *Making is Connecting: The Social Meaning of Creativity from DIY and Knitting to YouTube and Web 2.0* (Cambridge: Polity Press, 2011), 2.

39 Ibid., 226–8.

40 Bruno Latour, *Reassembling the Social: An Introduction to Actor-Network-Theory* (Oxford: Oxford University Press, 2005), 64–5.

41 Ibid., 71–2.

42 Ibid., 39.

43 Ibid., 217–18.

44 Processes of media transformation are always already inherent in any mediated expression since every medium responds to, contains, or reinterprets already existing media. Cf. Jay D. Bolter and Richard Grusin, *Remediation: Understanding New Media* (Cambridge, MA: MIT Press, 2002), 55.

45 David Fincher, *The Social Network* (2010).

46 Ben Mezrich, *The Accidental Billionaires: Sex, Money, Betrayal and the Founding of Facebook* (London: William Heinemann, 2009).

47 Thomas M. Leitch, *Film Adaptation and its Discontents: From Gone with the Wind to The Passion of the Christ* (Baltimore: The Johns Hopkins University Press, 2007), 282.

48 Carter Wood, *Facebook* 4 June, 2011.

49 James A. W. Heffernan, *Museum of Words: The Poetics of Ekphrasis from Homer to Ashbery* (Chicago: The University of Chicago Press, 2004), 7.

50 Latour, 249.

51 Hutcheon, 21.

6

Adaptation within the field of media transformations

Lars Elleström

For centuries, even millennia, scholars have studied different art forms, both in isolation and in collaboration. The age-old field of aesthetics has always involved a broad perspective on the common features of the arts. For the last two decades at least, art forms have been successfully subsumed under the heading of 'media,' in the broadest sense of the notion, and the field of intermedial research is now well established.[1] Nevertheless, an astonishing amount of research within the humanities is being performed without proper awareness of the wider, and, I would argue, fundamentally important perspectives of how art forms and media are interrelated. These are important for the simple reason that no branch of science can be thoroughly developed without comparative perspectives. Someone who wants to know Europe cannot pretend that Asia does not exist, and someone who wishes to understand mammals must have a good idea about the nature of fish. Likewise, someone who wants to be able so say something about music cannot ignore the existence of such things as film and literature. Even if the aim is not to make explicit and detailed comparisons, good research is always at least implicitly based on relevant comparisons.

Oddly, not even intermedial research (which includes a lot of research that does not refer to itself as intermedial) is always prone to widening its perspectives. Most studies of illustration are performed within the context of illustration only, and most studies of ekphrasis refer mainly to other studies of ekphrasis and are happy to keep the subject area delimited. Furthermore, most studies of adaptation prefer not to discuss anything but adaptation, which is generally understood as novel-to-film-adaptation. In spite of constant reminders from within the research field itself that adaptation could be so much more, there have only been a few serious attempts to understand in greater detail the nature of the theoretical framework into which adaptation must be placed: the transfer and transformation of form and content between all kinds of art forms and media.[2]

This may be a slightly unjust reflection. Surely, all areas of study must be delimited in a suitable way in order to retain the benefits of specialization. While that is true, specialization can be improved if at least the implicit contextualization is broadened. In the case of adaptation studies, this should initially include a simple shift of perspective. Although novel-to-film adaptation is certainly big business and a prominent feature of modern culture, it is neither historically nor theoretically unique. Other forms of transfer and transformation between media have been widespread since the dawn of history, and the media of film and written literature, like all media, share significant similarities and differences with other media.

From an adaptation studies perspective, therefore, it could be argued that the field should be expanded. However, I prefer the much more general perspective of humanities research at large: before expanding adaptation studies, they should be placed in the wider context of intermediality. Instead of inventing their own terms, adaptation studies should adapt to terminology that is applicable to general intermedial notions and phenomena. If such a strategy were applied, not only within adaptation studies, but in all research areas that involve multiple media types, it would be possible to communicate across the borders of specialization. At best, the discovery of significant similarities between media and media interrelations, in terms of media properties, analytical notions and research problems, might make the development of terms, notions and historical understanding much more effective. While such a goal is not easy to achieve, it is perhaps not utopian.

More specifically, the intermedial field of research includes a wide range of phenomena that are characterized by transfers of media characteristics; however, there has not yet been any systematic account of all of these. Most of the existing research is compartmentalized, which does not favour a general understanding of transmedial relations. Nearly all studies have focused either on only a few media types and their specific interrelations, or on delimited fields of study that are seldom properly related to each other, such as adaptation, ekphrasis and musicalization of literature. Without comparing a notion with others that also involve the transfer of media characteristics, there is a risk of becoming stuck in stiffened and isolated notions.

Presently, adaptation is probably the most vigorously researched area within the study of transmedial transfers. Many adaptation studies are engaged in issues of evaluation, focusing on what makes adaptations successful or unsuccessful, which explains why the issue of fidelity has become anathema. Fidelity is obviously a blunt and ambiguous notion upon which to base one's artistic evaluation. However, a discussion of similarities and differences between media products without normative aspects is quite a different thing. In fact, notions such as adaptation and media transformation collapse into nothingness if the aspect of similarity and difference is withdrawn.[3] Transmediating, transforming and adapting is equivalent to keeping something, getting rid of something else and adding something new.

The overall ambition of this article is to investigate transformations of media from a basic, theoretical point of view, and to place adaptation within that context. Instead of defining adaptation from an internal perspective, I will work through a set of crucial media notions, eventually reaching an idea of how adaptation can be understood in relation to and as part of transmedial issues at large. My aim is not to criticize the multi-faceted field of adaptation studies as such, or to evaluate or interpret its objects of study, but to point at possible and hopefully prolific ways of widening the field's frames of reference.

It should also be noted that I do not wish to isolate certain types of media products and label them as transmedial or as 'proper' adaptations. For me, transmediality is an analytical perspective. All media products can be investigated from a synchronic perspective, in terms of combination and integration, and also from a diachronic perspective, in terms of mediation and transformation. There is no doubt that the diachronic analysis of certain media products tends to produce remarkably fruitful meaning, with emphasis on their relations to other, previously existing media types and media products. However, there are no media products that cannot be treated in terms of transmediality without some profit.

State of the art and a new departure

One of the sources of stimulation for this article is Claus Clüver's 'On Intersemiotic Transposition' (1989), which was an attempt to sketch a more general approach to transmedial relations.[4] Clüver, in turn, was inspired by Roman Jakobson's brief remark that 'intersemiotic translation or *transmutation* is an interpretation of verbal signs by means of signs of nonverbal sign systems.'[5] Over the last decade, Jay Bolter's and Richard Grusin's *Remediation: Understanding New Media* (1999) has been influential and important for highlighting a much wider field of media transformation.[6] Although it is an inspiring study, full of interesting observations that are relevant for intermedial studies, it is hamstrung by its lack of distinction between various forms of 'representation', 'remediation' and simply 'similarity', as well as its vague notion of medium. According to Bolter and Grusin, all sorts of media can remediate almost anything. For example, 'our identity' can be remediated by the internet, 'the fatal stillness of Antonioni's films' can be remediated by a computer game and 'the printed book' can be remediated by hypertext.[7] Overall, their account gives a broad and stimulating, although somewhat confusing, view of the complexity of media relations, but no theoretical tools with which to deal with this complexity. Most importantly, I would argue that a distinction between representation (which involves the creation of meaning, or signification, by a media product) and mediation (which involves the process of realizing media content through technical media) is vital for the differentiation of phenomena that Bolter and Grusin treat as more or less identical. The present article is a preliminary attempt to develop more finely tuned notions that rival the popular and all-embracing idea of remediation, routinely referred to in non-committal wordings.

Irina O. Rajewsky's book-length study entitled *Intermedialität* (2002) is more conscientious. Rajewsky operates on different levels of distinction with three notions that I have found relevant when discussing media transformation. The first of these is *Transmedialität* (transmediality), which refers to phenomena that are not media-specific, such as parody. The other notions are *Medienwechsel* (medial transposition), which includes media transformations such as adaptation, and *intermediale Bezüge* (intermedial references), such as the narrativization of music or musicalization of fiction.[8] These three notions do not constitute Rajewsky's entire system of distinctions, and she is careful to separate each of them. Although I acknowledge Rajewsky's pioneering methodical approach, I prefer not to uphold her terminology because I feel that these notions are interrelated in important ways.

Some studies of adaptation have ventured to approach these wide intermedial and transmedial perspectives. Space limitations allow only a brief presentation of the most important ones here, in order to hint at a few possibilities of developing adaptation studies to a branch of the broad field of intermediality.

George Bluestone's influential study *Novels into Film* (1957) emphasized the differences between novels and films, an emphasis that is vital for making nuanced comparisons.[9] Bluestone's account nevertheless shows how tricky it is to compare two historically constructed media types without a systematic account of more basic media characteristics (material, sensorial and semiotic traits, for instance); novels and films actually share many essential qualities and the traditional critical idiom is often insufficiently precise to pinpoint the exact differences and similarities. The problem remains today, despite important discussions by Brian McFarlane (1996) and others about narration in novels and films.[10] Thomas Leitch's 'Twelve Fallacies in Contemporary Adaptation Theory' (2003) offers a crucial critique of the missing theoretical reflections and routine ideas about what literary texts and films actually are.[11] However, Kamilla Elliott's imperative study, *Rethinking the Novel/Film Debate* (2003), demonstrates a profound understanding of intermedial issues.[12] Elliott accurately spots many of the problems in traditional comparisons of novels and films. She problematizes and criticizes traditional but simplistic dichotomies, such as verbal–visual and word–image, and demonstrates their inapplicability for categorizing novel versus film; however, she still holds on to them as general categories for description. Elliott's study paves the way for a theoretical understanding of the intricate relations between overlapping media categories that extend far beyond written literature and film.

Robert Stam's theoretical introduction to the edited volume *Literature and Film* (2005) offers rewarding discussions on novel-to-film adaptations, although they are limited by the suggestion that the novel is 'a single-track, uniquely verbal medium', whereas film is 'a multitrack medium ... which can play not only with words (written and spoken) but also with music, sound effects, and moving photographic images.'[13] Although it may seem sensible to describe the novel as 'uniquely verbal', such a statement is one-dimensional and misleading. In fact, novels and films share many characteristics: they are presented visually on flat surfaces, they are spatially arranged, and, when decoded, they both unfold temporally. While it is true that novels are always dominated by verbal, conventional signs, this does not exclude the presence of iconic meaning-making of a kind other than what is produced by 'moving photographic images'. Although most films are more multimodal than most novels, *all* media types are 'multitrack' media, I would argue.

Finally, Linda Hutcheon's study *A Theory of Adaptation* (2006) is an important investigation of several kinds of media transformation. She limits her view to media representing 'stories', which is certainly defensible in the light of her ambitious expansion of the notion of adaptation. Unfortunately, however, she does not scrutinize the significant similarities and differences between media. Her approach is more pragmatic than theoretical, which is demonstrated by her three main categories of media capacities: 'telling', 'showing' and 'interacting'.[14] This distinction is too blunt to capture most of the complexities of different kinds of media transformation.

Compared to these studies, the present article aims to be both broader and more specific: on one hand, it gives a brief but wide-ranging overview of media transformations in general, and on the other hand, it narrows down on adaptation as a fraction of this extensive field. The following overview of media transformations is based on a fundamental distinction that is rarely, if ever, highlighted, that between mediation and representation. Conflating these two notions can result in a certain degree of obscurity, as is the case in Bolter and Grusin's notion of remediation. The term *mediate* is used here to describe the process of a technical medium realizing some sort of media content; for example, a book page can mediate a poem, a diagram or a musical score. If media content is mediated for a second (or third or fourth) time by another technical medium, I say that it is *transmediated*; the poem that was mediated by and therefore seen on the page can be heard later when it is transmediated by a voice. All transmediation involves some degree of *transformation*; the media content may be only slightly different and clearly recognizable, but it may also be profoundly transformed. *Representation* is basically the creation of meaning in the perceptual and cognitive acts of reception. I would submit that saying that a media product represents something is to say that it triggers a certain kind of interpretation. This interpretation may be more or less hardwired in the media product and how one perceives it with one's senses, yet it never exists independently of the recipient's cognitive activity.

I will first discuss what I refer to as simple and complex representations of media, and then transmediations. The difference between simple and complex representations is in no way essential, as the forthcoming discussions will make clear, but existing terminology makes it practical to uphold some degree of differentiation. Throughout these discussions, I will uphold two further distinctions. Both representations of media and transmediations can involve general characteristics of qualified media, on one hand, and specific media products on the other. The term *qualified media* is used here to denote all kinds of abstract media categories (both artistic and non-artistic) that are historically and communicatively situated, meaning that their properties differ depending on time, culture and aesthetic preferences (for instance music, television programmes, news articles and paintings).[15] A qualified medium constitutes a cluster of concrete media products. The final distinction is between unknown or fictitious media products and known media products.

Simple representations of media

Like many commonly used critical terms, the term *representation* is ambiguous. As used here, the term refers to the notion of signification in its widest sense. As soon as a human agent creates sense, meaning that sign functions are activated, representation is at work. When applied to the field of media, this means that all media products represent in various ways as soon as some sort of meaning is attributed to them. Following Charles Sanders Peirce, I maintain that there are three main types of sign function: symbolicity, which is based on conventions; indexicality, which is based on contiguity; and iconicity, which is based on similarity.[16]

Furthermore, I suggest three terms to denote the processes of symbolic, iconic and indexical representation. Although these terms are widely used for different purposes in diverse contexts, they fit the rationale of this article, which is to enable a systematic approach to media transformations. Therefore, I propose the term *description* to refer to symbolic representation, *depiction* to refer to iconic representation and *indication* to refer to indexical representation. Since sign types are rarely isolated, most media products create meaning with the aid of description, depiction and indication all in cooperation, although one sort of sign function usually dominates. It should be noted that the way in which these three terms are used here means that their significance is both wider and narrower than in many other contexts; I annex them only in order to efficiently distinguish verbally between the three main types of signification.

Media products can signify or represent almost anything. In this context, it is relevant to highlight one particular aspect of representation, namely, when one medium represents another. A specific media product can represent both qualified media as abstract categories and particular media products.

Representations of media may be marginal and brief, but they may also be crucial and elaborate or anything between. I call the former representations 'simple', the latter 'complex'. A number of terms may refer to simple representations. A media product may *hint* at, *allude* to or *refer* to another medium, it may *mention* or *name* another medium, and it may *quote*, *cite* or *comment* on another medium. References, allusions and hints are associated with iconic and indexical representation, as well as symbolic representation, whereas mainly symbolic representations (descriptions) can be said to mention or name other media. In addition, quotation, citation and commentary are chiefly associated with description: a quote or a citation is a verbatim reference. Recently, however, quotation, citation and commentary have also become associated with depiction; for instance, visual images are sometimes said to 'quote' other images.

Examples of media products that represent qualified media and general characteristics of qualified media in a simple way could be: a novel or a newspaper report that mentions 'music', 'melody', 'sonata form' or 'rock'n'roll', refers to the style of Renaissance painting, or comments on the narrative form of garden programmes on television and the typical personality types of their main characters; a pop song that mentions Beethoven or going to the movies, or momentarily sounds like a piece of Baroque music; a photograph of people in a living room where pictures can be seen on the wall in the background and out of focus. Representations of this kind may refer to known, unknown and even fictitious qualified media.

Examples of media products that represent specific media products that are unknown or fictitious in a simple way could include a short story that quotes a few words from a song that cannot be identified by the reader, or briefly describes the composition of a photograph taken by one of the characters of the story; a scene in a computer game that depicts a television screen mediating a sequence from an unidentifiable motion picture; or a movie clip that visually and auditorially depicts excerpts from an unknown song performed within the diegesis.

Examples of media products that represent specific, known media products in a simple way could include a poem that briefly refers to a particular song by Patti Smith, the national anthem of the Soviet Union or Michelangelo's statue of David; a symphony that quotes a few bars from 'Frère Jacques'; a documentary film in which fragments of popular songs can be heard and well-known commercial posters can be seen momentarily.

Simple representations of media may or may not have a major bearing on the significance of the representing media product. Details are sometimes important, but they are sometimes only details.

Complex representations of media

Complex representations of media occur when a media product can be said to convey representations that are more composite than simple references or comments. While a simple representation could easily have qualified media or general characteristics of qualified media as objects, I think that complex representations of media tend to represent specific media products: the more detail that is conveyed, the more one can expect that not only an abstract media category is being represented. Certain detailed descriptions may be the exception. Examples of this could include comprehensive accounts of general characteristics of gothic cathedrals or traditional blues songs. This kind of detailed description of qualified media, which is not also a description of a particular media product, is only possible if the qualified medium or submedium is formed by a set of truly rule-governed media products, or if the qualified medium is purely fictitious. I would argue that detailed iconic and indexical representations of media must have specific (existing or fictitious) media products as objects.

Therefore, full-fledged representations of media are generally representations of specific media products. These media products may be fictitious, unknown or known. One example of an unknown or fictitious media product represented in detail is an unrecognized painting that can be clearly seen in a movie. If the movie is based on photography, it could be argued that the painting cannot be truly fictitious, even if it is produced specifically to be part of the fictitious world of the movie. However, if the movie is computer-generated, for example, the represented painting could be either fictitious or simply unknown to the beholder. Similarly, a detailed description of a piece of music (what Steven Paul Scher calls 'verbal music'[17]) or of the story, plot or visual characteristics of a motion picture can represent both fictitious and unknown media products. This applies to verbal representations that are visual (in a scholarly article or a novel) as well as auditory (in a radio programme or a motion picture).

Complex representations of specific media products may be focused on all kinds of characteristics, from formal and abstract traits to features that are related to content. In practice, the form and content of a specific motion picture, for instance, are indissolubly interconnected, but a representation may still focus on one or the other. For example, one might describe the plot and dramatic turning points in detail without referring to specific characters or places, but one might also carefully describe the peculiarities of all the characters without paying a great deal of attention to the structure of the narrative.

There are many kinds of complex representations of specific, known media products. A verbal, visual text, such as a description on a website or a short story printed in a magazine, may represent in detail both a temporal media product, such as the hallelujah chorus from Handel's *Messiah*, and a non-temporal media product, such as the label on a can of Heinz baked beans. The content of Virginia Woolf's diary from 13 September 1925 could be described through both a monologue in a drama and the voice and gestures of a television news reporter. A still photograph could iconically and indexically depict and indicate the same text from Woolf's diary, but it could also represent Vanessa Bell's 1912 portrait of the author. A piece of music may iconically and indexically represent Martin Luther King's 'I Have a Dream' speech by way of including its recorded sound.

Some types of complex representations of specific media products are referred to generally as ekphrases. These constitute what Lydia Goehr refers to as the modern 'work-to-work ekphrasis' in order to distinguish it from how the notion was understood in classical rhetoric, that is, as any vivid description.[18] The notion of ekphrasis has a long history and has been delimited in different ways, including within the modern outline of work-to-work relation. Over the last century, ekphrasis has generally been understood as a verbal (symbolic) representation of an iconic representation, typically a poem representing a painting. Scholars have debated the proper delimitations of the modern notion of ekphrasis, sometimes allowing both the representing and the represented media product to be characterized by other media qualities. In its widest sense, ekphrasis can be said to include complex descriptions, depictions and indications of all types of media products. Even if one, for historical reasons, does not want to extend the notion of ekphrasis that far, it cannot be denied that complex representations of media products are possible, common and worth theorizing far beyond the conventional borders of ekphrasis. Under all circumstances, poems that describe paintings only constitute a tiny fragment of the wide field of complex representations of media.

Transmediations

Mediation is the communicative link between the surrounding world and the human receiver, and is a necessary condition for the sensorial perception of any kind of media content. Mediation and transmediation (the mediation of content that has already been mediated) are both fundamentally different from representation, which is a process of signification generated by media products that create meaning. From the perceiver's point of view, mediation always precedes representation. Mediation is the procedure of using a technical medium to realize some sort of media content. For example, the details and dramatic structure of the bombing of Pearl Harbor on 7 December 1941 have been mediated in many ways: by voices and other sounds, by journal and book pages, by television, cinema and computer screens, and so forth. These are different types of mediation that enable certain kinds of representation. The process of mediation could be described as firmly anchored in the material base of the medium, while representation is a semiotic aspect of the medium. As with all vital distinctions, the distinction between mediation and representation is a theoretical distinction that is helpful for analysing complex relations and processes that would otherwise be blurred. In practice, mediation and representation are deeply interrelated. Some kinds of mediation facilitate certain sorts of representation, while they render other sorts of representation impossible, and every single representation is based on the distinctiveness of a specific mediation.

Transmediation takes place all the time. The purpose of this article is not to find methods with which to categorically determine when a media product simply mediates something (which is the case as soon as one finds it meaningful to talk about a media product) and when it transmediates. Transmediation should be understood as a notion that is intended to help understand media processes that are sometimes clearly apprehensible and vital, sometimes indistinct but still crucial, and sometimes only vaguely discernible and of marginal magnitude. Many media products constantly transmediate general characteristics of qualified media that are not known to or observed by the recipients. In principle, characteristics of fictitious qualified media may also be transmediated, although it may seem far-fetched. For example, a novel might describe the structural traits of an invented musical genre (representation), and also use these traits as structural elements in its own narration (transmediation).

The media characteristics of qualified media that can be transmediated comprise many kinds of features, including aspects of both form and content. For instance, two qualified media or submedia may share narrative characteristics. Many novels and motion pictures tell stories about, say, people who are mistreated but struggle to achieve redress. Qualified media may also share structural elements of an even more general type. It is common in music and dance, among other media, to repeat elements of form, thereby creating distinctive types of structure. It is also common for several qualified media to represent similar motifs. For instance, photographs, poems and cartoons may all represent sleeping babies. Clearly, the transmediation of general characteristics of qualified media can be exemplified infinitely. Myriad transmedial characteristics can be realized in many ways by various qualified media that are mediated by different technical media.

Therefore, it could be said that some media characteristics circulate between several qualified media, or that transmedial traits can be transferred from one qualified medium to another in more or less covert ways. However, transmediations of general characteristics of qualified media can also include a specific media product as the receiver. For instance, a media product can have a structure that is similar to a conventional form associated with a qualified medium to which the media product in itself does not belong. Examples could include a poem that is structured in a way that makes it resemble a musical fugue; or an acrylic painting with properties of detail, perspective and colour that make it look like a photograph.

There is no overarching, established terminology for denoting these sorts of transmediation. It is common to simply talk about 'resemblance' or 'structural resemblance', and a few specialized research disciplines, such as the venerable 'stoffgeschichte', sometimes include a transmedial perspective. Lately, however, the phenomenon of transferring general media characteristics to media products that belong to other qualified media (covered by Rajewsky's notion of *intermediale Bezüge*, intermedial references) has been studied and aptly named as, for instance, 'musicalization of fiction'.[19]

Transmediation of specific media products is different from transmediation of general characteristics of qualified media in that it is the transfer of vital media characteristics that belong to one particular media product to (as a rule) another media product. This new media product is distinctly different from the existing media product, but based on its traits; it is a process of change that leaves a core intact. These media products can be named *original* and *version*, respectively, without being normative. In this context, *original* simply means the source and *version* means the new media product that can be relevantly compared to the original. No media product is an original per se. A media product that can be seen as an original in one specific case of transmediation may be a version of another original. One original may have many versions and it may ultimately be the case that most media products can be knitted together in a giant web of intra- and intermedial transmediations – an even larger system of interrelations than those exposed by theories of intertextuality.

Furthermore, it is not always possible, or even meaningful, to decide whether a trait or a set of traits originates from another specific media product, or if it is part of a more general pattern in one or more qualified media. Nevertheless, the distinction must be noted, not least because the difference may have hermeneutical consequences. For instance, it may be true, but perhaps not essential for its meaning, that a specific motion picture shares general structural and narrative traits with several qualified media. Stating that the motion picture has qualities that are normally associated more with, say, music than any other qualified medium, opens up certain interpretive possibilities. Concluding that the motion picture is actually a version of a specific painting or novel would push the interpretive impulse even further, since the original media product, for good or for worse, inevitably becomes part of the relevant interpretive context once its existence has been acknowledged.

It usually makes little sense to say that a media product transmediates the traits of a fictitious media product. However, a novel, for instance, could represent in detail a fictitious motion picture that is similar to the representing novel. It could then be argued that the novel also transmediates the fictitious motion picture, although such transmediation is, in itself, fictitious. Transmediations of actual media products, on the other hand, are certainly a real and widespread phenomenon.

All sorts of form and content can be transmediated from one media product to another. An example is a media product that represents the same thing as another media product that is already known. Consider the example of a motion picture that represents a man picking yellow flowers in the sunset while crying. The depicted content can be understood as a variation of an existing oil painting that depicts a similar scene. Thus, the represented media content (a man picking yellow flowers in the sunset while crying) can be said to have been transferred from one media product to another. The motion picture may actually represent the painting, while additionally transmediating its content, but transmediating a specific media product is distinct from representing it.

Another example of transmediating the characteristics of a specific media product would be a media product that has the same narrative structure as another media product that is already known. For instance, a novel might represent a pig that is transported to the abattoir, manages to escape and then meets a rabbit that reveals that the pig is actually a space traveler from Mars. This narrative structure could be seen as a variant of an existing comic strip about a woman who is sentenced to death, manages to escape from the prison and then meets a man who claims that her parents were actually monkeys. Thus, the narrative structure can be said to have been transferred from one media product to another.

Normally, then, transmediation of specific media products involves the transfer of media characteristics from one media product to another. Sometimes, however, it might make sense to say that one or more media products are actually transmediated to a new qualified medium or submedium. Sergei Eisenstein has argued that the narrative traits of Charles Dickens's novels were a seminal influence on early American film, particularly the prominent work of David Wark Griffith.[20] It could also be the case that a complex of media products, such as Ian Fleming's James Bond novels, is transmediated to a new media product: a motion picture that does not correspond to a single novel, but includes characters and narrative traits that are common to several novels.

Transmediated media products and their versions can belong to all kinds of qualified media and submedia, including old and new, artistic and non-artistic, motion pictures, documentary films, novels, essays, computer games, graphic novels, stage plays, comics and television series. The existence of various submedia that are designed especially for transmediation is evidence of the great importance of this process. For example, the libretto is a qualified submedium with which few people engage unless it is trans-mediated to the performance of an opera, operetta or musical. A musical score can be enjoyed by specialists, but is usually transme-diated to sounding music. The qualified submedium of drama text includes texts that work in their own right, as well as texts that require theatrical performances. Film scripts, screenplays and the like crave transmediation. Some people argue that written poetry is not true poetry until it has been transmediated by the technical medium of voice.

The general term for transmediation of media products is *adaptation*. The archetypical adaptation is a novel-to-film trans-mediation, although the term is not reserved exclusively for this type of transfer. Despite key research in the area of adaptation over the last few decades, it is unclear how adaptation fits into the wider field of transmediation. As noted, Linda Hutcheon's *A Theory of Adaptation* offers numerous examples of adaptation, including narrative qualified media such as novels, operas, films and computer games.[21] As another example, the writers of a collection of essays edited by David Francis Urrows focus on processes of adaptation from drama to symphony, from drama to opera, from novel to song, from novel to film to opera and from music to novel, among others.[22] Furthermore, Kamilla Elliott has increased our understanding of the problematic border zones of adaptation by introducing what I call general characteristics of qualified media into the discussion. As a rule, the term adaptation is reserved for transmediation of specific media products. However, when discussing individual examples of transmediation it is not always possible to distinguish clearly between general character-istics of qualified media and properties that belong to a certain media product. As Elliott points out, it is rare for common media characteristics to be properly treated as a part of the field that she prefers to refer to as adaptation.[23]

Notwithstanding several well-argued attempts to widen the

scope of the notion of adaptation, not all types of transmediation are generally referred to as adaptation, even considering only the transmediation of specific media products. As far as I know, libretti, scores and scripts are hardly ever discussed in terms of adaptation. The same applies to transmediations from non-temporal to temporal images, as analysed in, for instance, Angela Dalle Vacche's *Cinema and Painting: How Art is Used in Film*.[24] Transmediation from written, visual and verbal text to oral, auditory and verbal text (reading text aloud), or the other way round (writing down speech), is perhaps even less likely to be called adaptation.[25] The point is that even if many scholars, with good reason, have argued that the notion of adaptation should be expanded, few if any would favour the idea of extending the field of adaptation studies to all phenomena that have been analysed in this article in terms of media representation and transmediation.

Conclusion

It would appear that, to a certain point, the notion of adaptation can be rather firmly placed within the field of media transformation. Beyond that point, there is no consensus regarding where to draw the borderline. The following tendencies can be noted:

- Adaptation is not simply any kind of media transformation, but a sort of transmediation. Unlike ekphrasis, for instance, adaptation is never defined in terms of media representation, even though it can be combined with simple or complex representations of media.

- Generally, adaptation is not merely any kind of transmediation; it is transmediation of a specific media product. While Elliott has questioned this delimitation, her sophisticated analysis of the problem seldom has any bearing on adaptation studies.

- Rather than being just any kind of transmediation of a specific media product, adaptation is the transmediation of a specific media product into a new specific media product. To my knowledge, transmediation from specific media products to qualified media is not seen as adaptation.

- The field of adaptation generally does not include media products that belong to qualified media such as scripts and libretti, which are designed to be transmediated.

- Adaptation discussions seldom, if ever, mention transmediation from non-temporal to temporal images, reading written text out loud and many other kinds of transmediation. Indeed, there is a wide range of transmediation types that are not even discussed within the frame of intermediality.

However, there is no consensus regarding which media types the notion of adaptation should actually embrace. The relevance of expanding the view from novel-to-film-adaptation is not in question, but if and how certain media types should be systematically excluded has not been discussed at length. Similarly, there is no agreement regarding which traits are actually being adapted in adaptations. Although narrative features are highlighted, and there are many studies of narration in literature and film, no truly transmedial analysis has systematically investigated what kind of characteristics, in terms of both form and content, different media types can mediate.

I have no suggestions regarding the use of the term adaptation. It is certainly a good idea to delimit the frames of the notion or notions to which it should refer, and such delimitations should perhaps be done in terms of cultural history, socio-economic structures, expectations of the general public or something else that has little to do with theoretical media perspectives of the kind that has been presented here. Regardless of how one chooses to draw up the boundaries of the notion of adaptation, however, it should be done with a full awareness of the many other types of media transformation. Any adaptation studies that wish to highlight only a few sectors of this wider area must convincingly argue for the exclusion of other sectors; if this is not properly done, the notion of adaptation may become redundant. In any case, I think that some issues could be highlighted in a fresh way if the traditional restrictions associated with the notion of adaptation were put aside for a while.

The display of theoretical distinctions in this article could be a point of departure for further explorations into the nature of media representation and transmediation, as well as the place of adaptation in this wider context. In forthcoming articles, I will develop methods for analysing transmedial characteristics, regarding both form and content, which can be mediated, and hence transmediated, by different media types. The goal is to sketch a model for analysing media transformations that is applicable to all conceivable media types. This requires a deepened discussion of notions such as technical medium and mediation, as well as a much more detailed analysis of basic media characteristics.

Notes

1   See the comprehensive overview of the development of the research field intermedial studies in Claus Clüver, 'Intermediality and Interarts Studies,' in *Changing Borders: Contemporary Positions in Intermediality*, Jens Arvidson, Mikael Askander, Jørgen Bruhn, and Heidrun Führer (eds) (Lund: Intermedia Studies Press, 2007).

2   See the ensuing discussion of works by Kamilla Elliott and Linda Hutcheon.

3   My first attempt to systematically investigate media similarities and differences can be found in Lars Elleström, 'The Modalities of Media: A Model for Understanding Intermedial Relations,' in *Media Borders, Multimodality and Intermediality*, (ed.) Lars Elleström (Basingstoke: Palgrave Macmillan, 2010).

4   Claus Clüver, 'On Intersemiotic Transposition,' *Poetics Today* 10 (1989).

5   Roman Jakobson, 'On Linguistic Aspects of Translation,' in *Selected Writings, vol. 2, Word and Language* (The Hague: Mouton, 1971).

6   Jay David Bolter and Richard Grusin, *Remediation: Understanding New Media* (Cambridge, MA and London: MIT Press, 1999).

7   Bolter and Grusin (1999), 231, 268, 272.

8   Irina O. Rajewsky, *Intermedialität* (Tübingen and Basel: A. Francke Verlag, 2002), 12–13, 16–17.

9   George Bluestone, *Novels into Film* (Berkeley and Los Angeles: University of California Press, 1957).

10   Brian McFarlane, *Novel to Film: An Introduction to the Theory of Adaptation* (Oxford: Clarendon Press, 1996), 11–22.

11   Thomas Leitch, 'Twelve Fallacies in Contemporary Adaptation Theory,' *Criticism* 45 (2003).

12   Kamilla Elliott, *Rethinking the Novel/Film Debate* (Cambridge: Cambridge University Press, 2003).

13   Robert Stam, 'Introduction: The Theory and Practice of Adaptation,' in *Literature and Film: A Guide to the Theory and Practice of Film Adaptation*, Robert Stam and Alessandra Raengo (eds) (Malden, MA: Blackwell, 2005), 17.

14   Linda Hutcheon, *A Theory of Adaptation* (New York and London: Routledge, 2006), Ch. 2.

15   Cf. Elleström (2010), 24–7.

16   Charles Sanders Peirce, *Collected Papers of Charles Sanders Peirce, vol. 2, Elements of Logic*, Charles Hartshorne and Paul Weiss (eds) (Cambridge, MA and London: The Belknap Press of Harvard University Press, 1960), 156–73.

17   Stephen Paul Scher, *Verbal Music in German Literature* (New Haven: Yale University Press, 1968).

18   Lydia Goehr, 'How to Do More with Words: Two Views of (Musical) Ekphrasis,' *British Journal of Aesthetics* 50 (2010).

19   Werner Wolf, *The Musicalization of Fiction: A Study in the Theory and History of Intermediality* (Amsterdam and Atlanta, GA: Rodopi, 1999).

20   Sergei Eisenstein, 'Dickens, Griffith, and the Film Today,' in *Film Form: Essays in Film Theory*, (ed. and trans.) Jay Leyda (New York: Harcourt, Brace & World, 1949).

21   Hutcheon, 2006.

22   David Francis Urrows, (ed.), *Essays on Word/Music Adaptation and on Surveying the Field*, vol. 2 of *Word and Music Studies* (Amsterdam and New York: Rodopi, 2008).

23   Elliott (2003), Ch. 4.

24   Angela Dalle Vacche, *Cinema and Painting: How Art is Used in Film* (Austin: University of Texas Press, 1996).

25   However, see Thierry Groensteen, 'Le processus adaptatif (Tentative de récapitulation raisonnée),' in *La transécriture: Pour une théorie de l'adaptation*, (ed.) André Gaudreault and Thierry Groensteen (Québec: Nota bene, 1998), 276–7.

7

Imaginary museums, material refractions: André Bazin on adaptation

Eirik Frisvold Hanssen

This chapter examines the writings of French film theorist André Bazin (1918–59) and attempts to explore how his perspectives on intermediality and the properties of the film medium might be productive when theorizing and analysing adaptation. Film studies in general, and what is often referred to as 'classical film theory' in particular, has always to a great extent been a discourse on intermediality, at least since the Italian futurist Ricciotto Canudo's discussion in 1911 of cinema as the 'sixth art', a synthesis of already existing media.[1] In the film historiography of the past two decades, the intermedial dimensions of classical film theory have been instrumental for examining the role of cinema within a broader cultural, art historical and medial context. These historical and theoretical perspectives have, however, to a very limited extent been integrated in the contemporary theoretical debate on adaptation and cinema. This in spite of a fruitful renewal and expansion of the field in recent years.

More recently, however, Bazin has become somewhat of an exception to the general rule of overlooking the intermedial history of classical film theory. As Kamilla Elliott notes elsewhere in this volume, in current adaptation studies, the writings of Bazin suddenly seem to be everywhere.[2] From being absent as a theoretical reference in many of the most central works on the field throughout the 1990s and early 2000s,[3] the French film theorist has suddenly reappeared as one of the key writers on the topic. This happens simultaneously with a more general renewed interest in the aesthetical and philosophical dimensions of Bazin's extensive theoretical writings within film studies. A new, annotated translation of some of his most well-known essays appeared in 2009,[4] and anthologies and articles carrying titles such as *Opening Bazin* and 'Rethinking Bazin' suggest not only a renewed interest, but also an ambition to re-evaluate his writings.[5] A renaissance for Bazin was probably due, as a great portion of his massive theoretical output has been largely ignored by a majority of film scholars, but the fact that it occurs at this moment in time is probably not entirely coincidental. While discourses (both academic and industrial, in some cases strikingly overlapping each other) on cinema and media in the 1990s and early 2000s, propelled by the emergence of digital media, seemed to emphasize the alleged obliteration of media borders, their being replaced by convergence, a general discourse of intertextuality (where all media manifest-ations were reduced to 'versions' or 'content') and the 'post-medium condition', the last 5–10 years have shown an increased interest in media specificity and questions of ontology (perhaps related to the gradual disappearance of film on celluloid).[6] Rosalind Krauss has recently characterized the 'post-medium condition' as a 'monstrous myth', arguing that 'the abandonment of the specific medium spells the death of serious art.'[7] To ignore media differences is to ignore important formal and aesthetic properties; to overlook the way we perceive and reflect on different kinds of media, as well as central technological, economic and political mechanisms that inform how media are actually produced and distributed. Daniel Morgan claims that a significant part of the value of Bazin, and classical film theory in general, lies specifically in their interest in images as physical objects. The physical and material dimensions of media are fundamental to the way we think about them; this materiality has not become irrelevant because of digitization, as some suggest.[8] Bazin's writings on adaptation and intermediality could perhaps be understood as attempts to establish media ontologies and borders in a broad sense, including formal, psychological and cultural aspects. But, simultaneously, he is questioning and problematizing such ontologies and borders. As argued by Angela Dalle Vacche: 'Cinema's ontology encouraged Bazin to ignore all the standard modernist models [such as Lessing or Wagner]. Like a cultural anthropologist, Bazin pushes the arts well outside the library and the museum and into the unstable world of existence. Thus, he can study the arts' interaction with film in the context of living cultures and changing societies.'[9]

As indicated earlier, this survey of Bazin attempts to relate his wide-ranging writings (consisting of numerous brief essays) to the specific academic field of adaptation studies. Most importantly, texts that usually are discussed separately when applied to the question of adaptation, are combined and synthesized here. The chapter will begin with Bazin's discussion of adaptation in a broad cultural sense and then continue to examine his ideas about more formal and material (in particular spatial) dimensions of adapting (and *not* adapting) literature, theatre and painting in the cinema. Bazin's writings are to be understood historically, within the broader film theoretical and intellectual context in which it was written. In addition, I will throughout give some brief examples on more recent phenomena where Bazin's discussions on adaptation might be relevant.

Adaptation and repetition

In recent adaptation studies, two of Bazin's essays dealing specifically with literary adaptations have been given particular attention, two essays that to a certain extent seem to have offered new ideas on how to approach the question of adaptation as well as how to approach Bazin. The first is the classic essay on Robert Bresson's idiosyncratic adaptation strategies in his film version of Georges Bernanos' *Diary of a Country Priest*; the second is Bazin's essay on 'Adaptation, or Cinema as Digest' from 1948, which was first translated into English in 1997.[10] The former examines adaptation and the relation between cinema and literature from a formal, material perspective, the latter deals with the cultural status and implications of popular adaptations.

It is also the latter that has garnered the most attention in recent years. Here, Bazin defends the popular adaptation, the one designed for the audience rather than for the cinema, as he puts it, and attacks the 'clichéd bias according to which culture is inseparable from intellectual effort', and 'classical modes of cultural communication, which are at once a defense of culture and a secreting of it behind high walls.'[11] One of Bazin's points is that adaptations take part in creating and proliferating national and cultural mythologies, where narratives can first and foremost be regarded as immaterial mental constructs and fictional characters become 'part of our extra-literary mythology; they have a kind of independent existence, of which the original work has become an accidental or almost superfluous manifestation'.[12] The adaptations of, for example, Shakespeare and Mark Twain have been just as important in the formation of national myths as their literary originals, but are often overlooked because of what Bazin labels 'a rather modern notion for which the critics are in large part responsible: that of the untouchability of a work of art.' This modern conception is also linked to the constructedness of the notion of authorship, which Bazin problematized in several of his works. Bazin wrote, in 1948:

> The ferocious defense of literary works is, to a certain extent, aesthetically justified; but we must also be aware that it rests on a rather recent, individualistic conception of the 'author' and of the 'work,' a conception that was far from being ethically rigorous in the seventeenth century and that started to become legally defined only at the end of the eighteenth.[13]

This question of the 'fetishization' of the author and the work as rigorous entities have led various scholars to label Bazin as an early post-structuralist or postmodernist, or as introducing a 'proto-cultural studies idiom'.[14] Bazin envisioned a movement 'toward a reign of adaptation in which the notion of the unity of the work of art, if not the very notion of the author himself, will be destroyed.'[15] Robert Stam has also suggested that Bazin's call for a more open conception of adaptation would include what is now labelled 'intertextuality' and *transécriture*', and anticipated Foucault and Barthes' notion of 'the death of the author'.[16] Two years earlier, in his account of the first Cannes Film Festival, Bazin examined how a literary work of fiction 'simply tends to inevitably reproduce itself in the cinema (to some extent in the theater as well)' and the form of instability, with regard to medium identity and notions of origins, that such transfers produce: 'are we dealing with a play, a book, or a film? I see in it an esthetic trinity, a single work in three arts.'[17] Henry Jenkins established the term 'transmedia storytelling' when analysing how different narrative components of the diegetic universe of *The Matrix* are presented through a variety of media, including three live-action features, an animated television series, websites and comics.[18] Referring to André Malraux's *L'espoir*, executed by the author simultaneously both as a novel and a film, Bazin envisions a future where writers are working transmedially, just as Jenkins describes – 'theoretically there will be nothing to prevent the novelist of the future from writing his work simultaneously in cinema and in literature.'[19] Repeating this argument in the 1948 essay, he envisions a media landscape where the 'chronological precedence of one part over another would not be an aesthetic criterion any more than the chronological precedence of one twin over another'.[20]

In the introduction to the anthology *Film Adaptation* from 2000, James Naremore argues that greater attention to Bazin can free adaptation studies from an overemphasis on formalist aesthetics, as Bazin

> asks us to think of film adaptation in relation to commercialism, industrial modernity, and democracy. [---] The study of adaptation needs to be rejoined with the study of recycling, remaking and every other form of retelling in the age of mechanical reproduction and electronic communication. By this means, adaptation will become part of a general theory of repetition.[21]

Similarly, Dudley Andrew has recently emphasized Bazin's understanding of adaptations as an organic, ecological process, entailing 'to nourish culture via the circulatory system that spreads images to theatres and their audiences. Taken as one cultural form growing not in isolation but amidst many others, cinema grabs what it needs from its neighbors, often giving something back in an ecology of the "life of forms"'.[22] Still, in addition to the cultural and 'media ecological' implications of adaptation, it is nevertheless important to emphasize Bazin's great interest in the formal aesthetics of the phenomenon and the structural and material affinities between cinema and other art forms.

Adaptation and medium specificity

In the 1948 essay on cinematic adaptation as digest, Bazin points out how film adaptations in fact reinforce rather than eliminate the power of drama and novels, how words can bring about a 'longing' for the audio-visual, just as the film image produces a need to describe and talk about what we see through verbal language. Bazin wrote extensively on the relation between film and other media and his ideas on adaptation were not limited to the relation between literature and cinema. Thus, in this chapter I will demonstrate that there are reasons not to forget about Bazin's more general intermedial perspectives, taken from a variety of his theoretical output when discussing this relation.

Bazin starts his 1948 essay by comparing the display of paintings in the art museum with filmic adaptations of literature: 'one might even consider an art museum a digest, for we find collected there a selection of paintings that were intended to exist in a completely different architectural and decorative context.'[23] However, despite these processes of selection, as well as de- and re-contextualization, the paintings remain originals. Bazin again turns to Malraux, this time his vision of the role of painting within the 'imaginary museum', the museum without walls – in many ways a precursor to thinking about 'virtual' museums and the proliferation of images in digital environments overall.[24] Bazin describes how this envisioned museum 'refracts the original painting into millions of facets thanks to photographic reproduction, and it substitutes for that original images of different dimensions and colors that are readily accessible to all', in line with how engravings earlier had functioned as mass-reproduced 'adaptations' of visual artworks.[25] This quote is indicative of how Bazin emphasizes both the broader cultural implications and the formal and aesthetic changes brought about by the various practices of repetition: adaptation, reproduction, refraction, multiplication. The engraving of paintings, the popular novel-to-film adaptation or, for that matter, the proliferation of film through television, video, the web and various digital media, all provide new possibilities, new forms of accessibility, new ways of reception, new industrial and economic structures – but also important formal and material changes that need to be taken into account.

Bazin's most famous description of cinema in relation to other arts occurs in what is probably also his most famous essay, on the ontology of the photographic image. Here, the technical and 'psychological' properties of photographic images – the way they are produced and the audience's knowledge of their genesis – constitute a different relation to human subjectivity, a radical transformation of the psychology of the image and a notion of absence: 'All art is founded upon human agency, but in photography alone can we celebrate its absence'.[26] In addition to the phenomenological dimension of the experience of film found in Bazin's thinking, the emphasis of human absence, of the 'objectivity' and indifference of the photographic, indicates a non-human, or 'post-human', component that is essential in understanding how film and photography radically redefine the experience of artworks and, more importantly, the notion of art in general.[27] On the whole, Bazin's film theory is rooted in what might be described as an intermedial point of view with regard to cinema and other photographic media. The 'ontology' essay places film and photography within a broad art historical background, starting with the practice of embalming in ancient Egyptian culture, proceeding through medieval painting and the invention of the Renaissance perspective, and arguing that photography reveals how the 'history of the visual arts is not only an aesthetic history, but, above all a history of their psychology'.[28] The main difference between film and photography in relation to the existing visual arts is of a psychological nature rather than a material or aesthetic one, lying 'not in the resulting work but rather in its genesis'.[29] In addition, cinema extends the visual arts' drive to defend themselves against time through its temporality, the duration of time that is lacking in still photography: 'For the first time, the image of things is also the image of their duration, like a mummification of change'.[30] Cinema's specificity is nevertheless quite unstable and more susceptible to technological changes than, for example, that of literature. The aesthetics of cinema is continually transformed through the emergence of sound, colour, new forms of film stock, 3–D, etc.: 'every change of real importance, which enriches our cinematic heritage, is closely

linked to technology. Technology is cinema's infrastructure.'[31] In
addition, Bazin argues that analogies between cinema and other
arts often are deceptive, especially comparisons with media based
on individual creation such as painting or literature. Cinema is,
like e.g. architecture, dependent on extensive financing and a
large audience – it is a functional art, and an industrial art; Bazin
also paraphrases his contemporary Jean-Paul Sartre by claiming
that in the case of film, 'its existence precedes its essence'.[32] Bazin
acknowledges that technological and economic changes significantly influence the aesthetic development of all media, but argues
that cinema is fundamentally different from earlier art forms as
it appeared quite suddenly and very late within human cultural
history, as a product of a conjunction between specific economic
and technological circumstances. This bestows cinema with a kind
of 'mortality' that separates it from media such as music, literature
and painting; if these specific circumstances change, cinema might
disappear as suddenly as it came to being.[33]

Adapting textual realities

Bazin's discussion of cinema's relation to other media is informed
by the same notion of incompleteness and absence as his discussion
of cinema's general capacity to represent an external reality, and
the phenomenological aspects of the experience of film images.
Recurring in his work on filmic adaptation, whether of literature,
theatre or painting, are a number of spatial metaphors about the
specific materiality and fragmentation of the given work, and of
the medium presented through another medium – the cinema. For
example, Bresson's *Diary of a Country Priest* is understood not so
much as an adaptation of Bernanos' novel as a 'refraction', it is the
novel as the film medium sees it.[34]

With regard to the adaptation of the novel, Bresson declared
his intention to rigorously follow the book word-for-word. The
consequence of this strategy, according to Bazin, is that Bresson's
'fidelity takes the most insidious and discerning forms, the greatest
creative liberties. There can be no doubt … it is impossible to adapt
without transposing. The most faithful translations do not follow
the text word by word.'[35] Later in the analysis, he explains why:

its dialectic of fidelity and creation boils down to the dialectic of film and literature. Here it is no longer a case of translating, as faithfully and intelligently as might be the case, and even less of being freely inspired by loving respect, to create a film that will be the novel's double. The point, rather, is to construct on top of the novel, through cinema, a work in another state. Not a film which can be described as 'comparable' to the novel, or 'worthy' of it, but a new aesthetic existence, something like literature multiplied by cinema.[36]

What thus ensues from this faithfulness to Bernanos' text is, according to Bazin, a 'paradoxical effect.'[37] Textual elements, i.e. quotations taken directly from the novel, are presented as words being written on a page or as dialogue or voice-over performed in a deliberately monotone, non-psychological style. This specific style is in many ways contrary to the characteristics of the novel, which Bazin describes as 'full of picturesque descriptions – meaty, concrete, strongly visual.' Thus, in comparison, 'the film is literary and the novel teeming with images.'[38] Bazin suggests that Bresson's adaptation can almost be understood as 'a silent film with spoken subtitles', since 'speech here is in no way a realistic element of the image.'[39]

Dudley Andrew describes Bazin's reading of *Diary of a Country Priest* as the key text relating to a mode or attitude toward adaptation that he labels 'intersecting', where 'the uniqueness of the original text is preserved to such an extent that it is intentionally left unassimilated in adaptation. The cinema, as a separate mechanism, records its confrontation with an ultimately intransigent text.'[40] Bazin suggestively describes how the film relates to what he understands as two separate 'realities' that are dialectically confronted: first the diegetic reality of the fictional world, and then what he calls a second given reality, the literary text itself, as 'a raw aesthetic fact'. Since the literary text as it appears in the film is not condensed or edited, but rather cut and fragmented, what is left remains 'an original fragment. Just as a block of marble has been taken from a quarry, the words spoken in the film are still a part of the novel.'[41] Bresson demonstrates that it is 'more fruitful to examine their differences than the things they share, to bring out the novel's existence through film rather than to dissolve the novel in it.' Through Bresson, the film adaptation becomes a site for problematizing not only media borders but also realism, as literature itself is treated as a form of reality by being put on film.

Adapting theatrical space

In the preceding example, literature was conceptualized through spatial and material metaphors, and Andrew has identified the similarities between Bazin's description of the Bernanos adaptation and his elaboration on a metaphor by Baudelaire when discussing cinema in relation to theatre:[42]

'Theatre', Baudelaire remarked, 'is its chandelier. If I had to contrast another symbol with this crystalline, glittering, many-faceted, circular and artificial object, which refracts the lights around its centre and holds us spellbound in its aureole, I would say that film is the little flashlight of the usherette who crosses the night of our awakened dream like a fleeting comet. This is the diffuse space, without geometry or boundaries, which surrounds the screen.'[43]

With regard to theatre, Bazin emphasizes the importance of a specific dramatic *space*, of architecture, of the division presented spatially (albeit in different forms throughout theatre history) between the stage and the audience, relating to the audience and demonstratively existing in contrast to the rest of the world. The stage functions as

a physically enclosed space, a limited and circumscribed space that discovers only what our imagination sanctions. Its appearances are turned inwards, towards the audiences and the theatre apron. It exists by virtue of the fact that nothing lies beyond it, the way a painting exists by virtue of its frame. Just as a painting is never confused with the landscape it depicts – and neither is it a window in a wall – the stage and the set in which the action takes place are an aesthetic microcosm forcefully thrust into the world yet fundamentally different from their natural surroundings.[44]

While theatre thus emphasizes the boundaries of the action, cinema on the other hand denies these boundaries, the cinema screen is based on the notion that something always exists outside the frame, as in Bazin's recurring description of the film screen as a mask: 'The screen is not a frame like the frame of a painting, but a *mask* that reveals only part of an event. [---] The space of the screen, unlike the space of the stage, is centrifugal.'[45] Thus, the properties of the frame determine different directions of energy in images: a film image is directed outwards, beyond the frame, while the energy of a painting is directed inwards.

Just as Bazin admired the film medium's particular 'gaze' on the words taken directly from Bernanos' novel, he defended the display of theatricality through acting styles and painted sets in Laurence Olivier's Shakespeare adaptations. Bazin's theory on adaptation is in many ways a call for non-adaptation strategies, or 'intersectings' as found in Bresson's word-by-word fidelity, and prefigures an even more concrete realization in many of the works by Jean-Marie Straub and Danièle Huillet, such as *The Chronicle of Anna Magdalena Bach* (1968), *Moses und Aron* (1975) and *Une visite au Louvre* (2004),[46] as well as Jean-Luc Godard's montage and analysis of film (and other media, such as music and literature) through video in *Histoire(s) du cinema* (1980–98). Bazin's writings on film in relation to theatre and painting particularly accentuate and concretize the spatial dimension of his understanding of adaptation. Through emphasizing the spatial, he continuously links fidelity and faithfulness to a source text, or rather a source *medium* (spatially reconfigured through cinema), to a notion of 'paradox', which should first and foremost be read as a critique of contemporary preconceptions of cinematic 'purity'. One of Bazin's favourite examples in this respect is William Wyler's *The Little Foxes* (1941), based on a play by Lillian Hellman, where the director's use of *mise-en-scène* 'is pushed to the point of paradox'.[47] Here, most of the dialogue of the play is retained, the majority of scenes take place within the same interior, the cinematography is based on long, static takes; there are relatively few camera movements and cuts. According to Bazin, these are 'the paradoxical means by which Wyler has created one of the most purely cinematic films there is',[48] because of Wyler's controlled use of minimalist, or 'realist' cinematography, which never tries to alter the theatricality of the source text: 'The camera itself organizes the action, using the frame of the image and the mental coordinates of its dramatic geometry.'[49]

Bazin uses Wyler's films, and films employing similar adaptation strategies, such as *Les parents terribles* (Jean Cocteau, 1948), *Rope* (Alfred Hitchcock, 1948) and Laurence Olivier's Shakespeare adaptations, where we are constantly reminded of the theatrical nature of the source material, to criticize modernist (or 'formalist') film theories advocating cinematic purity as something that should be opposed to realistic reproduction, and that is radically different from literature and theatre in particular:

> It is madness to see cinema as something isolated that can be set down on a piece of celluloid and projected on a screen through an enlarging lense. Pure cinema exists in a weepie just as much as it does in Oskar Fischinger's coloured cubes. Cinema is not some sort of independent matter whose crystals must be isolated at all costs. [---] we must be aware of equating cinema with a given aesthetic or, even worse, with who knows what kind of style, some sort of substantialized form that the film-maker is obliged to use, at least as seasoning.[50]

As Philip Rosen puts it, Bazin criticizes the reduction of 'authentic cinema to something like the cinematic apparatus as such', as the cinematic apparatus is intrinsically connected to that which exists outside it, the nature of cinema is to encompass the external world: cinematic specificity would *'necessarily include the non-cinematic'*.[51]

According to Bazin, the main problem with most theatre adaptations is the concern to 'make cinema', a tendency to 'inject 'cinema' into theatre by force':[52] 'If the action is supposed to take place on the Riviera, the lovers, rather than chatting at an outdoor café, will be shown kissing behind the wheel of an American car while they drive along the La Corniche road with the cliffs of Cap d'Antibes in rear projection behind them.'[53]

Bazin instead defends what he polemically calls 'impure cinema', pointing out that the much-criticized practice of adaptation has been a constant feature of art history, both in terms of adapting techniques (Renaissance painting adapting Gothic sculpture, Michelangelo adapting Giotto, pre-classical tragedies adapting pastoral novels) and of themes and stories circulating between different forms of expression, and different media.[54]

The main purpose of a kind of 'radical' fidelity to the source material is to challenge established conventions and 'rules' regarding what constitutes the 'cinematic', the preconceived notion of pure art, the ready-made conclusions about what the language of cinema ideally should consist of. Fidelity can broaden the scope of cinema by breaking these established narrative and stylistic conventions, film can be renewed through the apparent negation of what one hitherto has believed to be cinema:[55]

> To view literary adaptation as a lazy practice from which true cinema – 'pure cinema' – has nothing to gain is thus a critical confusion contradicted by every adaptation of value. These adaptations are the least concerned with the sort of fidelity dictated by supposed cinematic rules which betray both literature and film.[56]

What is shared by the theatrical adaptations of Olivier, Wyler, Hitchcock and Cocteau is, just as in Bresson's film, a paradox: 'an almost provocative admission of their theatrical origins. It is almost as if a kind of faithfulness, not only to the original material but to its aesthetic specificity, to what most radically contrasts it with film, were an essential secret of its success.'[57] The radical fidelity, emphasizing the theatrical and the literary rather than hiding it, is based on an aesthetic inventiveness and a mastery of the film medium seldom found in more traditional adaptation strategies: 'There is a hundred times more cinema, and better cinema, in one immobile shot in *The Little Foxes* or *Macbeth* than there is in all the outdoor tracking shots, natural settings, exotic locations and glimpses behind the scenes with which film had previously strained in vain to try to make us forget the stage.'[58]

   Representing theatre through non-adaptation strategies offers a 'realism of space' rather than a realism of subject matter, where the play itself, its theatrical specificity, becomes the subject of the film, extending the language of cinema.[59]

Adapting the painterly frame

Bazin's film theory is in many respects an account of various processes of transfer where the physical and material existence and

qualities of film images have repercussions for how we understand and interact with what is being 'refracted' or 'multiplied' by the film medium. History and reality are materialized through the process of being captured on film; when discussing the newsreel, Bazin describes film in material terms as a form of physical substance, a type of 'skin', stripping the world bare, instantly peeling off the surface of history as soon as it is formed.[60]

The descriptions of absence, of incompleteness, of the uncertain movement within a diffuse, shapeless, borderless space, or of a fragmented, material world, when discussing cinema in relation to literature and theatre, are strikingly similar to another set of metaphors of spatiality and materiality presented by Bazin in connection with a discussion of the relationship between cinema and a third medium: painting.

Bazin points out that the only films that are comparable to the radical fidelity of Bresson's Bernanos adaptation are in fact certain films about painting, by among others Alain Resnais and Luciano Emmer: 'Their raw material is the work already formed in the highest degree by the painter, and their reality is not at all the subject of the painting but rather the painting itself, just as we have seen that Bresson's reality is the very text of the novel'.[61] In Bazin's famous analysis of art documentaries such as Resnais' film on Picasso's 'Guernica' (1950), he emphasizes how the painting, through cinema, functions just like a natural landscape, and how the film moves within this landscape but also outside of it. As was the case with theatre, the main difference between painting and cinema is defined through the properties of the frame: the 'centripetal' frame of painting is the limit of an enclosed space, 'the orientation of which is inwards, a contemplative area opening solely onto the interior of the painting.' This in contrast to the edges of the 'centrifugal' film image, which rather constitute 'the edges of a piece of masking that shows only a portion of reality.'[62] Thus, the fact that the film alters the painting in the adaptation process, in fact is unable to reproduce it in full, is not a limitation, as many contemporary critics of art documentaries suggested. The whole purpose of the film, according to Bazin, is the fragmentation and spatial disorientation of the original work, the 'othering' on a material level. A new analysis of Picasso's painting is achieved precisely because of the differences between cinema and painting with regard to formal properties such as duration, framing, editing and absence of colour. The novelty of Resnais' art documentaries was primarily linked to spatial dimensions, how the 'the abolition of the frame ... makes us equate the pictorial universe with the universe itself in all its tangibility' – through cinema, painting achieves a material existence just like any other part of reality. Henri-Georges Clouzot's *Le mystère Picasso* (1956), which demonstrates the process behind a number of drawings and paintings through a variety of material, cinematic means, uses the film medium to explore how temporal dimensions, like duration itself, can also be an integral part of a painting. Bazin claims that the film is 'Bergsonian' because it demonstrates how time and duration are a prerequisite for a creative process, and for freedom of the mind in general, here made visible through art.[63]

Representing a painting through cinema does not recreate the painting, it rather creates a new work – the art documentary is thus similar to earlier art criticism practices. The same goes for the representation of literature and theatre. Bazin understands cinema as neither opposed to other art forms nor as an absolute *Gesamtkunstwerk*-like fusion of already existing media. In general, a film cannot quote or encompass an entire work just as a film can never encompass the whole reality it is trying to represent. What is central here is, again, the extension of cinematic space beyond the boundaries of the image, and the screen as a mask.[64] Just as it relates to reality, cinema, and its screen as a mask, relates to the other arts by transforming them, and consequently also transforming the experience of specific artworks and the notion of art in general.

Adaptation and the invention of cinema

Bazin wrote specifically about developments in contemporary film culture in the 1940s and 1950s, and offered polemics to some of the established assertions of pre-WWII film theory. Bazin examined the implications of a cultural landscape that was changing fundamentally, and how cinema in particular affected the relationship between media and the concept of art in general. It would be futile to comprehend the discussions on cinema's relation to the other arts by Bazin, a theorist of cultural change and of the present, in terms of rigid, normative, ahistorical characterizations of what film, painting, theatre and literature is and is not.[65] As Angela Dalle Vacche points out, his understanding of the dialogue between cinema and older art forms is not 'systematic or prescriptive to the point of excluding recent developments, such as digital media, from pursuing new kinds of conversations with film.'[66] The usefulness of Bazin in the current media landscape, which of course has changed radically (and recurrently) since his death, is instead to be found in his original conceptualization of fidelity or faithfulness, his emphasis on the spatial dimensions of media and the properties of the frame, as well as his general recognition of adaptation as refraction, with aesthetic as well as cultural and economic implications. For example, Bazin's conceptualization of the distinction between the filmic frame as centrifugal and the painterly and theatrical frame as centripetal has been useful in the analysis of film screens outside the space of the cinema, for example in the gallery. Catherine Fowler has elaborated on this distinction and noted related functions of the frame in connection with the 'gallery film': it either appears to contain the image (that can be read centripetally, like a painting), or serves to connect the image to the gallery space, 'suggesting the spilling over of the image into the viewer's space', partly as a function of the centrifugal nature of the film image, its status as a partial representation, always implying an off-screen space.[67]

Likewise, current 3–D cinema seems to reinforce the usefulness of Bazin's film theory in general, and his writings on adaptation and intermediality in particular.[68] A striking number of the most successful and critically acclaimed recent films in 3–D deal with the spatial dimensions of other media, fitting almost perfectly with Bazin's conceptions of fidelity and realism of space as ways to expand the language of cinema in a format that questions and broadens established conventions of what cinema is and what its aesthetics should be like. Films such as *Pina* (Wim Wenders 2011) and *Step Up 3D* (Jon M. Chu 2010) represent dance in depth and in volume, not only through bodies moving in space but also through an emphasis on continuous space and a thematization of theatrical space relating to the world outside. The literary adaptation *The Three Musketeers* (Paul W. S. Anderson 2011) pays almost as much attention to the spatiality of hand-written documents, maps, heavily ornamented textiles and chessboards, with these becoming separate realities in themselves, as the rest of the diegesis. *Cave of Forgotten Dreams* (Werner Herzog, 2010) uses 3–D to highlight not only ancient cave paintings but also the uneven, curved material surfaces of the rocks they are drawn on. Films like *Avatar* (James Cameron, 2009) and *Tron: Legacy* (Joseph Kosinski, 2010) construct three-dimensional cinematic spaces from digital environments and media that did not exist during Bazin's lifetime. In *Hugo* (Martin Scorsese 2011), the inherent three-dimensionality of early cinema is explored, both in the multi-layered compositions of Georges Méliès' films and in the film material itself; in *Prometheus* (Ridley Scott 2012), the pixels of video images are given a physical, autonomous existence in space through 3–D.

'Cinema has yet to be invented!', Bazin famously proclaimed in 1946, more than 50 years after the alleged invention of the medium.[69] And almost 70 years after these words were written, the situation is basically the same: cinema retains a strong medium specificity and a distinctive ontology while having been in continual aesthetic and technological change the whole time. It is a medium that constantly needs to be invented and reinvented. And one of the most important arenas for the invention of cinema still is adaptation and refraction, cinema's persistent dialogue with other media, old and new.

Notes

1   Ricciotto Canudo, 'La naissance d'un sixième art: Essai sur le cinématographie' (1911), *L'usine aux images* (Paris: Éditions Séguier, 1995), 32–40. Agnes Petho's recent *Cinema and Intermediality: The Passion for the In-Between* (Newcastle: Cambridge Scholars Publishing, 2011) mainly draws her discussion on recent theorization on intermediality, but also includes and acknowledges the heritage from classical film theory with regard to the topic, referring to Bazin as well as e.g. Sergei Eisenstein, Vachel Lindsay, Siegfried Kracauer, and Rudolf Arnheim.

2   Elliott's chapter in this volume.

3   Bazin is not mentioned at all in oft-quoted publications such as Brian McFarlane, *Novel to Film: An Introduction to the Theory of Adaptation* (Oxford: Clarendon Press, 1996), Linda Hutcheon, *A Theory of Adaptation* (New York London: Routledge, 2006), nor

the anthology *Adaptations: From Screen to Text*, Deborah Cartmell/ Imelda Wheelan (eds) (New York and London: Routlege, 1999).

4 André Bazin, *What Is Cinema?*, (ed. and trans) Timothy Barnard (Montreal: Caboose, 2009).

5 See Daniel Morgan, 'Rethinking Bazin: Ontology and Realist Aesthetics', *Critical Inquiry* 32 (2006), 443–81, and *Opening Bazin: Postwar Film Theory & Its Afterlife*, Dudley Andrew, Hervé Joubert-Laurencin (eds) (Oxford and New York: Oxford University Press, 2011). See also Philip Rosen, *Change Mummified: Cinema, Historicity, Theory* (Minneapolis and London: University of Minnesota Press, 2001).

6 See e.g. D. N. Rodowick, *The Virtual Life of Film* (Cambridge and London: Harvard University Press, 2007) and Dudley Andrew, *What Cinema Is! Bazin's Quest and Its Charge* (Malden and Oxford: Wiley-Blackwell, 2010).

7 Rosalind Krauss, *Perpetual Inventory* (Cambridge, MA and London: The MIT Press, 2010), xiii–xiv.

8 Morgan, 443f.

9 Angela Dalle Vacche, 'The Difference of Cinema in the System of the Arts' (2011), *Opening Bazin, 142*.

10 André Bazin, '*Diary of a Country Priest* and the Robert Bresson Style' (1951a), *What Is Cinema?* (2009), 139–59. André Bazin, 'Adaptation, or the Cinema as Digest' (1948), *Bazin at Work: Major Essays & Reviews from the Forties & Fifties*, (ed.) Bert Cardullo (New York and London: Routledge, 1997), 41–51.

11 Bazin (1948), 44f.

12 André Bazin, 'For an Impure Cinema: In Defence of Adaptation' (1952), *What Is Cinema?* (2009), 107. See also John Bryant's chapter in this volume.

13 Bazin (1948), 46.

14 See James Naremore, 'Introduction: Film and the Reign of Adaptation', *Film Adaptation*, (ed.) James Naremore (London: The Athlone Press, 2000), 14. See also Andrew, (2010), 113.

15 Bazin (1948), 49.

16 Robert Stam, *Literature through Film: Realism, Magic, and the Art of Adaptation* (Malden and Oxford: Blackwell Publishing, 2005), 257.

17 André Bazin, 'The Cannes Festival of 1946' (1946), *French Cinema of the Occupation and Resistance: The Birth of a Critical Esthetic,*

(ed.) François Truffaut (New York: Frederick Ungar Publishing, 1981), 140.

18 See Henry Jenkins, *Convergence Culture: Where Old and New Media Collide* (New York and London: New York University Press, 2006), 93–130.

19 Bazin (1946), 140.

20 Bazin (1948), 50.

21 Naremore, 15.

22 Andrew (2010), 130. See also Jørgen Bruhn's chapter in this volume.

23 Bazin (1948), 41.

24 André Malraux, 'Museum Without Walls' (1947), *The Voices of Silence* (Princeton: Princeton University Press, 1978), 13–128.

25 Bazin (1948), 41.

26 André Bazin, 'Ontology of the Photographic Image' (1945/1958), *What Is Cinema?* (2009), 7.

27 See Angela Dalle Vacche, 'Introduction: A Cosmology of Contingency', *Film, Art, New Media: Museum Without Walls?*, (ed.) Angela Dalle Vacche (New York: Palgrave-Macmillan, 2012), 11–19.

28 Bazin (1945/1958), 4.

29 Ibid., 8.

30 Ibid., 9.

31 André Bazin, 'William Wyler, the Jansenist of Mise en Scène' (1948/1958), *What Is Cinema?* (2009), 53.

32 Bazin (1952), 133. For a discussion on the influence of Sartre in Bazin's writings, see e.g. Andrew (2010), 11ff.

33 André Bazin, 'Will CinemaScope Save the Film Industry?' (1953), *Bazin at Work*, 85f.

34 Bazin (1951a), 159.

35 Ibid., 141.

36 Ibid., 157.

37 Ibid., 141.

38 Ibid., 142.

39 Ibid., 153.

40 Dudley Andrew, 'Adaptation', *Film Adaptation*, 30.

41 Bazin (1951a), 150–1.

42 Andrew, 'Adaptation', 31.

43   André Bazin, ,'Theatre and Film (2)' (1951b), *What Is Cinema?* (2009), 194f.

44   Bazin (1951b), 195.

45   Bazin (1951b), 193.

46   For a discussion on the connection between Bazin's ideas about adaptation and the films of Straub-Huillet, see http://www.offscreen. com/index.php/pages/essays/timothy_barnard/ (accessed 3 January 2013).

47   Bazin (1948/1958), 47.

48   Ibid.

49   Ibid., 49.

50   Ibid., 67.

51   Philip Rosen, 'Belief in Bazin' (2011), *Opening Bazin*, op.cit., 111.

52   André Bazin, 'Theatre and Film (1)' (1951/1959), *What Is Cinema?* (2009), 171f.

53   Ibid., 172.

54   André Bazin (1952), 111.

55   Bazin (1952), 124. Bazin (1951), 146.

56   Bazin (1952), 125.

57   Ibid., 127.

58   Bazin (1952), 130. See also Bazin (1951/1959), 173–80.

59   Bazin (1951b), 200, 203.

60   Andre Bazin, 'On *Why We Fight*: History, Documentation, and the Newsreel'(1946), *Bazin at Work*, op.cit., 189.

61   Bazin (1951), 158.

62   André Bazin, 'Painting and Cinema' (1958), *What Is Cinema?*, Vol. 1, (ed. and trans.) Hugh Gray (Berkeley, Los Angeles and London: University of California Press, 1967), 167.

63   André Bazin, 'A Bergsonian Film: *The Picasso Mystery*' (1956), *Bazin at Work*, 212ff. How the temporal dimensions of painting relate to cinema has of course also been thoroughly examined in Sergei Eisenstein's montage theory. See e.g. Sergei Eisenstein, 'Yermolova' and 'Laocoön', both published in *Selected Works, Volume II: Towards a Theory of Montage (1937–1940)*, Michael Glenny, Richard Taylor (eds) (London: BFI Publishing, 1991), 82–202.

64   André Bazin, *Jean Renoir* (1957) (New York: Simon and Schuster, 1973), 87.

65 Bazin also includes this historical perspective, not only in relation to cinema but also with regard to theatrical space. See Bazin (1951b), 189.

66 Angela Dalle Vacche (2011), 142.

67 Catherine Fowler, 'Room for Experiment: Gallery Films and Vertical Time from Maya Deren to Eija Liisa Ahtila', *Screen* 45:4 (2004), 332f.

68 Bazin wrote briefly on 3–D or stereoscopy, see 'The Myth of Total Cinema' (1946/1958), *What Is Cinema?* (2009), 16; Bazin (1953), 88f. See also Grant Wiedenfeld, 'Bazin and the Margins of the Seventh Art', *Opening Bazin*, 262.

69 Bazin (1946/1958), 17.

8

What movies want

Thomas Leitch

This essay aims not to answer but to deconstruct the question its title implies. Although I shall indicate in due course what movies want, I am more interested in examining the proposition that they want, or could possibly want, anything at all. I understand that movies are different from the moviemakers from whom no one would think of withholding desire and agency. Even so, I intend in this essay – I had almost written 'this essay intends,' but that would have begged the question by assuming that essays can intend anything – to advance two highly tendentious arguments: that texts of all sorts can be seen as having some of the same drives and desires that are commonly imputed to their creators, and that movies – that is, commercially released narrative cinema – offer a quintessential example of these drives and desires in action. Because these are extravagant claims, I would like to approach them gradually and inductively, beginning by using Pier Paolo Pasolini's celebrated 1965 essay 'The Screenplay as a "Structure That Wants to Be Another Structure"' as the thin edge of the wedge.

According to Pasolini, screenplays, especially those screenplays that are not based on novels or translated into films, pose special problems for anyone who seeks to evaluate them. In addition to assessing each screenplay as 'a "type of writing" ... with its particular prosody and its own metrics,' judges must take into account its position as a blueprint for a potential film. The double status of every screenplay's language, contends Pasolini, means that its *primary structural element is the integrating reference to a potential cinematographic work.*' Every sign in a screenplay both refers to 'the meaning according to the normal path of all written languages' and *'hints at that same meaning, forwarding the addressee to another sign, that of the potential film.'* The distinctive doubleness of these signs makes the screenplay a unique kind of writing whose success depends on collaborative readers whose 'representational imagination', supplementing the words of the screenplay with a visual dimension the screenwriter has systematically excluded, 'enters into a creative phase mechanically much higher and more intense than when he reads a novel.'[1]

Although surprisingly little has been written about screenplays as a distinctive mode of writing, theories of screenwriting continue to be deeply influenced by Pasolini's analysis. Screenwriter Howard Rodman, for example, agreeing with producer James Schamus that screenplays are 'brutally instrumentalist', notes that 'an uncommissioned screenplay is referred to as a "spec," as if it were less an expression than a speculation. Even in other arts whose history is equally tinged with the notion of patrons, of salary, of the work for hire, there's far less emphasis on the teleology. One would not, for instance, speak of a spec fresco.'[2] Yet the amusing and unassailable distinction Rodman points out between screenplays and frescos may obscure a deeper kinship he does not consider that screenplays have with apparently more independent works of art, a kinship that is illuminated in surprising ways by recent work in adaptation studies – not, on the whole, by studies of textual adaptation, but by recent debates on the cultural implications of Darwinian models of biological adaptation that I will examine more closely in due course.

Even readers who think they are entering into exactly the sort of collaboration Pasolini reserves for the readers of screenplays by taking the trouble to visualize every image presented by the novels they read are likely to find his argument that screenplays are everywhere informed by the invitation for readers to complete them by adding their missing visual component enormously suggestive. In fact, Pasolini was far ahead of his time in proposing that screenplays cannot be judged as independent texts because each of them wants to be another text. But his formulation has dated in at least one respect. Pasolini contends that if a screenplay does not make continuous allusion to the movie it hopes to become, then 'its appearance as screenplay is purely a pretext (a situation that has yet to occur).'[3] He could not have known that the publication of unproduced screenplays, rare in the 1960s, would accelerate apace over the following half-century. Moviegoers can now read the complete 300–page screenplay Erich von Stroheim wrote for *Greed* (1924), the second draft screenplay Vladimir Nabokov wrote for *Lolita* (Stanley Kubrick 1962) – though not Nabokov's first draft, which reportedly ran to 400 pages – and *The Proust Screenplay*, Harold Pinter's still unfilmed adaptation of *A la recherche du temps perdu*.

Since 2006, Hollywood executive Franklin Leonard has been issuing annual editions of The Black List, under which he collects what a group of his fellow-executives consider the year's ten best unproduced screenplays. Many readers of these screenplays surely read them with reference to the movies they aspired to become. The Black List is aimed more or less explicitly at Hollywood producers, and a number of screenplays Leonard has considered, from *Inglorious Basterds* (Quentin Tarantino 2009) to *Sherlock Holmes* (Guy Ritchie 2009) to *Easy A* (Will Gluck 2010) have been made into successful films. But it also stands as an archive that preserves the screenplays it collects as screenplays and testifies to their tropism to be what they are rather than the will Pasolini ascribes to them to become something else. The ready availability of hundreds of unproduced screenplays online and the increasingly frequent publication of screenplays for films that have already been released make it likely that many other readers read the signs in screenplays on their own terms, without following Pasolini's forwarding address to another set of signs. For better or worse, a substantial audience that has arisen over the past half-century seems to regard screenplays as just one more discursive mode of storytelling, not at all the unique phenomenon Pasolini claimed.

But this essay is less interested (if essays can be said to be interested) in the evolution of the ways people read screenplays than in the distinctiveness Pasolini claimed for them. For screenplays are only the beginning of a long list of texts that want to be other texts. Pasolini himself notes that the poems of symbolists like Mallarmé and Ungaretti already 'require of the reader an operation similar to the one' undertaken by readers of screenplays by 'requir[ing] us to cooperate by "pretending" to hear [their] graphemes acoustically.'[4] The number of texts that ask to be read both on their own terms and as blueprints or recipes for other texts has grown exponentially since Pasolini wrote. Even more revealingly, Pasolini helps us see this invitation even in texts that had been extending it for many years before.

Although Pasolini most explicitly contrasts screenplays with movies, cinema is a medium whose desires have changed a great deal more than either music or literature since Pasolini wrote. In 1965, it made sense to regard individual movies as individual works of art, or, if you did not care to describe them as art, as individual products. It is much harder to regard them that way these days. Just as television pilots want to become television series, and each season of a television series wants to engender further seasons, an ever-increasing number of movies seek to generate sequels, prequels or franchises. Their highest aspiration would seem to be giving birth each to an intermedial franchise that included the most diverse possible media mix, from other movies to novelizations, television specials, comic strips, branded apparel and McDonald's Happy Meal figures. The exceptions to this imperialistic imperative are marketed, at least in the US, as 'niche' movies. These films, often 'counter-programmed' against summer blockbusters, are expected to reach limited audiences (e.g. tweens, teenaged girls, moviegoers over 21) and reap limited financial rewards.

Although the proliferation of intermedial franchises may be a relatively recent development, it suggests that the 1960s, when Pasolini was filming and writing, were more an outlier in this regard than today, especially in Hollywood. For until the decline of the studio system in the years just before Pasolini wrote, the unstated goal of every Hollywood product was to devise a new recipe for generic reproduction. Unlike theorists who 'have a vested interest in strong genres and single genre affiliation', contemporary producers like the fictitious Griffin Mill (Tim Robbins) in *The Player* (Robert Altman 1992) 'spend all their time listening to writers trying to identify their scripts with as many genres as possible' because they share with their grandfathers, the industry's founders, the primary goal of mass saturation that 'conceive[s] films as a mix of as many genres as called for by targeted audiences.'[5] In the process, these genre hybrids constantly stretch the formulas of their genres, sometimes producing travesties like *Billy the Kid Versus*

Dracula (William Beaudine 1966), sometimes renewing the genres in ways that insure their survival. In the mid-1950s, films like *The Far Country* (Anthony Mann 1954) and *The Searchers* (John Ford 1956) did not bother to generate sequels; instead, they focused on the more important business of establishing the formula for the widescreen Western (stark personal conflicts played out against picturesque natural landscapes filmed in Technicolor). Early and late, with important exceptions like the 1960s and early 1970s, the American film industry in particular has depended on producing cinematic texts that could in turn encourage the production of other texts, from movies to fan magazines to iPhone apps.

The fact that so many movies, from recent franchise kick-offs to classic genre films, aspire to be blueprints or recipes for other texts alerts us to the many other texts with similar ambitions. The most obvious of these texts are blueprints and recipes themselves. Like screenplays, these structures employ a set of signs that derive their meanings from the conventions of their representational genres while referring at the same time to the structures they hope to become. The same rule applies to self-help books, instruction manuals and volumes like *Sex for Dummies*. Advertisements, with their constant subtext *Buy this! Do this!*, belong in this category as well, along with other texts whose primary force is hortatory rather than representational: Dickens's Christmas books, *Pilgrim's Progress* and the Gospel According to St. John.

What all of these texts have in common is not formal openness or inconclusiveness but pragmatic and projective incompleteness. After sketching alternative visions of the future, both *A Christmas Carol* and *The Chimes* end with explicit pleas to their readers to work for the happy endings rather than settling for the sad endings. Advertisements are not effective unless they get their viewers to buy new products. St. John's Gospel will not rest content until its listeners accept Jesus as their messiah. *Sex for Dummies* has not achieved its goal until its readers are no longer dummies, at least not about sex. Each of these texts is therefore both a linguistic structure intelligible and complete in itself and a praxis that remains incomplete until it is imagined and enacted.

It might be objected here that hortatory texts commonly achieve their ends without creating new texts. But this objection would depend on a very narrow definition of texts. Like screenplays, dramatic scripts like those of *Oedipus the King* and *Spider-Man:*

Turn Off the Dark, musical scores for *The Messiah* and *Tristan and Isolde,* and Labanotations of ballets like *Swan Lake* and *Fancy Free* are intended first and foremost for performance, not for reading. The fact that their performance does not produce a tangible text we can hold or store or consult does not make them any the less performance texts. Such texts appeal to two kinds of readers: those who have a direct influence in bringing the work at hand to life by producing or performing it, and those accidental readers, like students stumbling through *Hamlet,* who happen to be reading a blueprint designed for quite another purpose. Indeed teachers of drama have long understood every play's primary status as a performance text that wants to be another text – or, more precisely, an indefinitely extended series of texts, nightly performances, each distinct from all the others, that playwrights and producers hope will run for years.

In the most prophetic passage in his essay, Pasolini makes this point himself. Observing that 'the sign of the screenplay ... *captures the form in movement'*, he argues that the structure of screenplays is both synchronic, every element existing simultaneously in textual space, and diachronic, unfolding not merely as an evolutionary 'passage from a phase A to a phase B, but ... a pure and simple "dynamism," ... a "tension" which moves, without departing or arriving, from a stylistic structure ... to another.' Just as the dynamic structure of screenplays resists reduction to spatial forms that can be transcribed and reproduced, the structure of performance texts and exhortations amounts to what Pasolini calls *'a structure morphologically in movement.'*[6]

A striking illustration of this suggestive idea is the four sculptures Michelangelo called *Captives,* statues of four incomplete human figures that seem to be struggling to emerge from the heavy stone that imprisons them. Richard Poirier, who reproduces a photograph of one of these sculptures on the cover of his 1971 collection *The Performing Self,* identifies as his subject the process of 'shaping a self out of the materials in which it is immersed.' The energy he locates in the activity of shaping a performing self, Poirier contends, is, like the nature of the sign in Pasolini's screenplay, 'an energy in motion, an energy which is its own shape', and one that therefore resists all '[e]fforts to institutionalize the study of literature.'[7] It is hardly surprising that Gary Taylor ends his monograph *Cultural Selection* by using one of these four figures to conclude in his final sentence: 'Culture is unfinished.'[8]

So radical are the claims of Pasolini and Poirier, and so wide is the range of texts that could plausibly be described as texts that want to be other texts, that Stephen Dedalus, that aesthetic radical from the opposite end of the ideological spectrum, makes a point of excluding all such texts from the category of proper art. As Stephen tells his friend Lynch in *A Portrait of the Artist as a Young Man*: 'The feelings excited by improper art are kinetic, desire or loathing. Desire urges us to possess, to go to something; loathing urges us to abandon, to go from something. These are kinetic emotions. The arts which excite them, pornographical or didactic, are therefore improper arts. The esthetic emotion ... is therefore static. The mind is arrested and raised above desire and loathing.'[9]

Stephen characterizes didactic works as improper art precisely because they are incomplete unless their audience responds to them in a certain way, creating a new state of affairs that Stephen calls a kinetic movement toward or away from something and that we may call another text. But attempts to exclude didactic and pornographic works from the proper realm of art merely end up opening, or closing, the gates to still more exclusions. Wayne C. Booth begins his Preface to *The Rhetoric of Fiction* with a forthright distinction: 'In writing about the rhetoric of fiction, I am not primarily interested in didactic fiction, fiction used for propaganda or instruction.' Yet the very next sentence utterly wrecks Booth's careful distinction: 'My subject is the technique of non-didactic fiction, viewed as the art of communicating with readers—the rhetorical resources available to the writer of epic, novel, or short story as he tries, consciously or unconsciously, to impose his fictional world upon the reader.'[10] Whether or not a storyteller seeks to point an explicit moral for the audience, he or she is always seeking to impose a fictional world on them – a very specific world, not any of the innumerable alternative worlds that might have been chosen, as more worthy of the audience's attention and understanding than those other worlds, and from a very specific point of view. Despite Booth's insistence that he is not writing about didactic fiction, his conception of his project ends by revealing the ways in which all fiction is rhetorical in the sense of wishing to persuade its audience to see fictional worlds and their own in some ways rather than others.

Although Booth is not as aesthetically conservative as Stephen is during his religious phase, he shares Stephen's desire to draw a bright line between propaganda, which tries to get readers and viewers to act on their newly awakened desires, and fiction, which is merely 'the art of communicating with readers.' *The Rhetoric of Fiction* is a classic of exactly the sort of close stylistic analysis that Pasolini rejects out of hand, at least when it comes to screenplays. What Pasolini calls a 'histological examination' of 'the infinitesimal detail that reproduces the whole' becomes impossible in considering screenplays, in which 'one can't "perceive" this "desire for form" from a detail of the form. This desire must be ideologically presupposed; it must be part of the critical code.' For Pasolini, the screenplay's dynamic structure, which embodies the 'clash between the by now traditional concept of "structure" and the critical concept of "process," reflects the ways in which 'men, as authors of history, react to a social structure by building another through revolution.' The same 'revolutionary will' is at work 'both in the author as creator of an individual stylistic system that contradicts the grammatical and literary-jargon system in force, and in men as subverters of political systems.'[11]

It is ironic to see a committed Marxist like Pasolini advancing his argument about the exceptionalism of screenplays as images of revolutionary will by implicitly conceding Stephen Dedalus's point that static emotion is the unmarked or zero-degree effect of artworks. Even when Pasolini was writing, it was already true that an extraordinary number of texts very much wanted to engender other texts. Novels hungered to spawn reviews, critical commentary and film adaptations. Histories and biographies lusted to become television miniseries or segments on The History Channel. Books of every sort ached to be translated, illustrated, abridged by Reader's Digest Condensed Books and reprinted in editions for young or blind readers. In my own professional corner of the world this process has accelerated sharply in recent years. Stanley Fish's notorious Introduction to *Is There a Text in This Class?* makes explicit what most collections of critical essays by a single author leave implicit: that each piece in the collection constitutes an errant and incomplete attempt at the next piece, and that the most recent pieces are less a summation than an indication of further work to be done on 'a whole new set of problems.'[12] Even literary and critical essays less self-celebrating than Fish's aspire to become footnotes in the essays by other hands they inspire – and no wonder, since a primary gauge of professional influence in the humanities is the frequency with which one's work has been cited, even by commentators who regard it as rubbish. More recently, the success of online blogs and videos has been most commonly measured by their going viral. The second-dearest wish of every blog is to record a stratospheric number of hits; its dearest wish is to engender an equally impressive number of hotlinks posted by other blogs or videos.

No wonder, then, that the novelist Anthony Burgess, dissenting from Stephen's celebration of static emotion in fiction, concluded that unlike musical notes and structures, '[w]ords can never be freed of their marketplace denotations ... and the subject matter of fiction is the marketplace.'[13] The most we can say in defence of Pasolini's wish to characterize screenplays as distinctive is that these other texts want to create new texts rather than transforming themselves into new texts. The currency of translations, adaptations and commentaries depends, after all, on the endurance and continued availability of the original text in its original form rather than its mutation into a final draft that supersedes or destroys its earlier drafts. But this apparent difference between screenplays and other texts is less important than Pasolini's deeper insight into the exemplary nature of screenplays as expressions of revolutionary will.

Just as the screenplay becomes, for Pasolini, a privileged example of 'the form in movement', there are at least three reasons that movies, out of the whole universe of possible texts, offer a particularly compelling example of texts that want to become other texts. Movies are apparently more synchronically stable than online texts – it's hard to think of a text that's less mutable, more clearly a *Ding an sich*, than *Avatar* (James Cameron 2009) – but their synchronic coherence increasingly comports with a frankly commercial dependence on their ability to generate other texts, from the successive Director's Cuts of *Blade Runner* (Ridley Scott 1982) and *Lord of the Rings* (Peter Jackson 2001–3) to reviews and feature stories to debates about their ideological implications and commentaries on their special effects to fan tribute mash-ups online and the obligatory 'Hitler Learns That the *Avatar* Trailer Sucks' YouTube video.

A second reason concerns the commonly held distinction between movies and all cinema. Documentary films offer a particularly instructive counterexample to the movies. With few exceptions, documentary films do not want to become other documentary films. Like all didactic texts, they want to generate other texts, but they mainly want those other texts, typically in print media, to validate their truth claims, not contest or complicate them. If W. J. T. Mitchell is correct when he says in 'Drawing Desire' that every 'picture is the intersection of two "wants"': drive (repetition, proliferation, the 'plague' of images) and desire (the fixation, reification, mortification of the life-form)',[14] then documentaries tend to be dominated by one or the other of these two wants, either the drive to preserve a series of moving pictures (or still pictures, in the case of Ken Burns's television series) or the desire to use them to advance or illustrate an argument. Even when documentaries have other goals than the didactic ends to which Wayne Booth professes indifference and Stephen Dedalus revulsion, these ends can adequately be described by the Horatian formula *dulce et utile,* strange though that formula may seem to turn in the hands of Michael Moore. Movies, on the other hand, want to generate other texts in the same medium along with the other texts in diverse media (print, television, online, etc.) they also want to generate.

It is harder to locate art films within a universe of cinematic modes that do or do not want to generate other texts like themselves because no matter how strenuously they insist that they are unique aesthetic creations that stand outside the mainstream of commercial cinema, they are deeply informed by their own relations to earlier visual artworks and contemporaneous visual culture. Even the most audaciously avant-garde films are shaped by their awareness of the *garde* they are *avant,* the aesthetic or representational traditions they define themselves by flouting. Nor does it seem likely that even the most revolutionary artists in cinema, as in any other medium, aim to create works that will have no influence on other artists' works. At the same time, because movies are such a culturally dominant mode of cinema, they provide an unusually ubiquitous set of representational conventions that art films can complicate, undermine or reject. In consequence, every given art film has the option of defining itself with primary reference to commercial cinema instead of as part of a continuous tradition of art cinema. So many art films, like most documentary films, do not share with movies, television programsmes and online blogs the distinctive tropism toward spawning later generations that closely resemble their progenitors.

Still a third reason that movies are exemplary in their desire to become other movies is rooted in their economic history. In the early days of the Hollywood studio system, movies sought by establishing generic norms and transformations to generate other movies and then perish in what was assumed, perhaps by analogy with newspapers and magazines, to be the natural order of things. One reason that the visual style of *Citizen Kane* (Orson Welles, 1941) so closely resembles that of *Stagecoach* (John Ford 1939), the story goes, is that when Orson Welles first arrived at RKO and asked to screen some old movies, the only print the studio could provide was a copy of *Stagecoach* because it did not archive its own productions. It had evidently never occurred to anyone at RKO that movies might have any residual value once they had gone out of release. Beginning when studio executives discovered ten years later that television created a lucrative new market for their old product, however, each new generation of each movie (remakes, most obviously, but other genre entries too) began to compete directly with earlier generations – if not in the original theatrical venues, then on other platforms like television, video and the Web. A closer study of the marketing of remakes, rereleases and genre films could well throw light on analogous but not precisely identical tendencies in book publishing as well as the more obvious analogue of periodical publishing.

Because he is intent on making screenplays rather than movies the exemplary texts that want to be other texts, Pasolini makes a sharp distinction between the gradual changes in textual genera-tions wrought by evolutionary processes and the sharp textual challenges offered by 'the screenplay-text's structure, which is "dynamic" but without functionality, and outside the laws of evolution.'[15] Every text may want to be another text, but the screenplay's revolutionary will, Pasolini maintains, is qualitatively different from the evolutionary processes that govern most textual production. But Pasolini is altogether too dismissive here of the evolutionary laws against which he sets the screenplay's revolu-tionary will. If the dynamic but incompletely enacted will Pasolini finds in screenplays is equally active in all movies and many other texts as well, then it makes sense to press the more fundamental question toward which this essay has been moving: What does it mean for a screenplay or a movie or any sort of text to want to be another text? This question is far more provocative and urgent than the question of whether all movies, or all cinema, or all texts in general, want the same things Pasolini claims screenplays want. Can texts, any texts, want anything at all?

Twenty-five hundred years of aesthetic theory says that they can't. Stephen Dedalus's take on proper and improper art may be Joyce's own, but it rests on a long tradition of aesthetics reaching from Aristotle to the Intentional and Affective Fallacies identified by William K. Wimsatt and Monroe C. Beardsley. Artists, these commentators agree, may have intentions, but works of art do not. In fact, it is precisely their freedom from the desires and intentions of their creators that makes them works of art. The most influential formulation of this aesthetic position is in Kant's *Critique of Judgment*, which distinguishes judgements about artworks from judgements about goodness or justice or practical reason in terms of their disinterestedness. Kant defines *taste* as 'the faculty of judging an object or a method of representing it by an *entirely disinterested* satisfaction or dissatisfaction. The object of such satisfaction is called *beautiful*' and famously rules that artworks are characterized by 'purposiveness without purpose.'[16] That is, even though their coherent form makes them seem to have been made expressly in order to be understood, neither they nor the pleasure they evoke serve any direct purpose. At least insofar as we consider them works of art, movies cannot want to become other texts because their disinterested lack of purpose prevents them from wanting anything at all.

Of course, you don't have to be Aristotle or Kant, or even Stephen Dedalus, to deny desire or purpose to inanimate objects like movies. It seems only common sense to reserve the faculty of desiring to agents like artists and writers, directors and screenwriters. Even Mitchell, who finds the question 'What Do Pictures Want?' so suggestive that he has used it as the title of both a 1994 essay and a 2005 collection in which that essay is reprinted, has acknowledged it to be 'a bizarre, perhaps even objectionable, question. I'm aware that it involves a subjectivizing of images, a dubious personification of inanimate objects; that it flirts with a regressive, superstitious attitude toward images, one that if taken seriously would return us to practices like totemism, fetishism, idolatry, and animism.'[17] Recent developments in the study of adaptation, however, have raised provocative questions about the commonsensical proposition that desire is limited to creators rather than shared by their creations – or rather that it inherently belongs to anyone or anything at all.

These challenges have come not from within the burgeoning field of adaptation study – that is, the study of how books and movies and other texts are adapted into still other texts – but from recent research and debate in the older branch of adaptation study Pasolini dismisses: the study of biological evolution. The chief provocateur is Richard Dawkins, whose 1976 monograph *The Selfish Gene* concludes with a chapter suggesting that human culture is passed on by the selective replication, transmutation and survival of cultural units closely analogous to the genes transmitted and adapted by DNA. Dawkins christens these cultural units – 'tunes, ideas, catch-phrases, clothes fashions, ways of making pots or of building arches' and so on – memes, micro-units of cultural knowledge and practice designed specifically to survive their conflict with other memes through 'longevity, fecundity, and copying-fidelity' in a cultural version of Darwin's natural selection.[18]

For Dawkins, the analogy between genes and memes extends to their potential agency. 'Just as genes propagate themselves in the gene pool by leaping from body to body via sperms or eggs,' he contends, 'so memes propagate themselves in the meme pool by leaping from brain to brain via a process which, in the broad sense, can be called imitation.... . As my colleague N. K. Humphrey neatly summed up an earlier draft of this chapter: " ... memes should be regarded as living structures, not just metaphorically but technically. When you plant a fertile meme in my mind you literally parasitize my brain, turning it into a vehicle for the meme's propagation in just the way that a virus may parasitize the genetic mechanism of a host cell.'[19]

Although he approvingly reproduces Humphrey's summary, however, Dawkins backs away from the more radical implications of his position that memes are parasites that infect brains. He warns that 'we must not think of genes as conscious, purposeful agents. Blind natural selection, however, makes them behave rather as if they were purposeful, and it has been convenient, as a shorthand, to refer to genes in the language of purpose. ... Just as we have found it convenient to think of genes as active agents, working purposefully for their own survival, perhaps it might be convenient to think of memes in the same way. In neither case must we get mystical about it. In both cases the idea is only a metaphor.'[20]

But Dawkins's caution in distinguishing the hypothetical agency, driven by an equally hypothetical desire to survive, he imputes to memes from the consciousness and intentionality he wishes to withhold from them has been taken as a challenge by several key philosophers and cultural theorists – including, in one important respect, Dawkins himself, who concludes that 'even if we look on the dark side and assume that individual man is fundamentally selfish, our conscious foresight – our capacity to simulate the future in imagination – could save us from the worst selfish excesses of the blind replicators. ... We have the power to defy the selfish genes of our birth and, if necessary, the selfish memes of our indoctrination.'[21] The problem with this ringing call to independence is that it is not at all clear how the thoughts and powers of defiance, imagination and wise foresight enter the human mind if not through the colonization of memes just as selfish in Dawkins's sense as the tyrannical memes against which they urge rebellion. Not surprisingly, Dawkins's more recent work has retreated from the claim that there is a '"we" that transcends not only its genetic creators but also its memetic creators.'[22]

The two questions Dawkins's analysis raises – are memes capable of desire and purposive agency, and what relation do they have to the human brains they colonize? – have sharply divided more recent commentators. On one side of the question is the philosopher Daniel C. Dennett, who proposes that 'consciousness is *itself* a huge complex of memes (or more exactly, meme effects in brains).'[23] Glossing the slogan 'A scholar is just a library's way of making another library', Dennett concedes that 'I am not initially attracted by the idea of my brain as a sort of dungheap in which the larvae of other people's ideas renew themselves, before sending out copies of themselves in an informational diaspora,' and wonders, 'Who's in charge, according to this vision – we or our memes?' He concludes: 'We would like to think of ourselves as godlike creators of ideas, manipulating and controlling them as our whim dictates, and judging them from an independent, Olympian standpoint. But even if this is our ideal, we know that it is seldom if ever the reality, even with the most masterful and creative minds.'[24]

On the other side of this debate is the philosopher Kate Distin, who maintains that memes cannot be conflated with consciousness because they are distinct from the physical vehicles into which Dennett and Blackmore collapse them. Because 'Dennett is mistaken in thinking that artefacts are the sources of memes rather than their effects,' she argues, 'he must be equally mistaken in thinking that the mind is the effect of memes rather than their source.' Instead, she concludes 'that the human mind develops as a result of acquiring memes, and many of its activities are dictated by its memes – but that the memes themselves cannot function independently of minds, and are always initially created by a mind.' Hence for Distin 'memetic evolution is quite consistent with a world of intentional, conscious and responsible free agents.'[25]

We might, like Dennett and Blackmore, include screenplays and movies as meme-vehicles, machines like the human brain designed for whatever purpose that also happen to have the subsidiary effect of insuring the survival and propagation of the fittest memes – though Pasolini would no doubt want to make a further distinction between movies, which just happen to insure the survival of their memes, and screenplays, which are designed for the express purpose of insuring the survival of their memes, whatever other purposes they end up serving. According to this account of meme machines, movies are no more or less capable of wanting anything than human brains themselves, and for exactly the same reason: because they have no independent sense of agency or purpose apart from the evolving complex of memes that colonize them. Or we might, like Distin, insist on a sharp distinction between screenplays and movies and brains, on the one hand, and the memes that populate these vehicles but do not colonize them. This account would endow all meme-vehicles with desire, agency and purpose whether those machines were human brains, screenplays or movies.

Sociobiologists like Dawkins share with more recent commentators who urge the 'consilience' of scientific and humanistic study a theory of cultural evolution that is closely analogous to biological evolution in recasting works of art as driven above all by the need to survive, adapt and replicate, if necessary through radical transformation. Edward O. Wilson, the naturalist responsible for the rebirth of consilience in our time, has announced that 'consilience is the key' to 'the attempted linkage of the sciences and humanities', which 'has always been and will always be … the greatest enterprise of the mind.'[26]

In an intellectual climate as sharply defined as ours by competing disciplines and their associated turf wars, it is hardly surprising that such calls have met with what Dennett calls 'a sort of immunological rejection'[27] from the humanities. Among leading scholars of textual adaptation, only Linda Hutcheon has emphasized the implications meme theory has for a theory of textual evolution when she observes that '[a]lthough Dawkins is thinking about ideas when he writes of memes, stories are also ideas and could be said to function in this same way. Some have great fitness through survival (persistence in a culture) or reproduction (number of adaptations). Adaptation, like evolution, is a transgenerational phenomenon. ... Stories do get retold in different ways in new material and cultural environments; like genes, they adapt to these new environments *by virtue of* mutation—in their "offspring" or their adaptations. And the fittest do more than survive; they flourish.'[28]

It is no wonder that few commentators on textual adaptation have followed Hutcheon into the thicket of sociobiology, for the disagreements between Distin and Dennett, and between Dawkins and the host of humanists arrayed against him, may seem too absolute to resolve without simply taking sides. But it may be possible to cut this Gordian knot by changing the terms of the debate from an argument about who or what has the capacity for agency to an argument about the nature of agency.

Bruno Latour forthrightly urges just such a change when he contends that it is fallacious and unnecessary to divide the world into agents and instruments, subjects and objects, and still more fallacious to set the freedom of self-avowed subjects against the determinism to which objects are assumed to be subject, opposing personal 'liberty, autonomy, mobility, and emancipation' to 'slavery, alienation, bondage, and attachment.' As an alternative, Latour urges the adoption of 'what the Greeks call "the middle voice," the verb form that is neither active nor passive', to describe the inescapable connections among entities that act on each other. Instead of conceiving action as a means by which agents exert their control over objects, Latour proposes the 'middle form' of the 'factish', which adds to the terms 'fact' and 'fetish', terms for describing 'what *makes us act*' in ways that are positively and negatively charged, '*the work of fabrication*'. To conceive actions as 'factishes', argues Latour, waives questions of control because it does not define the process of doing as active or the products of doing as passive. Hence subjects who are also inevitably objects can change the question of 'whether we should be free or bound' to the question of '*whether we are well or poorly bound*.'[29]

Developing this argument further, Julian Yates has proposed what he calls 'agentive drift' as 'a way of representing agency as a dispersed or distributed process in which we participate rather than as a property which we are said to own.'[30] Yates glosses Michel Serres's axiom 'There is no system without parasites'[31] and the system of relations Serres generates from this axiom as 'a way of reading events derived from cybernetics that eludes the usual agentive protocols of philosophy and social theory in an attempt to describe an open or dissipative system in which momentary deployments of force produce systemic orderings, local eddies or drifts, monopolizing the ability to act, to occupy, and so to own events.'[32] In Yates's reading, Michelangelo is not simply the creator of the captives that struggle to escape the stone in which they are imprisoned, for the agency is shared by the sculptor, the captive and perhaps even the stone itself as it tells the sculptor what shape it wishes to assume. The term 'agentive drift', which implies that agency has drifted, for example, from Michelangelo to the stone, applies more precisely to a shift in ways of thinking about agency than to the operations of agency itself. Instead of conceiving 'desire' as a finite verb, Yates invites us to conceive it as a gerund ('desiring') that indicates a state of affairs or an endless series of effects.

For Latour, agency is not a property of individuals but a function of relations, interruptions, interlopers and cascades. It is not, however, a property of systems in the Derridean sense that, for example, language is held to speak its speakers. Instead of 'hav[ing] to explain how a speaking subject manages to appropriate for himself that which in the end determines him', a theory of language as 'factish', Latour contends, holds that 'language does not control those whom it permits to speak, it *makes them those who can speak.*' Hence 'I no longer seek to sunder what makes and what is made, the active and the passive, because I am positioned to pursue a chain of mediators, each not being the exact cause of the next, but instead, each enabling the next to become, in turn, the originator of action: literally, each renders causal its successor.'[33]

This decentered, non-proprietary notion of agency is eminently consonant with recent work in consilience and adaptation. Yates's conclusion that '[p]arasitism as primary relation necessitates a new understanding of the human as one thing among many rather than as the transcendental subject of philosophy or phenomenology' is echoed by Brian Boyd in his defence of consilience: 'If we are evolved creatures, our brains are not guarantors of truth, citadels of reason, or shadows of the mind of God but simply organs of survival, built to cope with the immediate environment and perhaps to develop some capacity to recall and anticipate. Evolution has no foresight and no aims, least of all an aim like truth. It simply registers what suffices, what allows some organisms to last and reproduce better than others.'[34]

Indeed, evolutionary biology already provides a more satisfyingly complex notion of agency than adaptation studies has yet put to use because it acknowledges more fully the problematic relationship between individuals and species. The failure to come to terms with this relationship undermines Linda Costanzo Cahir's argument that textual adaptations are more properly understood as translations because translation is 'a *process of language*' through which 'a fully new text – *a materially different entity* – is made.' By contrast, Cahir avers, 'the term "to adapt" means to alter the structure or function of an entity so that it is better fitted to survive and to multiply in its new environment. To adapt is to move *that same entity* into a new environment. In the process of adaptation, the same substantive entity which entered the process exits, even as it undergoes modification – sometimes radical mutation – in its efforts to *accommodate* itself to its new environment.'[35]

Quite apart from the question of whether textual adaptations ought to be called translations, Cahir's proposal raises another question it does not resolve: whether a biological organism that successfully adapts to a new or changed environment is indeed 'that same entity' that began the adaptive process. Because Darwinian adaptation normally takes place over many generations, the product of any successful adaptation is not at all the same entity that initiated the adaptation. It is generations removed from that entity, which has acted as if on its behalf without ever knowing of its existence or making any plans more specific than assaying the widest range of possible adaptations from which the process of natural selection, not any generation of the organism, will choose the most successful. Just as new recruits to the armed services are drilled to value group cohesion above their own individual survival, the Darwinian will to survive through adaptation is exercised on behalf of an organism's descendants or, more precisely, its species, not itself.

Adopting a view of agency that is less anthropomorphic, less centered on individual control and ownership, less driven by a categorical distinction between active and passive roles, would have the salutary effect of decentring human agency in a world whose survival depends more and more clearly on a global rather than a merely human ecology. In addition, it would foster progress toward several less grandiose goals. It would shift the focus of Cahir's account of adaptation from individual mutations to the survival of species. It would allow scholars in adaptation studies to take account of recent developments in sociobiological adaptation that they have mostly ignored. It would return us to Pasolini's characterization of screenplays as structures that want to be other structures with a new and enriched understanding of the ways other discursive structures do and do not participate in the agency Pasolini reserves exclusively to screenplays – and would incidentally open the terms 'structures' and 'want' to productive debate. It would allow us to acknowledge more openly that essays like this one are written not to provide the last word on a given subject, but frankly to provoke further discussion. Finally, it would have the not inconsiderable benefit of allowing us to talk about what movies want without apologizing for sounding foolish.

Notes

1   Pier Paolo Pasolini, 'The Screenplay as a 'Structure That Wants to Be Another Structure,' in *Heretical Empiricism*, (ed.) Louise K. Barnett, trans. Ben Lawton and Louise K. Barnett (Bloomington: Indiana University Press, 1988), 188, 189.

2   Howard Rodman, 'What a Screenplay Isn't,' *Cinema Journal* 45 (Winter 2006): 86–7.

3   Pasolini, 187.

4   Pasolini, 189.

5   Rick Altman, *Film/Genre* (London: BFI, 1999), 128, 129.

6   Pasolini, 193.

7   Richard Poirier, Preface to *The Performing Self: Compositions and Decompositions in the Languages of Contemporary Life* (New York: Oxford University Press, 1971), xiv, xv, xiv.

8   Gary Taylor, *Cultural Selection* (New York: Basic, 1996), 292.

9   James Joyce, *A Portrait of the Artist as a Young Man* (1916), in *The Portable James Joyce*, with an Introduction and Notes by Harry Levin, rev. edn. (New York: Viking, 1966), 471.

10 Wayne C. Booth, *The Rhetoric of Fiction*, 2nd edn, (Chicago: University of Chicago Press, 1983), xiii.

11 Pasolini, 188, 193, 194.

12 Stanley Fish, 'Introduction, or How I Stopped Worrying and Learned to Love Interpretation,' in *Is There a Text in This Class? The Authority of Interpretive Communities* (Cambridge: Harvard University Press, 1980), 17.

13 Anthony Burgess, *This Man and Music* (Englewood Cliffs: McGraw-Hill, 1983), 159.

14 W. J. T. Mitchell, 'Drawing Desire,' in *What Do Pictures Want? The Lives and Loves of Images* (Chicago: University of Chicago Press, 2005), 72.

15 Pasolini, 193.

16 Immanuel Kant, *Critique of Judgment* (1790), trans. J. H. Bernard (New York: Hafner, 1951), 45, 55.

17 Mitchell, 'What Do Pictures Want?' in *What Do Pictures Want?*, 28–9.

18 Richard Dawkins, *The Selfish Gene* (New York: Oxford University Press, 1976), 206, 208.

19 Dawkins, 206–7.

20 Dawkins, 210–11.

21 Dawkins, 215.

22 Daniel C. Dennett, *Darwin's Dangerous Idea: Evolution and the Meanings of Life* (New York: Simon and Schuster, 1995), 366.

23 Daniel C. Dennett, *Consciousness Explained* (Harmondsworth: Penguin, 1991), 210.

24 Dennett, *Darwin's Dangerous Idea*, 346. See also Susan Blackmore, *The Meme Machine* (Oxford: Oxford University Press, 1999), 17.

25 Kate Distin, *The Selfish Meme: A Critical Reassessment* (Cambridge: Cambridge University Press, 2005), 82, 115, 5.

26 Edward O. Wilson, *Consilience: The Unity of Knowledge* (New York: Knopf, 1998), 8.

27 Dennett, *Darwin's Dangerous Idea*, 362.

28 Linda Hutcheon, *A Theory of Adaptation* (New York: Routledge, 2006), 32.

29 Bruno Latour, 'Factures/Fractures: From the Concept of Network to the Concept of Attachment,' *RES: Anthropology and Aesthetics*, no. 36 (Autumn 1999): 22–22. Emphasis in original.

30 Julian Yates, 'Towards a Theory of Agentive Drift; Or, A Particular Fondness for Oranges circa 1597,' *Parallax 8.1* (2002): 48.

31 Michel Serres, *The Parasite*, trans. Lawrence R. Schehr (Baltimore: Johns Hopkins University Press, 1982), 12.

32 Yates, 50.

33 Latour, 26.

34 Yates, 50; Brian Boyd, 'Getting It All Wrong: Bioculture Critiques Cultural Critique,' in *Evolution, Literature, and Film: A Reader,* Brian Boyd, Joseph Carroll, and Jonathan Gotschall (eds) (New York: Columbia University Press, 2010), 201.

35 Linda Costanzo Cahir, *Literature into Film: Theory and Practical Approaches* (Jefferson: McFarland, 2006), 14.

PART TWO

Theorizing the case study

9

The medium strikes back – 'Impossible adaptation' revisited

Hajnal Király

Although the study of adaptations lately has shifted under the authority of cultural criticism[1] and media/intermediality research,[2] the classical, comparative, hierarchical and critical discourse stemming from the *ut pictura poesis* principle still holds strong. In this pretheoretical discourse, adaptation appears unmistakably as a 'bad object' charged with tension and frustration, which makes the very term judgemental: a second-hand product, a copy, an originless entity. In a time when admittedly all media are mixed and new media technologies are melting into varied media, blurring boundaries and mirroring each other, the notion of original and 'adaptation' are irrelevant; yet works preoccupied with the issue of authorship, screenplay, genre and adaption process are still being published.[3] This occurs despite Robert Stam's efforts to discredit the traditional comparative discourse by deconstructing the term 'adaptation', which allegedly evokes the restrictions and taboos of a repressed Victorian society.[4] As Foucault pointed out in his essay 'We, "Other Victorians"',[5] the very term 'repression' stands for the authority of the word over the body, a notion we still reluctantly relate to as we find its discourses and representation transgressive. In terms of the fidelity principle of adaptations, this Puritanism is manifest in an ambivalent relationship to the 'word becoming flesh', that is, materializing in a mediated image.

As an alternative to these dead-end discussions, a shift to media studies and intermediality allows a better understanding of sociocultural and political phenomena – and of the medium itself – through transmedia processes. Bolter and Grusin's term 'remediation'[6] proves to be inspired not only in admitting the contradictory respectful and subversive attitudes of all new media to 'old' ones, but also in removing the emphasis from the original to the performative power of all media through their relationship to other media.

At the same time, in film studies, those preoccupied with medium specificity and the relationship of cinema with digital and new media propose a re-evaluation of cinema's narratological heritage. This advances the issue that narration is not inherent to film but a (well-) learned capacity, which has always been a major notion for many theoreticians and for non-mainstream cinema (vanguard and experimental, new wave and modernist films or simply what is traditionally called 'art cinema'). For example, Lev Manovich pointed out that joining the narratological and literary tradition was a simple detour in film history; with the advent of the digital, film seems to be returning to where it belongs, visual culture.[7] As a natural consequence of the 'visual turn,[8] the preoccupation with narratological issues among adaptation discourses shifted to visual anthropological and medium theoretical approaches. In terms of the 'impossible adaptation' concept, discussions no longer revolved around accurate narration techniques, but the performative power and opacity of the visual medium, the emergence of its 'body' through its ability to fill up gaps and reveal taboos of the written text, or resist certain narratives. In other words, the interest seems to have turned towards the problems of 'suture', demasking the mechanisms of film narration and acting against a perfect diegetic effect. Similarly, the visual uncanny – the excesses and gaps in visual representation – constantly confront the spectator with the disturbing presence of the visual medium. On the basis of these considerations, without trying to replace the term adaptation with remediation, I propose using 'adaptation' for the films solving merely technical, narrative issues and 'remediation' for those connecting the literary text into the actual visual tradition, both in a respectful and subversive manner, and at the same time revealing the workings of the film as medium.

This reasoning also fits into the actual film theoretical preoccupation with visual effects, a 'cinema of the senses' tackling the sensual relationship between the spectator and the visual medium. In this theoretical framework, the literary visual also must be reconsidered because its powerful appeal to the reader's imagination gives it a psychological load[9] that cannot be avoided when talking about adaptation or remediation in film. As a kind of 'therapy', also meant to elucidate the taboo of the 'impossible adaptation', this discussion also aims to give an overview of film solutions for the main visual paradigms of nineteenth-century literature. I argue that by comparing different ways in which female characters from nineteenth-century novels have been represented in film, one can identify not only various tendencies in film-making, but also a history of a medium gradually breaking with narrative restrictions of adaptations (aiming at transparency) and 'looking back' to its spectator as remediation (see Table 9.1 below).

I also demonstrate how remediation on film appears as an ekphrastic 'other'[10] of the literary text. According to a more general interpretation, ekphrasis is not only an aesthetic figure, but also an artistic practice in which an artwork becomes the *object of* or *a mirror for another*. For instance, a recent revival of interest in ekphrasis offers adequate background both for the theory of remediation and a re-evaluation of the 'impossible adaptation' concept, related to the inhibition caused by so-called 'visual literature'.

Ekphrasis: Managing the literary visual

In his *Ekphrasis: The Illusion of the Natural Sign*, Murray Krieger offered a detailed overview of the modes of sensual descriptions and the picturesque identifiable in the nineteenth-century novel, ranging from the fashion of *couleur locale* to the ekphrastic attitude of the characters in Henry James' novels.[11] He also argued that this literature defines itself as presentation instead of representation, solely aiming at the reader's imagination. This is, we can add, at the core of all spectatorial resistance to all kinds of visual remediations and, consequently, the myth of impossible adaptation. On the other hand, the issue of spectatorship (looking, the gaze), often a theme in literary works starting at the end of the nineteenth century, is essential to the theory and self-understanding of all visual media. In writings by Joseph Conrad, Henry James, Oscar Wilde, Edith Wharton, Gustave Flaubert and Marcel Proust – just to mention some of the more prominent authors who are traditionally considered impossible to adapt – the visual medium (painting, photograph or film) often appears as uncanny compared to imagination and memory. For example, *Anna Karenina*, *The Age of Innocence* and *Madame Bovary* contain numerous examples of how the picture of a woman alters the memory of her. In *Madame Bovary*, one of Emma's lovers experienced this:

> Near it, chipped at all the corners, was a miniature given him by Emma: her toilette seemed to him pretentious, and her languishing look in the worst possible taste. Then, from looking at this image and recalling the memory of its original, Emma's features little by little grew confused in his remembrance, as if the living and the painted face, rubbing one against the other, had effaced each other.[12]

This experience can be described as what W. J. T. Mitchell called 'ekphrastic fear', strongly related to 'ekphrastic hope/desire', in *Ekphrasis and the Other*.[13] Although Mitchell used these terms to describe pictures, they seem applicable for this characterization of the views in adaptation studies mentioned above. There is a strong desire to see the inner image become an outer picture, which, when seen, appears odd, uncanny. According to Merleau-Ponty and Hans Belting,[14] there is nothing more normal because they are not our own images: *They are created by somebody else.* But we also can avoid the fear of facing the new, physical image with *ekphrastic indifference,* assuming that a perfect visual representation of mental images is impossible. The fear also stems from the power the physical presence of a technical picture has to neutralize the imagination and replace its images: When talking about a book, we remember pictures of its adaptation and sometimes we simply don't know *if we've read or seen something.* As Belting has rightly stated, there is a constant exchange between the medium carrying the outer images and our bodies, the natural medium.[15] The expansion of our inner images depends on the limitations set by the 'visible,' physical images. And, of course, new remediations constantly correct these images: A picture from a film is replaced or adjusted whenever it is digitally remastered or refracted, for example, in a video game.

The archetypical story of Perseus and the Medusa elucidates not only remediation or refraction and the peculiar interaction between inner and outer images it involves, but also the phenomenon of the visual uncanny that makes us turn our gaze and become aware of our role as spectators and, consequently, of the medium. Furthermore (and most relevant to this essay), this story makes Medusa's mirrored female body a prototype of all visual remediation. Perseus' protectors warn him about the danger represented by Medusa's image and gaze, and at the time of the encounter, he has a mental image of Medusa. When Perseus places a medium – a mirrored shield – between himself and Medusa, he turns the inner image into a mediated, outer picture, killing the former along with the fear associated with it. The dead body is reduced to a mere picture of its former existence. Thus the painting Medusa's Head (ca. 1600, by an unknown Flamish painter) originally attributed to Leonardo is a reflection on the *body becoming a picture*. This Medusa is not looking back, but being a 'feminine object' par excellence, is exposed to the spectator's voyeuristic gaze (an allegory of all visual representation).

Caravaggio's Medusa (ca. 1598) goes one step further when representing the medium of the shield. Through this self-reflexive gesture, a mythical allegory of the genesis of the portrait genre becomes accessible: The head and the face replace the body, whose presence is thus extended in space and time. In this painting, 'picture' and 'woman' become synonyms: *The woman appears as picture and the picture as woman*, that is, irresistibly attracting the gaze and activating the voyeuristic and scopophilic mechanisms of spectatorship. The fact that the head of the dead Medusa could not be mirrored in the shield points to a paradox of the visual medium, namely that its images are actually not those of the body, but are deliberately manipulated, appropriated, refracted by the medium. (In the case of film, think of stars' images, those of *femme fatale* or the *vamp* as variations of the Medusa image.) Consequently, in the case of adaptations, the film functions as a medium-mirror, letting the images of the literary narration appear while refracting it.

Representations of women in film – beyond the tradition of visual arts implying the gaze – are always active in theoretical considerations of the medium's very mechanisms, mostly conceptualized by feminist theorization. These representations are strongly connected to the issue of the body and its picture, the mechanisms of emerging media images, inseparable from a whole discourse of the gaze and spectatorship. For example, the movie star represents not only a character, but also the medium itself and the sociocultural needs and abilities it responds to. The star's image not only projects, multiplies, 'uses off' the unique mental images activated by the auratic descriptions of literary works (the standpoint of the defenders of the literary original), but also guarantees the aura of the film, according to Walter Benjamin, a defender of popular culture.[16] Thus, the auratic descriptions of characters in a novel survive as the aura of star image, when transposed from the reader's imagination into the imaginary of the collective unconscious. Consequently, in the (movie) star image, the reader/spectator recognizes her/his own inner image.

In my view, these medium theoretical and visual anthropological approaches represent a framework susceptible to a re-evaluation of critical, spectatorial and directorial inhibitions when facing the literary visual.

À la recherche of 'impossible adaptation'

As Hippolyte Taine rightly put it in 1867, woman and the (visual) work of art can be seen as metaphors of each other in that they both are 'objects of desire', upon which the beholder gazes: 'One wants to own them and put them on display.'[17] Moreover, in the case of film, television and new media, the star system constructs the technical image of the woman, again with a strong influence on interpretation. The modes of visual details used when representing female characters can define a sort of typology of adaptations, and to the extent these representations depend on narration, define a certain style or become part of the meta-narration, that is, they make the medium 'visible' through (cultural or even cross-cultural) remediation.

Table 9.1 contains a typology of adaptations for relevant historical moments of visuality in literature of the nineteenth through the beginning of twentieth centuries: the *couleur locale* (first part of the nineteenth century) characterized by decorative, atmospheric descriptions and represented by Walter Scott, Jane Austen and the Brontës, among others; *milieu* (mid-nineteenth century) standing for an art of realistic detail in which character and environment mirror each other, as represented by Honoré de Balzac and Charles Dickens; 'the Flaubert-turn' (later nineteenth century), introducing multiplied points of view and characterized by an adventure of the eye and impressionistic visual effects; and finally, an 'adventure of the gaze' and observation as synonymous with the learning process (late nineteenth and early twentieth centuries), as in the literature of Henry James, Joseph Conrad, Edith Wharton, Oscar Wilde and Marcel Proust.

Accordingly, three types of adaptations can be identified in these main paradigms of the literary visual: 'the woman in the picture', 'the woman as picture' and 'the picture as woman'. The first paradigms contains all the historical adventure and costume dramas, TV dramas in which visual detail – sceneries, interior spaces, costumes and the look of the female figure – is subordinated to the rules of genre and narration, being simply one of the many visual details. The characters' physical appearance – physiognomy, make-up, symbolism of costume and colours, and so forth – is important only to the extent that it is relevant to the plot (romance, adventure, seduction, good-bad conflict). 'The woman in the picture' paradigm reduces all visual detail – even those thematizing observation, learning process and visual techniques, characteristic of the 'adventure of the gaze' type – to a simple decorative element of the plot or the genre, as in Minnelli's *Madame Bovary* (1949) and Volker Schlöndorff's *The Love of Swann* (1984). The second paradigm, 'the woman as picture', integrates the visual detail in an easily identifiable style – painting, photograph, film. Thus, *couleur locale* is translated into tableau-like compositions in Zeffirelli's *Jane Eyre* (1996); milieu is represented as realistic style in Lean's *Great Expectations* (1946), and painting compositions and style imitations are characteristic of Chabrol's *Madame Bovary* (1991) and Scorsese's *The Age of Innocence* (1993). This kind of 'framing', mostly characteristic of the so-called 'pictofilms'[18] that use compositions like portraits or tableaus or employing mirrors, is equivalent to literary descriptions. As a result of this effort to remain faithful to the literary original through stylization, visual invention remains subordinated to narration, never breaking narrative illusion. Most 'false adaptations' belong to this group, that is, those films that can be mistaken as adaptations because of their pictorial style (standing for the 'literary style'). The most prominent example is *The Piano* (Jane Campion, 1993), with a thoroughly Victorian style and symbolism. *Elizabeth* (Shekhar Kapur, 1998), with its exquisite, often oriental-style decorations, costumes and pictorial compositions, is also a 'pictofilm', although it easily can be confounded with period/costume dramas and adaptations of literary classics.

Finally, the third paradigm, 'picture as woman', involves a self-reflexive gesture: The visual becomes a pretext for the thematization of the gaze, looking and spectatorship. As in the previous group, the 'object of the gaze' often appears framed as a painting. But in this third paradigm, the act of looking is central either because of a doubling of the position of the spectator or the uncanny appearance of the visual, which may be a strikingly stylistic excess or a disturbing absence acting against the diegetic effect. Many of the BBC adaptations can be listed in both of these two latter paradigms. For example, the latest adaptation of *Madame Bovary* (Tim Fywell 2000) is not only 'pictorial', but there also is something more striking, more elementary in its use of colours, especially yellow, which is an impressionistic detail as well as a visual effect of the film medium, involving lighting, photogeneity and digital treatment.

Paradoxically, what has been widely considered 'impossible to adapt', is literature in which the visual has a similar role: looking becomes a synonym for exploring and learning and, therefore, a central topic of narration. As Mieke Bal pointed out, the main feature of the Proustian epistemology – that reality and its visual representations are equal – is valid for all the literature from the end of the nineteenth and beginning of twentieth centuries, represented prominently by Joseph Conrad, Henry James, Oscar Wilde, Marcel Proust and Edith Wharton. For example, in James's *Portrait of a Lady*, the men look at Isabel (and try to understand her) from the very start *as if at a picture* – thus, the title; in *The Picture of Dorian Grey*, the portrait and Dorian are interchangeable and the portrait is a source of self-understanding; in Edith Wharton's *The Age of Innocence,* Newland's love for Madame Olenska is substantially influenced by the fact that she has been painted eight times. Similarly, the other characters of *The House of Mirth* see and remember Lily, the protagonist, as an image 'staged' in the 'tableau vivants', a fashionable amusement of American high society at that time. Most studies on the adaptations of these novels are preoccupied with the limits and limitations of the intertwining cinematic literature and literary cinema.[19]

There is nothing surprising about this because the so-called 'visual literature' and the emerging cinema have the same sociocultural background: taking 'captures' of, framing and thus exploring the outer world which is changing at an unprecedented pace. Despite a large number of classic 'woman in the picture' adaptations, which turn these so-called 'ultravisual' works into costume dramas, there are also films dealing with the same self-mirroring mechanisms of the medium. Raúl Ruíz in his *Time Regained* (1999) even uses the same visual techniques and devices identifiable in Proust's gigantic work: the *laterna magica,* the augmenting glass, peepholes, zoom-in, which serve to turn the inside outside and make it easier to explore, as Mieke Bal pointed out in her in-depth analysis of the novels.[20] Ruíz also manages to establish a connection between the voyeurism and memory of the character and those of the spectators: The figure of Catherine Deneuve like a petit Madeleine reminds us of her other roles. The gaze is not only thematized, but narrativized, and is in constant movement. Similarly, Chantal Akerman's film *La Captive* (2000) concentrates on the obsession with love as a theme and mirrors this with Hitchcock's *Vertigo* (1958). Thus, as Melissa Anderson put it, the movie is presented as 'Proustian' and Proust's novel as 'Hitchcockian'.[21] This film, as an example of the jealousy drama intertwined with a detective story, becomes an original interpretation of the Proustian learning/knowing process and a self-mirroring of a typical film genre in which the gaze becomes a main factor in unfolding the story. These two films bring enough counterarguments to the myth of the impossible adaptation, which is a mere narratological issue that disappears once the suitable techniques are found. A fidelity discourse and the very term 'adaptation' are characteristic of this effort to prove again and again the place of film in the 'big narrative tradition'. For example, Ruíz manages to deal not only with the

Table 9.1: A Typology of Film Adaptations for Visuality in 19th–early 20th century Novels

Film Solutions to Literary Visuality	'Woman in the Picture'	'The Woman as Picture'	'The Picture as Woman'
The Visual Paradigms of the Nineteenth-Century Novel	Films converting literary descriptions into motifs and decors prescribed by the plot and genre.	A type seeking for a similar visual effect by using technical and stylistic tools of photography, paintings, other film styles (framing, lights, colours).	The self-reflexive type, thematizing (inter)mediality, spectatorship, its own making process, mirroring and redoubling itself in other films, etc. Remediation: the medium as 'object of desire'.
Couleur Locale First part of nineteenth century – decorative, atmospheric descriptions (Walter Scott, Jane Austen, the Brontës).	Historical/Adventure films, costume dramas, 'heritage films', almost all BBC adaptations, TV adaptations.	'Pictofilms' ('Zeffirelli's *Jane Eyre*, 1996), 'noir' and expressionist adaptations of the 'gothic style' (William Wyler's *Wuthering Heights*, 1939).	Surprising, unusual use of some decorative detail(s), drawing attention to the 'third meaning' as medium specificity and our role as spectators.
Milieu Mid-nineteenth century – an art of realist detail, character and environment 'mirroring' each other (Honoré de Balzac, Charles Dickens).	Adventure films, social dramas, melodramas, costume dramas (Mario Soldati's *Eugénie Grandet*, 1946).	Documentary style imitations, filmic expressionism, realism and naturalism (David Lean's *Great Expectations*, 1946).	Ironic and/or parodic style imitation.

The Flaubert-turn After mid-nineteenth century – points of view multiplied, an adventure of the eye, impressionist visual effects.	The visual effect as genre specificity (Minnelli's *Madame Bovary*, 1949, a musical).	A filmic realism, a preoccupation with details, pictorial compositions (Claude Chabrol's *Madame Bovary*, 1991).	Seeing/watching as perception and impression becomes a central preoccupation, reflecting the position of the film spectator (Manuel de Oliveira's *Abraham's Valley*, 1993).
The Adventure of the Gaze Late nineteenth and early twentieth centuries – observation as learning process (Henry James, Joseph Conrad, Edith Wharton, Oscar Wilde, Marcel Proust).	'Classic' adaptations of Proust, costume dramas (Schlöndorff's *The Love of Swann*, 1984).	Frames, mirrors, painterly style imitations (Scorsese's *The Age of Innocence*, 1993; Jane Campion's *The Portrait of a Lady*, 1996).	Raul Ruiz's *Time Regained*, 1999; Chantal Akerman's *La Captive*, 2000; Martin Scorsese's *The Age of Innocence*, 1993

narrative bravura involving frequent shifts in time and space and
the blurred distinction between the character, narrator and author,
but also with the meta-narrative resulting from a constant thematization of writing. But, most important, through a presentation of
visual techniques, devices, types of observers and ways of observation, Ruíz also realizes a historiography, and accordingly, a
gnoseological narrative[22] of the medium itself, similarly to Chantal
Akerman. This quest for identity of the film as medium is shown
not as renarrativization, but as a series of remediations. Characters
and scenes appear through different media (photos, film, *laterna
magica*), revealing at times some of the basic visual mechanisms
that film language relies upon. Most prominently, the examination
of the photos with an augmenting glass can be seen as the origin
of both the close-up and blow-up. Furthermore, through this intertextual link to Antonioni's *Blow-Up* (1966), this film participates
in the ongoing discourse on the issue of illusion and reality in film
representation.

If we take a closer look at the literary-visual paradigms reflected
in the three types of adaptations (see Table 9.1), the apparently too
easy types – the *milieu* and *couleur locale* – are the real impossible
adaptations. Self-reflexive, 'picture as woman' solutions of these
are very rare, as all visual details are subordinated to the narrative
illusion. Most often they remain 'the film of the novel', a kind
of extension or illustration of the literary text to which they are
thoroughly faithful. However, in the last two decades, as a result
of feminist film theory, gender discourses and cultural criticism, a
tendency has begun to show the sexual and moral taboos underlying
these literary texts. In most cases, an unusual (because unfaithful)
use of a visual (decorative) detail draws attention not only to the
sensual body of the character, but, because of the surprise effect,
to the medium of film, its sociocultural role and spectatorship.
For example, this is how the 1995 BBC adaptation of *Pride and
Prejudice* (Simon Langton) revealed the repressed sexual body
(the wet clothes of Darcy sticking to his body after swimming,)
or *The Scarlet Letter* (Roland Joffé 1995) confronted the reader-
spectator with Demi Moore's sumptuous body (as opposed to
the completely closed, asexual, black Victorian dress). But these
remain isolated moments, as if the tradition of the big epic with
its repressed image of the body would be too heavy to get rid of.
Actually, because of this duplicity of obeying the literary text while

deliberately making fissures in it, most BBC adaptations oscillate between the narrative tradition and the visual culture, adaptation and remediation. Tim Fywell's *Madame Bovary* is an eloquent example of this phenomenon. In the following section, I argue that Manoel de Oliveira's *Abraham's Valley* (Vale Abraão, 1993) is a cross-cultural remediation of Flaubert's *Madame Bovary*. On the one hand, it 'colonizes' the original text (Thomas Leitch's terminology[23]), imposing new cultural meanings on it, such as the image of the modern woman in a pseudomodern, moralizing, patriarchal society. On the other hand, the film subversively reveals, with the Portuguese intermediation of the literary text *Vale Abraão* by Agustina Bessa-Luís, the narratological and spectatorial mechanisms of the medium.

Madame Bovary Remediated. Manoel de Oliveira's *Abraham's Valley* (1993)

In an analysis dedicated to adaptations of Flaubert's novel, Robert Stam pointed out that no film director has attempted to realize the relativization of the narrator's position in *Madame Bovary*.[24] Moreover, apparently the equivalent of the famous statement 'I am Madame Bovary' – which Robert Stam interpreted as Flaubert's attitude towards the sentimental literature to which Emma is addicted – is also missing from existing adaptations. (Emma's death is a metaphor of this ritual break with a literary tradition and the omniscient narrator.) However, Manoel de Oliveira's *Abraham's Valley*, besides conferring a Portuguese cultural interpretation on the story (with the 'intermediation' of Bessa-Luís' homonymous novel), seems to incorporate this contradictory relationship (both respectful and subversive) between the film and the 'old' medium, which Stam suggested and which Bolter and Grusin maintained is characteristic of all remediation.

Intriguingly, all criticism of the film, including interviews with the director, emphasized the effort for complete fidelity to the literary text, the novel of Bessa-Luís, with obvious and numerous intertextual connections to Flaubert's novel, transforming it into a Portuguese version of *Madame Bovary* (Ema, the adulterous protagonist, has read the novel many times, and is called 'Little

Bovary' by her entourage). But this excessive fidelity, manifested
in a suffocating voice-over narration, turns subversive as it acts
against all diegetic effect as a result of the extremely long shots
and the film's length of more than three hours. The voice-over
stops the action repeatedly and unexpectedly, characters freeze in
their positions, and the moving picture is turned into a *tableau
vivant* (an intermedial figure used in many Oliveira films). This
authoritarian gesture not only works as a metaphor of a traditional, hierarchical and patriarchal society, but also functions
as an allegory of the feminine picture ('picture as woman')
being controlled by the male, omniscient narration, an ekphrasis
repeating the myth of Philomena.[25] The same mechanism of
ekphrasis works in the frequent monologues of different men who
analyse Ema's beauty and recall the story of patriarch Abraham,
who took advantage of his wife's beauty. During these descriptive
monologues (often in voice-over), Ema appears as a blank surface,
an expressionless, statue-like entity, in many respects similar to
Bressonian models on to which the male characters project their
views on women, Ema and femininity in general. The protagonist's puppet-like appearance is emphasized in every aspect of the
narration: She looks like the mannequins in the European shops,
and, at the end of her life, like an 'antiqued mannequin.'[26] This is
not only an alternative to Flaubert's narration technique – Emma
appears as *she is seen by different men* – but also an act revealing
the medium in the striking contrast between the aggressive, noisy
voice-over narration and the passive, placid and silent picture.
Ritinha, Ema's deaf-mute servant, a Portuguese beauty whose
story is told by the same narrator, represents the same ekphrastic
principle. As Ema emphasizes, Ritinha is a constant presence in
her life, who has been with her since childhood, ceaselessly
washing the laundry in an old stone pool by the house, while
nothing escapes her attention. At the same time, she's obviously a
literary *topos* representing the adulterous mistress' consciousness,
relentlessly washing the laundry (or spots of shame).

The secret life of images revealing unexpected cultural connotations is beyond the control of the big narrator,[27] as they become
a symbolic, mythical story of femininity, resisting the male gaze.
Her father finds Ema 'a bit frightening', men think that she's
gorgeous and try to avoid her, and in general she triggers a 'sudden
inquietude' in others.[28] There also is a rumour that whenever she

appears on the veranda, her unusual beauty causes cars to crash, crippling or killing the drivers.

The thematization of the visual uncanny – recalling the myth of the Medusa – is a recurrent topic in both the novel and film. Ema, for example, is not a perfect object of desire because she limps. This fault obviously disturbs male contemplation, and as an unconventional representation of feminine beauty, becomes the 'uncanny' making the medium visible. Pedro Dossém, one of her lovers, turns his eyes 'as if seeing a nude', when Ema lies down on the sofa revealing her defective leg.[29] This subversive detail recalls Impressionist paintings, especially those of Manet's that represent women in bizarre, often puppet-like positions and settings,[30] and specifically his *Baudelaire's Mistress, Reclining* (1862) which depicts poet and art critic Baudelaire's semi-invalid mistress, Jeanne Duval. Duval lounges like a stiff doll, her left foot oddly protruding from her oversized skirt. The narrator in both the novel and the film repeatedly depicts Ema as a *tableau vivant*, posing as an odalisque or even as a movie star/character – Lola Montès, Greta Garbo or Marlene Dietrich – representing the vamp or *femme fatale*.[31] But, interestingly enough, the same narrator doesn't forget to mention that Ema's hands *were not beautiful* – a detail recalling, again, the sketchy, unconventional representation of Duval's hands in Manet's painting.[32]

Ema's limp is, at the same time, an obvious allusion to that of the horseman Hippolyte from the novel *Madame Bovary,* who underwent surgical intervention carried out by Emma's husband. According to Mary Donaldson-Evans' interpretation,[33] at that time a limp was considered a sign of increased sexual drive, and thus would be nothing but an allusion to Emma's sensuality through transposition and her last effort to control it by encouraging her husband to do the surgery. In Oliveira's film this is the only sign of Ema's predilection to promiscuity, contrasting with her expressionless, rather innocent look. The limp becomes a crack, both in the image of the woman and in the medium, revealing the (imperfect) body of the female character and of the medium as well.[34] In other words, both the modern woman (as opposed to the mythical feminine) and film, as a modern medium par excellence, are flawed. (Not irrelevantly, the imperfection of Ema's body is carefully put in an intercultural context in both the novel and film by allusions to other physically imperfect mistresses, such as

La Vallière or the Lady of the Camelias). To illustrate and further reinforce this subversive gesture, in one of the *tableau vivant* scenes, depicting a dinner and the moment when everybody rises for a toast, the characters freeze as if waiting for the voice-over narrator to finish his overwhelming tirade, and Ema (because of her limp) makes a tiny movement, sufficient to break the hypnotic effect.

The influence of the Impressionists, Manet in particular, on Flaubert's writing has been pointed out several times: His work is not only impressionistic because of the detailed descriptions, but also because of his ability to convey the *visual effect* of the scenes through light and colours. As already noted, the BBC adaptation created the same effect with Emma's strikingly yellow dresses that function as source of light and a constant attribute of hers. Besides preserving this 'dress code' and an impressionistic style, Oliveira's film, relying on the Portuguese novel, also adapts the subversive gestures of both Flaubert's and Manet's art, producing a noise in representation. As Susan Strauber pointed out in her essay, Manet's portrait of Jeanne Duval is also 'Manet's dialogue with Baudelaire about aesthetics, modernity, femininity, and politics, and his continuation of their exchange about picturing and writing' … in which 'Manet contradicts customary idealizing prescriptions for portraiture and especially for the portrayal of femininity.' This subversive act draws attention to the medium instead of the object represented: 'The visibility of the presentation functions here to begin to draw our attention away from the model as portrait to the painting as entity.'[35] The same subversive principle applies to the image depicting Abraham's Valley (the valley of the Douro River, where the famous port wine, a symbol of fertility and vitality,[36] is being produced). The scenery has the physiognomy of the female body, which is repeatedly disturbed by the intrusion of a white boat, driven by Ema and her lover. Throughout the film, we witness the *body becoming a picture,* through ekphrastic descriptions, *tableaux vivants* and the protagonist's puppet-like appearance – a mechanism recalling Manet's paintings, the myth of Medusa and represented in the painting originally attributed to Leonardo.

Finally, a denial of all realism produces the same effect of anti-transparency, as it is impossible to detect the story's time period. The costumes, decorations and cars represent different ages, trends and social backgrounds. This lack of reference is typical of all fashion: It is not compensated by a symbolic level of meanings, but produces a third meaning, a noise revealing the medium.[37] The film also is Oliveira's original discourse on fashion – a central subject of modernity, as Baudelaire emphasized in his *The Painter of Modern Life*[38] – and on the new trends in the visual representation of women. Its futility and excesses also involve new techniques of representation (fabrics ranging from heavy to light and transparent), harmonizing with the mannequin-like appearance and addressing the different spectator groups. The uncanny visual effect relies on the striking discrepancy between the 'eternal feminine' and, in the words of Bessa-Luís's narrator,[39] the woman turned into pure spectacle (*uma mulher-espectáculo*).

Theorizing the 'resistant medium'

While the traditional discourse on literary adaptations has been primarily preoccupied with the resistance of the original narration – thus considering the main goal of adaptations as the realization of an equivalent of literary narrative techniques – the most recent trends in visual anthropology, medium theory and intermediality research focus on the new medium performing an oedipal turn by renouncing the exclusivity of the literary heritage. Accordingly, the concept of 'impossible adaptation,' propagated by the narratological approach, is being replaced with 'remediation', preoccupied with the self-definition of a medium (in this case film) through its relationship to other media. As Gaudreault and Marion stated, 'A medium's identity is a very complex affair. Moreover, specificity by no means signifies separation or isolation. A good understanding of a medium thus entails understanding its relationship to other media: It is through intermediality, through a concern with the intermedial, that a medium is understood.'[40] According to Gaudreault and Marion, the new research area of narrative mediatics focuses on the resistance of a medium when meeting a certain narrative.[41] With the concept of *fabulae* of the Russian formalists, independent of all media, as their point of departure, they argued that even before their incarnation on film, all *fabulae* already have some media characteristics that can be named 'mediageneity' or 'media sensitivity'. At the same time, in the case of literary adaptation, the moving picture has a sort of inner narrativity facilitating the transposition of the narrative in question. But, despite these circumstances, as seen in Oliveira's film, in the effort to get closer to the *fabulae* by using an omniscient narrator, the medium produces a *sujet-reaction* that resists narrative transparency. This is actually the essence of the so-called mediativity: the answer of the combination of forms of expression to the technical apparatus meant to emphasize them. The narrative diegetics would investigate all these factors of the imaginary or real narrative that are obeying film narrative.

A similar reasoning can be identified in Joachim Paech's description of the medium as being 'only recognizable in the contingency of the formation it makes possible.'[42] The medium can be observed in its 'other' as an oscillation, a 'parasitic third'. a 'background noise', in the 'breaks, gaps, and intervals of the form processes'.[43] Besides the too noisy, intruding narrator, Oliveira's film presents endless examples of breaks and gaps mostly because of an excessive use of long shots. This definition of the medium as either excess of the form or an absence and gap shows striking similarities with the enigmatic, never completely clarified 'third meaning' of Roland Barthes and is closely related to his 'punctum' concept:[44] Something uncanny, unexpected, a *'je ne sais quoi'* in a (visual) representation (the too thick layer of the paint in a painting, for example) that strikes us as something that is beyond referential and symbolic meaning. The striking brightness of Emma's dresses in Fywell's version of *Madame Bovary,* as well as the eclecticism of the fashion elements in Oliveira's film accurately exemplify this concept. We might be tempted to identify this third or obtuse meaning as the emergence of the medium, acting against illusion and making us aware of our position as spectator.

As we have seen, all these considerations are stemming from the discourse of modernity on representation, initiated by Baudelaire's *The Painter of Modern Life.* The preoccupation with the medium instead of the represented object is present in linguistic, semiotic, psychoanalytical and philosophical trends of film theory, which emphasizes the qualities of film as text, sign system or a sensual presence confronting spectators with the visual uncanny. Along this modernist theoretical line is Jacques Rancière's view on a 'regime of the sensible that has become foreign to himself', a characteristic of the aesthetic regime of the art. This view 'strictly identifies art in the singular and frees it from any specific rule, from any hierarchy of the arts, subject matter, and genres.'[45] Not surprisingly, one of Rancière's examples is the art of Robert Bresson and his model theory, revealing truth through alienation. As we have seen, this mode of thought specific to the Modern Age is represented by Oliveira, one of the last representatives of the European modernist film. Ema, the protagonist of his *Abraham's Valley*, is a descendant of the puppet-like women represented in Impressionist paintings and Bresson's films, asexual and anarratological, removed from all mythical and romantic stories. In both Impressionism and modernist films, this change in the representation of women coincided with a change of paradigm and the advent of a high cultural and even political awareness of visual media. For Oliveira, film is the modern medium 'par excellence', breaking with all mimetic and narratological tradition and defining itself through remediation and not adaptation of literary texts. The contradictory concept of 'impossible adaptation' can be easily discredited – we should rather reformulate the statement to say that adaptation *as such is impossible* (as long as it requires a mimetic attitude, solving merely narratological issues).

Bolter and Grusin's proposed term 'remediation' fortunately avoids a hierarchical and judgemental approach activated by the notion of 'original'. Similarly, 'hypermediacy', as opposed to immediacy, stands for the active, narcissistic presence of an opaque medium – literary or visual – in any mixed media configurations.[46] The curse of the impossible adaptation is lifted by the new theoretical paradigm of the medium and intermediality: The medium is no longer something to hide (by making the 'sutures' invisible), but the 'other' as 'object of desire' and a constant source of fascination.

Notes

1   For example, see the latest themes of the Association of Adaptation Studies' conferences and the articles published in *Adaptation*. Similarly, Linda Hutcheon called adaptation a cultural or transcultural phenomenon of 'indigenization' or 'colonization' in her recent book, *A Theory of Adaptation* (New York and London: Routledge, 2006), 33.

2   A discipline taking shape in international conferences, workshops, and essay collections. Playing a pioneering role in this respect are Lars Ellestrom (ed.), *Media Borders, Multimodality and Intermediality* (Houndmills: Palgrave and Macmillan, 2010) and Ágnes Pethő, *Cinema and Intermediality. The Passion for the In-Between* (Cambridge: Scholars Publishing, 2011).

3   See Jack Boozer (ed.), *Authorship in Film Adaptation* (Austin: University of Texas Press, 2008) or Greg Jenkins, *Stanley Kubrick and the Art of Adaptation. Three Novels, Three Films* (McFarland and Company, Inc., 2007).

4   See the books written and edited by Stam in 2004–5: *Literature through Film: Realism, Magic, and the Art of Adaptation* (Oxford: Blackwell Publishing, 2005); *A Companion to Literature and Film* (Oxford: Blackwell Publishing, 2004); and Robert Stam and Alessandra Raengo, *Literature and Film. A Guide to the Theory and Practice of Adaptation* (Oxford: Blackwell Publishing, 2005).

5   Michel Foucault, 'We "Other Victorians,"' in *The History of Sexuality, vol. I, The Foucault Reader: An Introduction to Foucault's Thought*, Paul Rabinov, (ed.) (London: Penguin Books, 1992), 292–326.

6   Jay David Bolter and Richard Grusin, *Remediation: Understanding New Media* (Cambridge, MA: MIT Press, 1999).

7   Lev Manovich, *The Language of New Media* (Cambridge, MA: MIT Press, 2001).

8   See W. J. T. Mitchell, 'The Pictorial Turn,' in *Picture Theory* (Chicago: University of Chicago Press, 1994), 11–34.

9   The literary visual is a taboo of the pretheoretical discourse of the *ut pictura poesis* concept that leads to the inhibition of the 'impossible adaptation.' This tradition is represented in adaptation studies by George Bluestone's book *Novels into Film*, followed by a long line of *neo-laokoönians*, accurately delimitating the abilities of literary and film media: Literature addresses the cognition, while pictures and film the senses. Although this principle can be and has been easily discredited by film history and theory (not to mention Eisenstein's films and views on film-making and recently cognitive theory that that visual media activate mental processes as well), the fear and deception (or fear from deception) bursting out every time a mental image turns into a physical one remains unchanged. See Ralph Stephenson and J. R. Debrix, *Cinema as Art* (London: Penguin, 1978); Keith Cohen, *Film and Fiction: The Dynamics of Exchange* (New Haven: Yale University Press, 1979); J. Dudley

Andrew, *Concepts of Film Theory* (Oxford: Oxford University Press, 1984), 107–32, and McFarlane, *Novelto Film: An Introduction to the Theory of Adaptations* (Oxford: Clarendon Press, 1996).

10 See W. J. T. Mitchell, 'The Ekphrasis and the Other,' in *Picture Theory: Essays on Verbal and Visual Representation* (Chicago and London: University of Chicago Press, 1994), 151–81.

11 Murray Krieger, *Ekphrasis: The Illusion of the Natural Sign* (Baltimore and London: Johns Hopkins University Press, 1992), 197–206.

12 Gustave Flaubert, *Madame Bovary* (London: Penguin Classics, 2003), Chapter 13.

13 See p. 154.

14 See Merleau-Ponty, 'Eye and Mind,' in *The Merleau-Ponty Aesthetics Reader: Philosophy and Painting*, Galen A. Johnson, (ed.) (Evanston, Illinois: Northwestern University Press, 1996), 121–50, and Hans Belting, *Bild-Anthropologie: Entwürfe für eine Bildwissenschaft* (München: Fink, 2001).

15 See Hans Belting, *Bild-Anthropologie: Entwürfe für eine Bildwissenschaft* (München: Fink, 2001), 85.

16 See Walter Benjamin, 'The Work of Art in the Age of Its Technical Reproducibility', in *The Work of Art in the Age of Its Technical Reproducibility and Other Writings on Media*, Michael W. Jennings, Birgid Doherty and Thomas Y. Levin, (eds), (Cambridge, MA: Belknap Press of Harvard University Press, 2008), 19–55.

17 Hippolyte Taine, *Notes sur Paris. Vie et opinions de M. Frédéric-Thomas Graindorge* (Paris: L. Hachette & Cie, 1867), 76.

18 On pictofilms see Ágnes Pethő, *Cinema and Intermediality: The Passion for the In-Between*, 36.

19 See Nancy Bentley, 'Conscious Observation: Jane Campion's Portrait of a Lady,' in *Henry James Goes to the Movies*, Susan M. Griffin, (ed.) (University of Kentucky Press, 2001), 127–46; Ken Gelder, 'Campion and the Limits of Literary Cinema,' in *Adaptations. From Text to Screen, Screen to Text*, Deborah Cartmell and Imelda Whelehan, (eds) (London and New York: Routledge, 2000), 157–70; Brigitte Peucker, 'The Moment of Portraiture,' in *A Companion to Literature and Film*, Robert Stam and Alessandra Raengo, (eds) (Oxford: Blackwell, 2004), 258–65.

20 See Mieke Bal, *Images Littéraires, Ou Comment Lire Visuellement Proust* (Toulouse: PUM, 1997)

21 Melissa Anderson, 'In Search of Adaptation: Proust and Film,' in

Literature and Film. A Guide to the Theory and Practice of Film Adaptation, Robert Stam and Alessandra Raengo, (eds) (London: Blackwell, 2005) 100–10.

22 Tzvetan Todorov distinguishes between mythological and gnosseological narratives, these latter focusing on the discovery of the former. See Tzvetan Todorov, The Two Principles of Narrative,' in *Genres in Discourse* (Cambridge: Cambridge University Press, 1995), 27–38.

23 See Thomas Leitch, *Film Adaptation and its Discontents: From Gone with the Wind to The Passion of Christ* (Baltimore The Johns Hopkins University Press, 2007), 109–10.

24 Robert Stam,'Introduction: The Theory and Practice of Adaptations,' in *Literature and Film. A Guide to the Theory and Practice of Film Adaptation*, Robert Stam and Alessandra Raengo, (eds) (London: Blackwell, 2005), 2–52.

25 According to legend, Philomena represented the story of the rape on a white silk cloth she had woven herself, which become the silent accusation against Tereus, her perpetrator, who loudly propagated another version of the story.

26 See Agustina Bessa-Luís, *Vale Abraão* (Lisboa: Planeta DeAgostini SA, 2000), 13–15, 48.

27 André Gaudreault used the term 'grand narrateur,' along with 'grand imagier,' in his *Du Littéraire au Filmique. Le Système du Récit* (Paris: Méridiens Klinksieck, 1988).

28 Ibid., 217, 279.

29 Ibid., 206: 'Ema estendeu-se pelo sofá, e a perna defeituosa ficou em evidencia. Pedro Dossém desviou os olhos, como se surpreendesse uma nudez.'

30 See Sidsel Maria Søndergaard, 'Women in Impressionism: An Introduction,' in *Women in Impressionism. From Mythical Feminine to Modern Woman*, Sidsel Maria Søndergaard, (ed.) (Milano: Skira, 2006), 11–28.

31 Ibid., 140, 247, 272.

32 For a detailed analysis of this portrait see Susan Strauber, 'Manet's Portrait of Jeanne Duval: Baudelaire's Mistress Reclining,' in *Women in Impressionism. From Mythical Feminine to Modern Woman*, Sidsel Maria Søndergaard, (ed.) (Milano: Skira, 2006), 99–131.

33 Mary Donaldson-Evans, 'A Medium of Exchange: The Madame Bovary Film,' *Society of Dix-Neuviémistes*, no. 4 (2005): 21–34. She is quoting an Italian proverb, translated by Montaigne as 'Celui-lá

ne connaît pas Vénus en sa parfaite douceur qui n'a pas couché avec la boiteuse.'

34 The same directorial subversive gesture applies to Buñuel's Tristana (1971). *Jørgen Bruhn* discussed the limp *in* Changing Borders: Contemporary Positions in Intermediality, Jens Arvidson, Mikael Askander *et al.*, (eds) (Lund: Intermediality Studies Press, 2008).

35 Strauber, *'Manet's Portrait of Jeanne Duval: Baudelaire's Mistress Reclining'* 102, 117, 130.

36 See Gilbert Durand, *Les Structures Anthropologiques de L'imaginaire* (Paris: Bordas, 1960), 249.

37 See Roland Barthes, 'Le Troisième Sens,' *Cahiers du Cinéma*, no. 222 (1970): 12–19 and Joachim Paech, 'Artwork – Text – Medium. Steps en Route to Intermediality.' http://www.uni-konstanz.de/FuF/Philo/LitWiss/MedienWiss/Texte/interm.html [accessed 17 April 2011]

38 Charles Baudelaire, 'The Painter of Modern Life,' in *Baudelaire: The Painter of Modern Life and Other Essays,* Jonathan Mayne, (ed.) and trans. (New York, 1964), 31–3.

39 See Agustina Bessa-Luís, *Vale Abraão*, 245.

40 Gaudreault, André and Philippe Marion, 'The Cinema as a Model for the Genealogy of Media,' *Convergence*, no. 8 (2002): 12–18.

41 See André Gaudreault and Philippe Marion, 'Transécriture and Narrative Mediatics: The Stakes of Intermediality,' in *A Companion to Literature and Film*, Robert Stam and Alessandra Raengo, (eds) (Oxford: Blackwell, 2004), 58–64.

42 He is citing Niklas Luhmann, *Die Kunst der Gesellschaft* (Frankfurt/Main: Suhrkamp, 1995), 165–214.

43 Joachim Paech, 'Artwork – Text – Medium. Steps en Route to Intermediality.' http://www.uni-konstanz.de/FuF/Philo/LitWiss/MedienWiss/Texte/interm.html [accessed 17 April 2011]

44 See Roland Barthes, 'Le Troisième Sens,' and *Camera Lucida* (Hill and Wang, 1993).

45 Jacques Rancière, *The Politics of Aesthetics* (London: Continuum, 2005), 23.

46 Bolter and Grusin, *Remediation. Understanding New Media*, 155.

10

Auto-adaptation and the movement of writing across media: Ingmar Bergman's notebooks

Anna Sofia Rossholm

In today's media culture, where private and public forms of expression merge, there is an increased interest in the diary genre throughout history and various media: personal diaries, diary novels, diary films or online diaries represent the trajectory of a heterogeneous genre of self-construction on the boundaries between intimate and public realms. Like adaptations, the diary genre raises questions about authenticity and fidelity, and also addresses issues regarding the relation between source text and rewriting or revision. However, discourses on diaries understand the notions of the original and authenticity differently than discourses on adaptations: when we refer to an 'original' diary, we generally mean a singular trace of a singular moment of writing or creation, whereas the 'original' in a process of adaptation is another version of the story, generally a novel written prior to a film adaptation. Put simply, an adaptation is truthful or untruthful to the content or form of another text, whereas a diary is truthful or untruthful to life itself or to the actual moment of writing. These different understandings of original, source and fidelity entangle in diary adaptations and in diaries used in the process of artistic creation. For instance, film adaptations of written diaries (fictional or non-fictional) often include images of writing that somehow point back to the (imaginary or real) unique moment of creation. The most emblematic example is perhaps Robert Bresson's *The Diary of a Country Priest* (1951) where close-ups of the action of handwriting integrate the 'aura' of the moment of writing into the adaptation.[1] The adaptation here displays an image of the original (which is of course not an actual original) as a process of writing and as physical movement.

This essay deals with a kind of diary that is particularly interesting, yet rarely discussed in this context, namely the notebook used in artistic creation. With Ingmar Bergman as my case in point, I examine the personal creative diary in the process of film-making. As pretexts to films or plays, Bergman's notebooks allow for a discussion on the creative diary as a 'source' of fiction, as well as on how the personal writings of the artist resurface in the final work and pose aesthetical questions about the relation between words and images or art and life.

The artist's notebook is in itself a heterogeneous genre that can take many forms and have various functions: scrapbooks, creative diaries, drafts, sketches, photos or other imprints. A notebook can be born from spontaneous note-taking or be a product of more elaborate methods and aesthetics framing and forming the whole process of creation. The artists' notebooks are often the missing link in the studies of the different versions of a work of art. This not only because they are rarely preserved to the same extent as other pretexts, versions or adaptations, but also because the identity of these notebooks seems to be difficult to define and reflect upon. Shall the notebook be considered 'art' or primarily a biographical document? Can it be considered a version of a work of art or is it merely a pretext that documents the process of creation? The specificity of the creative diary lies in the transgressive character of the genre: it is a text somewhere between the personal and the shared, between the fictional and the real, between aesthetic practice and reflection. A study of the notebook in the process of film-making therefore sheds light on diaristic aspects of film and writing beyond what is usually labelled 'diary film' or adaptations of diary fiction between film and literature. It also bridges the division between 'real' diaries and diary fiction.

Ingmar Bergman's notebooks played a particularly important role in his film-making: throughout his career, Bergman kept creative diaries where fragmentary and searching drafts for films or stage plays merged with reflections on the creative process or notes on everyday matters. Today The Ingmar Bergman Archives, where these documents are preserved, provide access to this previously invisible yet central dimension of Bergman's creation: over 60 notebooks from the 1930s until the end of Bergman's life are preserved in the archives.[2] Bergman often argued against the literary adaptation by advocating the common idea that film and literature are fundamentally different forms of expression.[3] His use of the written notebook as a source text consisting of personal writing, rather than a work of 'literature', represents an adaptation practice where writing and cinema intersect beyond the comparison between two separate works of art. Bergman's notebooks can be compared with the dream diaries of the surrealist artists or James Joyce's notebooks; even if the diary or the notebook itself is not produced as a work of art, its aesthetics specificities form later stages of the work of art. The notebook is beyond the realm of art, but at the same time it raises perhaps the most essential aesthetical questions. On the one hand, it is a form where the author can write freely, test ideas and reflect on the creative process in an intimate sphere protected from the judgement of readers, audiences and critics. On the other hand, the artistic diary turns the aesthetic process of rendering the subjective into a shared experience. As such, it makes the process of creation itself visible.

My study of this particular form of adaptation is informed by studies on drafts and versions in genetic criticism and textual criticism, theories where drafts, manuscripts or other pre-texts are understood as instances of the work of art, as multiple texts or versions rather than steps on the way towards a 'final' materialization of the work. Instead of regarding the notebooks as a mere pre-text to the screenplay and the film, I argue that the notebook forms a movement of what I call 'auto-adaption' across media.

Auto-adaptation and the movement of writing

Auto-adaption in this case refers to a continuous movement of writing and transposition that takes place on two levels: first the materialization of the author's 'self' in the process of writing, and then the transposition from one form of inscription, the notebook, to another, a film or a screenplay. This study thus understands adaptation in a double sense, as a movement of writing (transforming the self into writing) and writing as movement (towards new mediations).

I employ the term adaptation in this broad sense as I argue that the aesthetics of the notebook, as a materialization of the personal experience in writing, is also reflected in Bergman's films. The notebook thus offers a point of entry for a 'diaristic' approach to Bergman's films. It sheds new light on the diaristic elements of his films, such as the confessional monologues, the autobiographical elements merged with the fictional and the oscillation between public and intimate forms of expression. The relationship between film and notebook is read as a mirror image in the Bergmanian sense: a doubling that is both opposite and alike, something that shares fundamental characteristics through differences.[4] The mirroring between film and notebook is primarily visible in the recurrent images of intimate writing in Bergman's films, images of letters, diaries and notebooks. In her study of *The Silence* (1963), Maaret Koskinen offers an approach to Bergman's integration of writing in the movie in terms of 'mixed media'.[5] Via the notebook, I suggest that the merging of writing and cinematic forms of expression as 'mixed media' also intersects and bridges other dichotomies or categories, such as intimate and public, fictional and non-fictional, memory and present.

Understanding Bergman's films as adaptations of his notebooks draws on the notion of the *avant-texte*, as the term is employed in the tradition of genetic criticism. In *Genetic Criticism: Texts and Avant-Textes*, Jed Deppman, Michael Groden and Daniel Ferrer write that genetic criticism 'examines tangible documents such as writers' notes, drafts and proof corrections, but its real object is something much more abstract – not the existing documents but the movement of writing that must be inferred from them.'[6] This

approach differs from the traditional notion of intentionality and
from textual approaches that proclaim 'the death of the author' as
a condition of textual production. Instead it regards the writing as
a materialization that constructs the author in the text through an
act of separation. Ferrer argues that the study of the *avant-texte* in
a concrete and material way shows that 'the text is not produced
by the author but the author is produced by the text'.[7] This process
of materialization by separation is explicitly revealed and even
reflected upon in Bergman's notebooks. For instance, in a passage
from the notebook for *Persona*, Bergman reflects on the process
of writing with the following words: 'I can think only when I am
speaking. If I am thinking in silence or write down things that
come to mind the words on the paper inhibit me horribly.'[8] The
notebook itself cannot answer the inevitable questions raised by
such remarks, whether Bergman actually spoke his thoughts out
loud when writing or if he here merely reflects upon the questions
of silence and speech; instead it tells us that what we read is not
the process of creation itself but the materialization of it in written
form. These hastily written words appear as incomplete, silent and
visual imprints in the absence of the voice, separated from and the
unique moment of writing.

Ferrer further argues that the *avant-texte* is a 'hyper-text' or
'hyper-medium' rather than a 'text' in the strict sense of the term:
it is a document written to be transformed, that also reflects on
the mode of transposition itself.[9] Even if it is true that drafts, notes
and other pretexts are highly self-reflexive this distinction between
text and avant-texte is somehow problematic: not only pretexts
but also works of art in the public domain visualize their process
of becoming, not least self-reflexive works like Bergman's films.
Persona is perhaps the most striking example of this: as the title
indicates, the film is about masking the self and as such it reflects
the creation of the work of art itself. In contemporary studies
of textual criticism, the terms 'version' or 'variant' are typically
employed to bridge the differences between drafts, manuscripts
and published editions. The pretext is here understood as a version
similar to a re-edition or an adaptation. John Bryant's notion
of the 'fluid text' understands the work of art in a broad sense,
including pretexts, re-editions and adaptations in other media or
art forms. Bryant argues that 'the surviving variants of texts, when
put together, give us a vivid material of the *flow* of creativity, both

authorial and editorial, constituting the cultural phenomenon of writing'.[10] This links to the question of whether screenwriting can be regarded in terms of a literary adaptation. Steven Price questions Thomas Leitch's description of the screenplay as exclusively 'a performative text' in the production process by pointing out that screenplays 'circulate in other forms and to other readerships than the immediate production team'.[11] So do all 'surviving variants' of a work of art: personal notebooks, drafts or diaries are accessible to readers outside the original process of creation through their preservation in archives, libraries or databases. We may, of course, argue that the text is *created* as a personal text rather than a text addressing a reader in the public sphere. However, the diary is a particularly revealing example of a private text that problematizes the personal address. Even the personal diary has an ambiguous recipient, as the diarist addresses the self as another or the diary itself as a reader (as in 'dear diary'). It is a kind of personal writing that often indirectly addresses an anonymous reader in a future public domain. The diary is a genre that reconciles the immediacy of the moment of writing with an address 'in dialogue with the future'.[12] This is particularly important when analysing Bergman's notebooks, diaries written by a film-maker who was fully conscious about the potential future interest in his personal notes, and who also perpetually reconstructed his public *persona*, in his art and in interviews, essays and autobiographies.

The personal notebook is of course not an 'original' in the sense that it functions as a literary reference for film viewers. Instead it draws on the Benjaminian notion of the original as an authentic trace of the actual moment of creation, an 'aura' that gives the text a unique presence in time and space. The French literary theorist Philippe Lejeune defines the diary genre in terms of such a physical presence of the inscription, as 'a series of dated traces' formed by the diary's temporal succession of entries.[13] Through the repetition of entries the diary is conceptualized as a series of traces capturing movement: 'the diary begins when traces in a series attempt to capture the movement of time rather than freeze it around a source event.'[14] In Bergman's case, the notion of the trace is central when understanding the written notebook in relation to the cinematic medium. Lejeune's definition is perhaps mainly applied to written diaries but it clearly lends itself to a comparison between writing and film or photography: as the cinematic succession of photographic images creates movement, the diary is a series of traces that forms a continuous movement in time, i.e. the movement of writing itself.

In the preface to an edition of a selection of his screen-plays, Bergman describes the initial phase of the making of a film as impressions, images and rhythms coming to his mind, fragments that he perceives as somehow more 'cinematic' than the narrative form they are given in a screenplay. The writing of a screenplay becomes 'an almost impossible task', an attempt to transform 'rhythms, modes, atmosphere, tensions, sequences, tones and scents into words and sentences of an understandable screenplay'.[15] These 'words and sentences', he explains, are mainly dialogue; what is essentially cinematic, the rhythms, tensions and tones, remains absent in the script's literary form. This description is perhaps not an accurate description of how all Bergman's scripts were actually prepared and developed, but it sheds light on a paradox in Bergman's film-making, namely that the transposition between words and images is a necessary yet impossible process in the making of a film. The notebook captures this paradox in a particularly conspicuous way: on the one hand, in the absence of a coherent narrative, the notebook text is further away from the film than the script versions, but on the other, these fragments of impressions, situations, images and memories seem to be closer to what Bergman considers 'cinematic'. Is it perhaps a form of writing that challenges the 'literary' dimension of the screenplay to the same extent as the film does? If so, it is also a kind of writing that in itself represents a form of 'mixed media', intersecting the written and the cinematic.

Unframed writings

Bergman kept notebooks from the beginnings of his career in the 1930s. It was, however, in the 1950s that the notebooks began to form a specific aesthetic that remained relatively consistent throughout the rest of his career. The earliest notebooks preserved at the archives, from the 1930s, seem to function more as blueprints for staging a play or writing a screenplay, whereas the notebooks from the period from *Through a Glass Darkly* (1961) and *Winter Light* (1963) until the end of his career consist of open searching reflections on the threshold of the emerging fictional world. This period also represents a personal turn in Bergman's film-making and a beginning of a film-making that shares similarities with the confessional, self-reflexive or autobiographical mode of the diary genre. From this period, diaries and other forms of intimate writing also play a significant role in Bergman's films. In *Through a Glass Darkly,* the author in the story keeps a diary to register the illness of his daughter, a diary where he also confesses the pleasure that this documentation gives him. This is an example of how diaries and personal letters in Bergman's films allegorize the integration of life and art in the form of a critique of art as intrusive, voyeuristic or confessional.

At first glance the notebooks seem far from what one might expect from a film-maker's creative diary: there are few drawings and pictures. In contrast to many film-makers' notebooks, such as Agnès Varda's media hybrid notebooks where photos and writing are merged, or Federico Fellini's dream diaries with colourful drawings, Bergman's notebooks consist almost exclusively of handwritten pages.[16] The writing used as a means to develop a cinematic expression is a method in line with the negative aesthetics that we find in Bergman's modernist films from the 1960s, a form of expression that reflects on itself and its own limitations as representation. In the notebooks from the period when *Persona* (1966) and *The Silence* (1963) were created, Bergman paradoxically examines a silent, wordless cinematic expression through long, wordy, often frustrated but sometimes cheerfully chatty, written reflections.[17] Descriptions are often interrupted by phrases such as 'words are unnecessary, you say what you want but not what you mean'.[18] In moments of despair over creative impasses, he can express his frustration with repetitions that fill the blank paper as if the writing itself would dispel his lack of inspiration: 'Patience, patience, patience, patience, patience, pace. Patient. Patience. No panic, don't be afraid, take it easy, don't get tired, don't think that it is all boring.' Bergman struggles with both the absence and the presence of words. At times he uses the blank paper to the express himself wordlessly. A straight line following the heading 'exercise in simplicity' occurs several times in the notebooks from this period. Writing itself is also not only a verbal but also a *visual* and *silent* form of representation. Bergman's notebooks often make the duality of voice and silence as well as the visual inscription of the written word explicit. The notebook's reflection on the necessity of speaking cited above is an example of when Bergman's writing makes the silence of the written word as visual imprints on paper perceptible.

The notebooks are radically different from a screenplay or even an outline for a coherent story: the writing is fragmentary, searching and self-reflexive. Instead of dialogue the story is presented through prose fragments written in the present tense; descriptions of actions, situations, characters or impressions are merged with thoughts and ideas on the writing or creation itself, and sometimes also minor everyday matters unrelated to the fictional story. Sometimes different projects are merged in one notebook. Every notebook is also full of revisions of older passages: there are underlinings, overcrossings, corrections and sometimes even whole rewrites of sections.[19] The revisions reveal the non-linear structure characteristic for the *avant-texte* with multiple layers of writing side by side. The notebook often begins as a draft of a story, continuing as a diary of the process of the writing of the screenplay. It takes the form of a diary in Lejeune's sense of the term as the text is structured by day-to-day entries, a temporal continuity that stands against the fragmentary form. The dating, which is of course unrelated to the drafted story, shows that Bergman does not only use the notebook to develop a story; it is also a means to trace, document and remember the personal development of the creative process. The documentary function is crucial for Bergman, who also documented the shooting of his films through amateur films.[20] The difference between the notebook and other means of documentation is the various functions of the notebook, simultaneously a phase of the work of art and a documentation of, and reflection on, that process.

Even if the address of the notebook is personal (Bergman talks to himself), the notes inevitably raise questions about to what extent the author addresses an outside reader, or if the writing only represents notes for personal memory making. Notably, Bergman edited a few personal diaries for publication and also used personal diaries as a source for fiction. His most explicitly autobiographical screenplay, *The Best Intentions* (made into a film by Bille August in 1992) was partly based on his mother's diary; the book *Three Diaries* is a compilation of personal diaries by Bergman, his last wife and their daughter.[21] Another example of a published diary is the preface to the programme of *Virgin Spring* (1960) in the US and French distribution, with an extract from his notebook labelled 'A page from my diary'.[22]

The notebooks are part of the collection donated by Bergman himself, first to film scholar Maaret Koskinen and later to the foundation responsible for the archive.[23] The very gesture of donating these documents is in itself an ambivalent act, somewhere between making public and preserving the private. Bergman did not publish his notebooks, he made them public as private documents, as traces of the moment of creation to become memories for the future. With exhibitions such as *Ingmar Bergman: Truth and Lies* in Los Angeles or Berlin, the notebooks circulate in an even wider public domain today.[24] The broader public interest in pre-texts and material around film-making in books and exhibitions is, of course, not exclusive to Bergman, but can be placed in a context of contemporary film culture, where the becoming of a film attracts attention through DVD bonus material or making-of films.[25] According to Daniel Ferrer and Jean-Loup Bourget, the attention to the genesis of cinematic works can be linked to cinema as mechanical reproduction in a Benjaminian sense: the interest in source texts in the film-making process is understood as a compensation for the loss of an 'aura' of cinema as a reproduction medium.[26] The handwritten notebook is a particularly conspicuous example of when a pre-text takes the form of an original enunciation or 'aura', as a trace of the hand in the process of film-making.

The notebook is a trace of the materialization of thoughts into writing, but it does not in itself explain the process. We cannot see whether the initial spark of a film is a mental image, a situation or a personal memory. Instead the transgressive character of the notebook is manifested through the absence of a beginning or a coherent narrative. The story in the notebook for *Winter Light*, for instance, opens with an attempt to clarify and capture thoughts in writing: Bergman begins with the problem of the initiation of writing, by saying that 'I will try to write this as simply as I can but I don't know if it is possible.' The notes continue with: 'This I know:' followed by a description of a situation where an 'I' enters the church to encounter God.[27] The notes are neither the beginning of a fictional story nor the beginning of the creation as such, it is the beginning of writing an intermediate phase in the process of developing a narrative.

The ambiguous address characteristic of the diary genre takes various forms in Bergman's notebooks. Reflections are often expressed by searching questions posed to himself as another, often addressing himself as 'you' but sometimes, more ironically, 'Mr. Bergman', 'IB' or 'Ingmar'. In other cases he talks to the fictional characters in the process of creating. These forms of ambiguous address, similar to the make-believe games a child would play, trace the process of fictionalization and document his method of testing and forming characters and situations.

As often pointed out in recent research, Bergman's work can be seen as constructions of a public 'persona' or as a merging of the fictional and autobiographical:[28] Bergman's portrait of 'Bergman' the film-maker, written under a pseudonym in the Swedish film journal *Chaplin*, his interviews with himself, his vocal cameos (like the voice of the photographer heard off-screen in *Scenes from a Marriage*) and the use of his proper initials in fiction (such as I.B. for 'Isak Borg' in *Wild Strawberries*) exemplify a *mise-en-scène* of the *auteur's* life in fiction and in constructions of the public self.[29] The notebook foregrounds the creative act in these processes of self-construction. It documents the playful dimension of merging the authentic with the fictional and also shows to what extent the construction of the self as another is less a staging in the public realm, in contrast to the private, than a condition for all phases in the process of creation, that the personal writing in itself is a process of masking and transposing the self.

In a notebook from the period of the self-reflexive films *Persona* and *The Hour of the Wolf* (1968), this playfulness with the levels of the fictional is particularly striking. For instance, in a notebook from this period, Bergman begins writing in the first person, but then interrupts himself and asks:

> Who is this secret 'I'? That is something to think about. I think it has to be an ambiguous split in wishes and dreams. Whole series of interesting characters. They come and go – very surprising. But this is clear: He does not keep very good track of them. I guess he is careless with them.[30]

The 'I' in this passage oscillates between the narrating agent, Bergman, as a writer and as a fictional character. Notably, it is the ambiguous self rather than the answers to the questions posed in this passage that is transposed into the film: the divided 'I' mirrors *Persona*'s multiple masks of the dual subject as well as the ambiguous subjective visions in *The Hour of the Wolf*. Elisabet, the woman in *Persona* who remains silent throughout the story, emerges in the notebook through a similar interaction with the fictional realm. Bergman pushes the boundaries of the division between life and fiction by speaking to the character in the moment of creation: 'How can I experience and feel you more than in short moments', he asks and continues by reversing the question: 'How can you experience me as real'.[31] In the notebook for *Persona* we also find several remarks on the inscription of writing, such as 'now I think that this blue pen is so alive and its pin jumps around as hell' or 'it's so nice to write with a pencil, it reminds me of my childhood'.[32] Such reflections on writing as material inscription, almost alive in itself, could be a chatty remark by an author in a good mood, but they also document media inscription in an analogue way, as the film *Persona* displays the cinematic medium as material inscription.

If these examples show writing and cinema as analogue forms of inscription, in later periods, the reflections in the notebooks are to a greater extent integrated literally and reframed in the cinematic work. In *Scenes from a Marriage,* for instance, Bergman's reflections on the characters' psychological and emotional characteristics in the notebook's development of the story are in part integrated literally into the fiction, either in the short résumés introducing each chapter of the story, or transformed into dialogue. From the autobiographical turn in Bergman's work in the 1980s to his last film *Saraband* (2003), the notebooks are increasingly used to revisit the past through a double movement of remembering his own personal past and retracing his fictional *oeuvre*.[33] In this period Bergman also seems to have become more familiar with his own methods of creating, playing with them in a self-conscious, sometimes ironic, way. A notable example is the partly auto-biographical screenplay for the film *Faithless* (Liv Ullmann 2000), which begins with a prologue that we also find in the beginning of the notebook, where the author reflects on the term 'imagination' through a dialogue between the 'I' (the writer) and a fictional character in the moment of creation. Gradually, an unmistakable portrait of Liv Ullmann as 'Marianne' emerges, a development of a character reflected upon in a playful manner throughout the dialogue.[34] Here the method of creation from the notebook is explicitly and literally transposed into the published screenplay.

Cinematic intimate writing

The diary in the process of creation is also explicitly reflected upon in the films. *The Hour of the Wolf* is an apt example of Bergman seemingly pointing towards his own diary as a source of fiction: the prologue of the film states that the story we are about to see is based on the diary of 'the artist'. Significantly, the diary shown in the film is a notepad similar to Bergman's notebooks. This use of the fictional diary as a transgression of the fictional and the real is further accentuated in an earlier version of the story in an unfilmed script called *The Cannibals*. Here Bergman uses the day-to-day entry structure of the diary: the story is told through a fictional diary continuously dated throughout the script, with dates that correspond to the time when Bergman wrote the script, an ambiguity between fictional time and the moment of writing. Bergman, voiced by the fictional 'artist', uses the diary to disguise or mask the real explicit. At one point the artist in the story even makes an almost sarcastic comment about the impossibility of reaching the truth behind the words in the diary: 'Read what you want, interpret what you wish', he says to the female protagonist who has been reading his diary. He continues by saying 'don't think that you own me, don't think that I will be grateful and certainly don't think that I will be honest.'[35] The masking of the real in *The Cannibals* and *The Hour of the Wolf* is less about the truthfulness of the content in the diary in relation to life than it is about the act of writing as fictional disguising of the author.

Bergman's final film, *Saraband*, shows a similar integration of the *auteur*'s authentic writing: several close ups on a letter, in the story written by the deceased Anna, show Bergman's own handwriting written on the kind of notepad paper that he favoured. Such handwritten traces in the fictional work represent an *auteurist* signature that points in two directions: it creates a link between the fiction and Bergman himself, but also shields the author behind the mask of fiction. The diary and the letter in *The Hour of the Wolf* and *Saraband* are authentic *messages* only in the fictional realm, yet they are authentic *traces* of Bergman's hand beyond the fiction. Such integration of traces of Bergman's hand is an archival gesture in the double sense of the term, simultaneously a gesture of memory making and playing with these personal souvenirs in the present moment of creation.

In Bergman's films there are other autobiographical objects than his handwritten notes, but the images of writing are particularly revealing as they point to the movement of creation as a movement from words to images. As mentioned above in regard to the diary in *Through a Glass Darkly*, images of intimate writing that are not necessarily written by his own hand also display a particular diaristic depiction of the written trace and the intrusive or voyeuristic side of reading and writing diaries. Examples of such intimate writing in Bergman's films, besides the diaries in *The Hour of the Wolf* and *Through a Glass Darkly* and the letter in *Saraband*, are the letters in *Winter Light, Persona* and *The Passion of Anna* (1969), and the diaries or notebooks in *Scenes from a Marriage* (1973) and *The Silence*. The scenes or sequences with letters and diaries are key narrative turning points where secrets are revealed through intrusion or confession, yet these revelations often remain mysterious. They also often stand out in relation to the mode of storytelling and make the relations between various forms of media inscriptions explicit. For instance, in *Persona* and *The Passion of Anna*, the letters' material dimension are emphasized through a display of the cinematic apparatus as a *dispositif* of visual perception: in the letter scene of *The Passion of Anna* the camera is following each word one by one, letter by letter, in an extreme close-up, a movement simulating a reading eye. In *Persona*, the typed sheets of paper of the letter are exposed in long close-ups as if the letters were typed on the screen itself. The cinematic representation here makes the visual dimension of writing appear, and as such it relates to the notebooks as material traces of the movement of writing.

In the scene in *Scenes from a Marriage* where Liv Ullman's character reads her diary to her husband yet another form of mediation intersects the movement of reading and writing, namely still photography. As Ullman reads her diary, where she reflects on her childhood memories, we see a series of still photographs, mirroring and contrasting the writing as subjective expression. The sequence comments on the mode of representation by making the process of adaptation from words to images visible. On the one hand the photographs are juxtaposed with the voice: subjective reflection stand against objective impression, authentic testimony against the staged portraits. On the other, the opposed media also mirror and inform each other in a process of memory making. The scene shows that the diary, as a series of dated traces, is in its relation to time more similar to a collection of photographs than a literary narrative: without beginning or end, like the genre of reconciling memory and immediacy, the diary is a collection of mnemonic signs that trace and construct the remembering subject.

Significantly, in the process from notebook to script or film, the way these fictional letters or diaries are integrated into the stories often undergoes considerable changes. For instance, in the notebook for *Scenes from a Marriage*, the diary scene is absent, but the words Ullman reads in the movie are present as Bergman's own reflections and interpretations of his characters. In the screenplay, the reading of the diary is integrated, but the photographs are not mentioned. A handwritten note next to the typed text in the shooting script indicates that the idea of the photographs came to Bergman's mind late in the process. Bergman writes: 'This is too long. No one will listen. I will have to find a solution to shorten it.'[37] Instead of shortening, he extended the passage and added the series of photographs. The development of the idea of the photographs is in one way a progression towards a cinematic form – moving from words to images – but at the same time a form that points back to the diary as a series of traces similar to a succession of photographic imprints.

In *Saraband*, the letter in the film is the result of a particularly complex process of transpositions of intimate writings that not only represents a movement across media but also a transgression of the authentic and the fictional diary, even of life and death. The notebook begins with Bergman's personal reflection on how he remembers reading his wife Ingrid's diary after her death, and this is followed by attempts to integrate passages of his own personal diary from the period when Ingrid was dying into the fiction. He then changes his mind and replaces the transcriptions of the real diary with the fictional letter, leaving his actual handwriting as a sign transgressing the fictional realm. In the notebook, he first rewrites a passage from his earlier diary: 'I see clearly how I can use my grief for constructive creativity,' he says and continues with a reflection on the strength and skills needed to describe such personal experiences. The passage is crossed out in red pen and followed by this capitalized comment:

IT IS A TERRIBLE STUPID MISTAKE TO USE MY OWN DIARY. HOW THE HELL COULD I BE SUCH AN IDIOT![38]

The radical revision is obviously a reaction to how Bergman, paradoxically, exposes himself and his private life in his films through a gesture of disguise that attempts to shield and protect the intimate. It is significant that the ethical critique of art as voyeuristic intrusion turns against Bergman himself on such a personal level in the making of his final film. This passage shows that the personal diary is simultaneously a central part of the artistic creation and an intimate sphere that should be protected from it. The display of letters, notebooks and diaries in the cinematic expression performs a dual gesture that both reveals and exposes the intimacy of the artist's self in the moment of creation.

Conclusion

As a genre that foregrounds the inscription itself, the diary in the process of adaptation intersects media beyond the transposition of a narrative from one form of expression into another. Bergman adapts the drafted stories in the notebooks, but even more so he adapts the diaristic writing that materializes the self in media. The transpositions of the notebooks into film can be thought of as reframing the original movement of writing in film. The relations between film and writing are negotiated differently in different films and periods of Bergman's film-making: he moves from emphasizing on the cinematic language in relation to writing, in films such as *Persona,* towards foregrounding the archival trace, in his later films, especially *Saraband.* Throughout his career, Bergman's filmmaking shared characteristics with the written diary, and in his films the written word is framed by cinema as a screen medium that transforms the personal drafts into visual film art. This kind of adaptation represents the relation between film and writing as an intersection of media inscription and 'art', beyond the notion of writing 'as literature'. The notebook has a double status as, on the one hand, a search for an aesthetics that in itself forms and conditions the artistic creation, and on the other, personal writing beyond the realm of art.

The diary as a source text to the film problematizes the notion of original as such. Both film and writing draw attention to their own materiality and inscription as a unique movement, but both film and writing are intermediate stages in the process of creation. Even the initial act of writing is a process of transposition, a transposition of the experience into writing that inevitably bears the trace of separation from that experience. Separate from the writer, the silence and the visual dimension of writing becomes visible. It is this dimension of writing that is transposed into the cinematic representation of intimate writing. The duality of the uniqueness of the inscription and loss, separation or transposition is crystallized in the cinematic images of intimate writing, images where writing and cinema mirror each other.

The diary as a genre that shields and unfolds what is real through continuous processes of masking and de-masking, ultimately addresses the actual reader of the notebook, a researcher like myself or a visitor to a museum where Bergman's personal writings are exhibited. Reading these drafts on the computer screen at the archive in itself gives a kind of voyeuristic pleasure of which one has to be suspicious. Is the reading an intrusion on a secret sphere or is it voiced by Bergman himself, as the creator of the archive? Deciphering the barely legible handwriting where Bergman talks to himself in what seems to be the most intimate moment of creation gives us the impression that we will reveal the mystery of his genius and unfold what is behind the fictionalization of the self. But each answer that the notebooks provide leaves new questions behind: questions on the selection of material for the archive, on the parts of the process of creation that were never materialized in writing, and questions of how to frame the words we read. We find ourselves in a situation similar to the fictional characters who secretly read letters or diaries that reveal fragments of the past or of identities, as indices without clear answers, as words spoken with a silent voice. Still, it is in this way that the notebooks say something significant about the nature of creation, where each materialization is an intermediate phase, and about the work of art as a process from the personal to the shared, across versions and media.

Notes

1   Most famously discussed by André Bazin in his classic essay '*Diary of a Country Priest* and the Robert Bresson Style' (1951), *What Is Cinema?*, (ed. and trans.) Timothy Barnard (Montreal: Caboose, 2009), 139–59.

2   www.ingmarbergmanarchives.se [accessed 3 January 2013].

3   See, for instance, the preface to Ingmar Bergman, *Four screenplays of Ingmar Bergman: The Seventh seal, Wild Strawberries, The Magician, Smiles of a Summer Night* (New York: Simon and Schuster, 1969).

4   Bergman's mirror figure takes various forms and is explicitly displayed in the *mise-en-scene* by the frequent use of mirrors, see Maaret Koskinen, *Spel och speglingar: En studie i Ingmar Bergmans filmiska estetik* (Stockholm: Stockholms Universitet, 1993).

5   Maaret Koskinen, *The Silence: Pictures in the Typewriter, Writings on Screen* (Washington: University of Washington, 2010).

6   Jed Deppman, Daniel Ferrer and Michael Groden (eds), *Genetic Criticism: Texts and Avant-textes* (Philadelphia: University of Pennsylvania Press, 2004), 2.

7   Daniel Ferrer, 'Production, Invention, and Reproduction: Genetic vs. Textual Criticism', *Reimagining Textuality – Textual Studies in the Late Age of Print*, E. Bergmann Loizeaux and N. Fraistat (eds) (Madison: The University of Wisconsin Press, 2002), 57.

8   Ingmar Bergman, Notebook *Persona* (arbetsbok 22), The Ingmar Bergman Foundation: The Ingmar Bergman Archives (1964–6). Quotes from notebooks and scripts are my translations.

9   Ferrer (2002), 55.

10 John Bryant, *The Fluid Text: A Theory of Revision and Editing for Book and Screen* (Ann Arbor: University of Michigan Press, 2002), 6.

11 Steven Price, *The Screenplay: Authorship, Theory and Criticism* (New York: Palgrave Macmillian, 2010), 57.

12 Julie Rak, 'Dialogue with the Future: Philippe Lejeune's Method and Theory of Diary', in Philippe Lejeune (ed.), *On Diary* (Honolulu: University of Hawaii Press, 2009), 16–26.

13 Philippe Lejeune, 'The Continous and the Discontinous', in *On Diary* (2009), 179.

14 Ibid.

15 Bergman (1969), 16.

16 See Federico Fellini, *The Book of Dreams*, Tullio Kezich and Vittorio Boarini (eds) (New York: Rizzoli, 2008).

17 Also see Koskinen (2010), 67–83.

18 Ingmar Bergman, Notebook *De skeppsbrutna* [*The Stranded*] (arbetsbok 21), The Ingmar Bergman Foundation: The Ingmar Bergman Archives (1962–1964). This notebook contain fragments of a story transformed into the script *The Cannibals*, which is a preliminary version primarily of *The Hour of the Wolf*, but also to a certain extent *Persona*. In the Swedish original text the repetition of the word 'patience' continues with a word play through separation between 'tåla' (withstand or bear) and 'mod' (courage) as the two parts of the word 'tålamod' (patience).

19 In the notebook for *Through a Glass Darkly*, for instance, Bergman has revised the text several times: some phrases are underlined others are crossed and a selection of extracts are even rewritten on the last pages. Notebook *Tapeten* [*Såsom i en spegel, Through a Glass Darkly*] (arbetsbok 18), The Ingmar Bergman Foundation: The Ingmar Bergman Archives (1960).

20 A documentary film with footage from Bergman's amateur films from film productions: *Bergmans lekstuga* (Stig Björkman, 2011).

21 *Tre dagböcker*, Ingmar Bergman and Maria von Rosen (eds) (Stockholm: Norstedts förlag, 2004).

22 Ingmar Bergman, 'A Page from my Diary', film program for *Virgin Spring*, SF, 1960.

23 Maaret Koskinen, *I begynnelsen var ordet: Ingmar Bergman och hans tidiga författarskap* (Stockholm: Wahlström och Widstrand, 2002).

24 *The Ingmar Bergman Archives*, Paul Duncan, Bengt Wanselius (eds) (Taschen Books, 2008).

25 Thomas Elsaesser, 'Ingmar Bergman in the museum? Thresholds, limits, conditions of possibility', *Journal of Aesthetics and Culture* 393 (1,615).

26 Daniel Ferrer and Jean-Loup Bourget, *Cinéma, Genèse* (Paris: Jean-Michel Place, 2007).

27 Notebook *Nattvardsgästerna* [*Winter Light*] (arbetsbok 19), The Ingmar Bergman Foundation: The Ingmar Bergman Archives (1959–61).

28 Janet Staiger's interpretation of Bergman's 'self fashioning' or Jacques Aumont's reading of the films shot at Fårö as a merging of life and

fiction represent approaches to Bergman's life as fictional creation or public media construction: Janet Staiger, 'Analysing Self-fashioning in Authoring and Reception', *Ingmar Bergman Revisited: Performance, Cinema and the Arts,* Maaret Koskinen (ed.) (London: Wallflower Press (2007); Jacques Aumont, *Ingmar Bergman: Mes films sont l'expliquations de mes images* (Paris: Cahiers du cinéma, 2004).

29　Ingmar Bergman, 'När lägger du av Ingmar?', *Dramat* no. 3 (1994); Ingmar Bergman, 'Ingmar Bergman intervjuar sig själv inför premiären på Sommaren med Monika', SF Program (1953); Ernest Riffe [Ingmar Bergman], 'Schizofren intervju med nervös regissör', *Chaplin* 10:84 (1968).

30　Bergman (1962–4).

31　Bergman (1962–4).

32　Bergman (1964–6).

33　Koskinen, Maaret, 'Out of the Past: Saraband and the Ingmar Bergman Archive', in *Ingmar Bergman Revisited,* op.cit., 19–34.

34　Ingmar Bergman, *Trolösa,* in *Föreställningar* (Stockholm: Norstedts, 2000).

35　Ingmar Bergman, *Människoätarna* [*The Cannibals*], The Ingmar Bergman Foundation: The Ingmar Bergman Archives (1964).

36　Philippe Lejeune, (2009) 'Auto-Genesis: Genetic Studies of Autobiographical Texts', in *On Diary* (2009), 228.

37　Ingmar Bergman, *Scener ur ett äktenskap* (shooting script), The Ingmar Bergman Foundation: The Ingmar Bergman Archives (1972).

38　Ingmar Bergman, Notebook *Saraband* (arbetsbok 47), The Ingmar Bergman Foundation: The Ingmar Bergman Archives (1998–2001).

11

Tracing the originals, pursuing the past: *Invictus* and the 'based-on-a-true-story' film as adaptation

Sara Brinch

I am the master of my fate:
I am the captain of my soul.

WILLIAM ERNEST HENLEY, 1875

The emotionally laden words of the Victorian poem 'Invictus' by William Ernest Henley have been a source of consolation and inspiration for countless people over the years, including Nelson Mandela.[1] In 2009, filmgoers widely recognized the poem's significance for Mandela because of Clint Eastwood's film *Invictus*. The feature film tells the story of how, prior to the 1995 Rugby World Cup, Mandela convinced the South African national rugby team – the Springboks – to join him in his quest for a unified nation, and of the team's success in that very competition.

Invictus is an adaptation of the 2008 non-fiction book *Playing the Enemy: Nelson Mandela and the Game That Made a Nation*, by

British journalist John Carlin.[2] In Anthony Peckham's screenplay, a little twist was added to the story about Mandela and the Rugby World Cup: the poem 'Invictus' and its significance for Mandela was included in the story about the relationship and friendship evolving between the South African president and the Springboks' captain, Francois Pienaar. With its character-driven narrative, the added twist and the presence of two Hollywood stars – Morgan Freeman and Matt Damon – playing the major roles, the film is a rather typical example of the historical fiction film. This type of film usually stresses some actual matters and historical events, while at the same time utilizing a creative license in a highly interpretative fashion.[3] When addressing the question of what constitutes an original in relation to the concept of adaptation, the genre of the historical fiction film is particularly interesting because of its double reference, to existing representational artifacts and to the past itself.

Similar to adaptation studies being regarded traditionally as a subdivision of literary studies, studies of historical fiction film has been conducted by historians – with some important exceptions. As adaptation studies for a long time was ruled more or less exclusively by the question of fidelity, studies of historical fiction films have been dominated by the historian's evaluation of the particular film's capacity to represent the past accurately or truthfully, according to the standards of the discipline. However, parallel to a growing interest in the genre among film scholars, the historical film has over the last few years also been given an increased attention within the field of adaptation studies. This would not have been the case had it not been for a reorientation of the field during the last two decades, opening the way for a broader understanding of adaptation as a concept. Advocating this new direction, Christine Geraghty claims that the range of theoretical methods and topics found in conferences as well as in print these days are nothing but encouraging, demonstrating among several things 'a flexible approach to both the source text and the adaptation.'[4] The source text no longer has to be a canonized work of literature to make an adaptation worth studying – it does not even have to be a *literary* text. Including new types of originals and methods of relevance results in a broader range of approaches for study, such as addressing adaptations in a visual perspective.

The case of *Invictus* exemplifies that a historical fiction film never will be an adaptation of just a single precursor text or one original. Furthermore, the case also demonstrates that the ontological status of a film's sources can differ highly. After a short presentation of the variety of originals on which the film is based, I focus on one original in particular and discuss *Invictus* as an adaptation from a visual perspective. That original is a photograph of Nelson Mandela and Francois Pienaar taken at the moment when Mandela greets Pienaar after the South African victory in the 1995 World Cup final (see illustration). Prior to the film's release, a newspaper article noted that this photo was the core of the film itself – meaning the film was about this image as such. I elaborate on this perspective to some extent, but first and foremost, show how the press photo represents the sources constituting the visual originals of the film. The aim is to discuss the various ways that sources of this kind are transposed in the adaptation process and the means they serve in regard to the film-makers' aspirations for a realistic look, the resemblance between the actors and the historical persons and the overall feeling of authenticity, despite being a feature film. Geraghty's use of the term 'recall' in her book, *Now a Major Motion Picture*, informed my approach to the press photography as one of the film's originals. Based on Catherine Grant's elaboration on the importance of recall in her discussion of how to make the audience aware of a film's status as an adaptation, Geraghty argues that studying an adaptation 'involves both textual and contextual analysis', an approach that includes studying reviews as well as publicity materials.[5] The material constituting the basis of my specific study counts beside Eastwood's *Invictus* a selection of promotional material, news paper articles and reviews of the film, all providing information about the film's adapted sources.

According to Thomas Leitch, case studies of films based on non-literary or non-fiction source texts aim to 'enlarge the range of adaptation studies by revealing the parochialism of theories that restrict their examples to films based on fictional texts.'[6] In other words, studying adaptations of non-fictional sources may expand the scope of theories of adaptation, illuminating the understanding of adaptation in general. In the final part of this essay, I discuss adaptations of non-fiction sources in more general terms, with *Invictus* as an example of a 'based-on-a-true-story' film. The reorientation of adaptation studies expresses not only a flexible

approach to the source text, but to the concept of adaptation as well. Whereas questioning what is an original broadens the horizon of prolific perspectives to pursue, I argue that a (too) flexible approach concerning what is adaptation may potentially undermine the concept altogether. My understanding of adaptation aligns with Linda Hutcheon's definition: 'an extended, deliberate, announced revisitation of a particular work of art.'[7] With *Invictus* as my case, I argue that 'based-on-a true-story' films exemplify borderline cases in which one encounters the danger of draining the concept of adaptation of any substantial meaning and leaving it without much explanatory power.

A short inventory of the originals

With its focus on personal matters and one specific event, *Invictus* can best be described as a hybrid of a biographical drama and what Robert Burgoyne labels the 'topical historical film', focusing on a narrow slice of history.[8] The story is organized in a rather traditional, linear narrative, depicting the historic time span of about one-and-a-half years after the film's initial prologue, which presents the years from Mandela's release from prison in 1990 until he won South Africa's first free election and was inaugurated president in 1994. The film encloses the historical events with the scenes of the Springboks' victory in the rugby final, and in so doing separates the World Cup incident from the steady stream of history. It uses no device, such as an epilogue – often used in historical fiction films – to describe any possible effects the victory had on the society at large. In other words, *Invictus* focuses on the World Cup drama and the immediate reactions to it, not the social or political implications of the event.

In addition to telling a story that represents actual historical events, *Invictus* is the sum of a myriad of transposed originals, with John Carlin's *Playing the Enemy: Nelson Mandela and the Game That Made a Nation* being its main source text. From this, the film has brought the story about Mandela's quest to the screen, an account based on Carlin's interviews with the former president. In addition, the multi-faceted focalization and the juxtaposition of black and white South Africans' point of views also were transposed from Carlin's work into the film. However, in Eastwood's telling of his version of the event, another story intersects Carlin's: the story of the importance of the poem 'Invictus' to Mandela. The use of Henley's poem as a recurring theme throughout the story heightens the impression of a well-forged drama, connecting Mandela's resistance and willpower to Pienaar's determination, and enclosing the narrative around itself. Besides lending its title to the film, the poem 'Invictus' surfaces as part of the narrative on several occasions, implicitly when the characters talk about it, and explicitly when it is shown in writing or recited in a voiceover. The poem holds a central position in several of the encounters between Mandela and Pienaar, gradually replacing the political agenda that motivates Mandela's engagement in rugby. The poem provides a threshold to the audience's indulgence in the 'human factor' (which for some time was the film's working title).[9] In the end, the poem becomes the expression of Mandela's quest to unify his country.

As a result, the film relates an 'out of this world' true story, partly because the story is isolated from the years following the events of 1995, and partly because the poem as the thematic core makes the story complete in itself. At the same time, great effort was taken in *Invictus* to display audio-visually the referentially authentic; for example, photos and recordings were restaged and elaborated impersonations and compiled news footages (although manipulated) were included to signal the authenticity of the historical events the film depicts. Press photos and photographic portraits, TV news and the 1995 World Cup coverage were transposed with great variety, serving many means – some intended to support the realism of the film's diegesis, some intended to underline the story's reference to an actual past. Although fictional and staged in every way, all in all the film presents a complex referential discourse in which the film-maker himself claims to be telling the true story of the events.

The creative transposing of a telling handshake

Like most directors of historical fiction films and biopics telling a story of events taking place after the birth of photography, Clint

Eastwood sought to re-enact scenes found in visual sources such
as photographs or recorded film. *Invictus* includes references to
several audio-visual sources that are particularly interesting to
consider when the film is studied as an adaptation. The Springboks'
games in the World Cup, televised and later released on DVD,
and clips of news accounts and interviews constitute important
source texts for the film's diegesis.[10] Press photos are used to set
up scenes, like the ones showing cheering crowds of rugby fans,
black and white united. Others are compiled in their original form
in the film's credits sequence, identifying the Springboks' players.
However, one image stands out with an emblematic character: the
photo of President Mandela congratulating Captain Pienaar after
the South African victory in the World Cup finals (see illustration).
By examining the ways the film relates to and quotes this image,
I underscore the importance of studying the complexity of (audio)
visual sources in adaptations that relate stories of historical events
and show how the act of recalling constitutes an important strategy
for creating authenticity in historical fiction films.

The photo of Mandela and Pienaar (or rather photos, as several
versions are in circulation, credited to various photo agencies)
taken at the awards ceremony, shows Mandela dressed in a green-
and-yellow Springboks' rugby jersey greeting the captain after
having presented the World Cup trophy to Pienaar. This image
became emblematic of Mandela's quest for national reconciliation.
It has been widely distributed in the aftermath of the World Cup,
visually expressing the rainbow nation, and was originally used as
cover illustration of Carlin's book, *Playing the Enemy*. In his film,
Eastwood makes the photo the original for shooting the trophy
sequence in which Mandela greets Pienaar with the words, 'I have
to thank you for what you have done for our country', to which
Pienaar replies, 'No, Mister President, I have to thank you for
what *you* have done for our country.' Certainly, in a scene told
by shifting camera angles and with the actors moving, no attempt
was made to create a 1:1 transposition of motif from photo to film.
Nevertheless, the scene quotes the motif in full, depicting that very
moment. This is, however, not the only version of the photo seen
in relation to the film. In the film's promotional still, shown here
and used in articles and reviews, Freeman and Damon are captured
in a middle-key, medium-shot framing, similar to the original press
photography.

In the film's trophy sequence, the point of view is mirrored 180 degrees, with the camera positioned at an angle pointing down on the two, the crowd of press photographers visible in the background, below the podium. This is a minor detail, but nevertheless, it can be interpreted as the film-maker's intentional joke, staging the scene and directing the promotional still photo's framing and point of view to create an impression of a blurred boundary between the fictional diegesis and the film set, while at the same time quoting the motif of the emblematic photo.

Quoting images in historical fiction films

When accompanying articles about *Invictus*, the press photo of Mandela and Pienaar, which has been part of journalistic discourses for many years, underlined the authenticity of the historical matters and events the articles presented. Needless to say, the restaging of the scene in its photographic representation is not marked as such in the film, and while watching the movie, only those who already know of the image's existence will recognize the trophy scene as a palimpsest. Although filmgoers may recall the film's intertextual and referential relations to the image only after seeing the film, the strategy to connect *Invictus*' depiction of the past to the actual event nonetheless heightens the impression of an authentic representation and strengthens the film's overall realism. The stylistic application of mediated images serves the same purpose by another means – through remediation of the grainy expression of television news. The prologue of the film gives a telling example of this in the form of a compilation of authentic video recordings from Nelson Mandela's election as president and scenes recorded for the film in the same audio-visual style showing Morgan Freeman as Mandela greeting people, depicted on the voting bill and being inaugurated. In this type of visual mash-up, authentic footage of actual historic situations are digitally merged with restagings of the same situations, and a graphic filter is applied to add the *expression* of authentic news clips to the material. This strategy of indexing something as authentic by presenting it as mediated is highly common in historical fiction films when the story is set in the age of mass media. And even though we know definitively that what we see is either staged or the result of visual effects, we believe it to be a true rendering of the events depicted, within the fictional frame set around the story.

An image can serve several other purposes in a historical fiction film to support the film's more general verisimilitude to the actual past. Documentation of appearances, ways of dressing and milieu or surroundings are all aspects revealed in a picture that can be used for various purposes – casting, rehearsing roles, mise-en-scène and cinematography. Designing a mise-en-scène to have verisimilitude to one or several originals is a crucial part of the adaptation process, whether it involves turning a fictional story set in an identifiable time and place into another medium, or a non-fiction account of past events into an audio-visual representation. Christine Geraghty addresses this matter in the last chapter of *Now a Major Motion Picture*, asking 'how are ideas about faithfulness and adaptation worked through when we focus on the physical appearance of a set that aims to represent the past?'[11] Basically, there is little difference between the set design for a film adapting a novel with a story set in the historical past and a historical fiction film. To present a film with an authentic rendering of the past, the film-maker uses visual sources for inspiration or for specific quotations. Geraghty points out that Hollywood studios are equipped with reference libraries of photographs, paintings, drawings and recorded film, which are important sources for realistic representations of the past.[12]

Since the past is being designed, whether it be on a set or at an actual location, the 'look' of the past will always have short-comings – either because the designer has missed some detail or because designing a set is necessarily based on simplifications or stylizations to some extent. The negative side of these shortcomings is the potential for weakening the historical accuracy and authenticity. Natalie Zemon Davis describes the difficulty in getting the right look this way:

> For the historical eye, the flaw in a period look would not just be the obtrusiveness or staginess of the props and costumes. Worse, an overdone period look is static. It ignores the mixture of goods, clothes, and buildings found in documents from the past: the old and the hand-me-down along with the new, the

archaic with the fashionable, the inherited with the purchased, a dynamic mixture expressive of central processes in a society.[13]

These are the words of a historian and film consultant, aiming for a higher degree of sensibility when trying to capture the complexity of the past. At the same time, what Zemon Davis presents is an ideal that a set designer will have a hard time matching within the limits of production time and budgets. And, filtered through the adaptation debate, what Zemon Davis' argument expresses is nothing but the old wish for fidelity.

If we regard adaptation as Catherine Grant does – as belonging to the reception process and recalling the adapted work or the cultural memory of it – a quoted picture can be used to make the audience aware of the relationship between the film and the original, with the intent of either highlighting the film's attempted authenticity or of identifying specific references or allusions in the film for the audience's enjoyment. Historians often make use of visual originals to illustrate or underline their arguments about a feature film's shortcomings or inaccuracies in representations of the past; these criticisms are levelled sometimes without reflecting on the fact that every historical representation by definition will diverge from its referent. However, Geraghty takes a positive angle to this matter: An 'awareness of a gap, between what is being referred to in the work of recall involved in the adaptation and what we see on the screen' has the potential for allowing the audience to enjoy the similarities as well as the differences, and for highlighting the actors' achievements in their performances.[14] This is never truer than with historical fiction films starring well-known actors.

Quoting through portraying

In biopics and historical fiction films, a lot of effort often goes into creating verisimilitude between the leading actor(s) and the historical person he or she impersonates. Such a verisimilitude is based partly on the acting and partly on the manipulation of physical appearance. The casting constitutes one of the most powerful marketing assets related to the historical fiction film.

It also can prepare the ground for recalling the original when watching the film, highlighting the feature film's references to an actual past. Long before a release, the producers promote a film by focusing on the casting and the likeness between the actors and the actual persons they portray. If there is only a faint likeness to begin with, the focus most often is on the effort to make the actors look more like the historical persons, through acting and appearance. *Invictus* presents telling examples of both. Morgan Freeman as Mandela made celebrity news from the very day the film project was announced. His resemblance to Mandela, especially in charisma, was reported as stunning. On the set, journalists reported that Freeman seemed to exude the aura of the former South African president, resulting in repeated remarks from other actors and people on the set.[15] Matt Damon as Francois Pienaar also got attention, but never due to any physical likeness between him and the rugby player.[16]

The focus on verisimilitude between the actor and the historical person impersonated is highly relevant to the adaptation process. However, when Jean-Louis Comolli addressed the issue in the late 1970s, it was as part of his reflections on how cinematic fictions work as such. When an actor impersonates a famous person who is known to the public through depictions of various kinds, the viewer will have two persons in her mind – the historical person and the actor playing him or her.[17] In his article, 'Historical Fiction: A Body Too Much', Comolli discusses the strategy that most historical fiction films use to make the fiction more convincing as historical past: the attempt to erase the image of the actor from the spectator's mind through a combination of the actor's close impersonation and the makeup artist's handiwork. However, in Comolli's view, what makes a cinematic fiction work is not verisimilitude, but the very bodily presence of an actor combined with our knowledge of the historical character he is playing. According to Comolli, the actor's presence summons us to 'the delicate exercise of a double game: It is him and it is not, always and at the same time; we believe in it and we do not, at the same time.'[18] Instead of being disappointed and dissatisfied over any potential flaws in verisimilitude, the best actors combined with the effects provided by the narrative cause us to invest enough emotions to engage with the presence of the historical body, even though we see only the actor's body, performing.[19] In the film *Invictus*, we know for sure that Mandela is not the one on the screen, and we know Freeman is not Mandela, but we still can appreciate and be fascinated by Mandela as portrayed within the fictional framework of the film.

Using historical fiction as his case, Comolli's reflections on how cinematic fiction works parallel the way adaptation relies on recalling the adapted work or the cultural memory of it. His reflections also are in the same vein as Linda Hutcheon's thoughts on the pleasure of adaptation springing from 'repetition with variation, from the comfort of ritual combined with the piquancy of surprise.' At the same time, Hutcheon continues by noting '[r]ecognition and remembrance are part of the pleasure (and risk) of experiencing an adaptation; so too is change.'[20] One could easily claim the same for impersonations and the phenomenon of the 'body too much'. The risk of impersonating a historical person is rooted in a complex set of transpositions: of audio-visual appearances, of gestures, movements and acting, but also the story itself, attracting the audience. However, whether an actor succeeds with his performance is, in the end, a matter of reception. Some find it delightful to watch the similarities and the differences which one and the same performance express, while others will have a hard time engaging in the story, regardless of how well performed the impersonation is.

Is there such a thing as an adaptation of an image?

My reflections so far generate at least one question that begs an answer: Should the act of quoting an image or an audio-visual recording be considered an *adaptation* of that very image or recording? According to Linda Hutcheon, most adaptation theorizing assumes that what is adapted is the story, that the story is 'the common denominator, the core of what is transposed across different media and genres'.[21] Furthermore, the story is the sum of its various elements: 'its themes, events, world, characters, motivations, points of view, consequences, contexts, symbols, imagery, and so on.'[22] When a story is adapted, all these elements are subject to transpositions, each of them contributing to an overall process of adaptation, transforming the story into a new version. What discussions on adaptation do not address to the same extent, however, is that the *outcome* of an adaptation process has to be a story as well. When reflecting on what is not to be regarded as adaptation, Hutcheon argues that shorter, intertextual allusions to other works should not be included.[23] But then, what are fragments clearly showing the characteristics of a palimpsest to be regarded as, and when does a fragment expand into an adaptation?

The problem embedded in operating with a normative distinction, as Hutcheon does, is where to draw the line between adaptation and allusion. David T. Johnson's study of the documentary film *Dogtown and Z-boys* (Peralta 2002), which addresses the concept of 'adaptations of the image', is an illustrative example.[24] In discussing the various uses of the works of photographer and essayist Craig Stecyk in a film about an influential group of American skateboarders in the 1970s, Johnson deliberately notes that the film is an adaptation of Stecyk's photographs.[25] The documentary film is based on current-day recorded interviews with members of the group and people related to it, intersected with archival material. To Johnson, 'adaptation of the image' implies the act of quoting the photographs' style and motives in the interviews conducted. That is, the film applies the grainy look and the black-and-white palette of Stecyk's photos in the framing of the motives, and sometimes even using locations depicted in the photos as backdrops for recording the interviews. In this way, *Dogtown and Z-boys* is an adaption, in Johnson's opinion.[26]

Johnson's focus on the visual presents a refreshing perspective, and his case draws attention to aspects of transpositions that indeed exemplify the relevance of a broad understanding of adaptation. However, I part with him when it comes to regarding intertextual and stylistic references alone as sufficient basis for considering the documentary an adaptation *as such*; the film's specific story is about the phenomenon seen in retrospect, and not an evocation of Stecyk's photos or photo essays. According to Julie Sanders, adaptions 'constitute a more sustained engagement with a single text or source than the more glancing act of allusion or quotation, even citation, allows.'[27] Film-maker Peralta clearly quotes the motive of several photos, and alludes stylistically to both the graininess of the analogue photographic medium and to

Stecyk's personal style, but that does not make the documentary's discourse an adaptation.

Not until one can identify an openly quoted image as *mise en abyme* in a film's discourse can one regard a film as an adaptation of the image, at least according to the 'story-argument' Hucheon presents. The photo of Nelson Mandela and Francois Pienaar quoted in *Invictus* is doubly an example of *mise en abyme*. First, the trophy scene without question constitutes the film's core, its culmination, in which the quotation is the abyme – the emblematic motif at the centre – according to the terminology of heraldry. However, when a journalist, writing before the film's release, presented the film as based on the iconic image of the president and the team captain, he was referring not to the picture itself, but the meaning inscribed in its motif – the story of Mandela's quest and its glorious outcome.[28] The quotation of the image, which refers to the historical event (the actual congratulatory handshake) as well as the story behind that very handshake (known through Carlin's account and paratexts commenting on the film), becomes an emblematic expression for the film's textual whole. As a consequence, the film can be regarded as an adaptation of this very image, being the film's most important visual original.

Numerous pictures are quoted in *Invictus*, pictures whose motifs have been transposed into fragments of the visual design of the film, aiming for authenticity. The originals quoted or otherwise implied in the film, contribute to the overall adaptation process which produced the film. When viewers experience the quotations embedded in the film and recall the original, they potentially enjoy identifying the original as well as the recognizing of the differences. (Or, if they recall the photo after seeing the film, they may enjoy the quotation they experienced unknowingly when watching the film.) However, as noted above, the picture of Mandela and Pienaar not only communicates authenticity, but also a symbolic content: As the emblematic expression of a united South Africa at a time when the country was on the edge of civil war, the image represents the very unifying national narrative that President Mandela sought – the narrative adapted by Eastwood in his film.

When does a historical fiction film become a film based on a true story?

The question 'what happens to our understanding of the historical fiction film when regarded as adaptation?' ignited this essay. Of course, the flip-side of that question is 'what happens to our understanding of adaptation when the historical fiction film is seen as such?' However, in the wake of these questions, yet another breaks the surface: *When* do we actually think of a historical fiction film as adaptation? The answer is that most people never do, except when recalling an account's *specific perspective* on the past by reading a book or seeing an image they already know to be the film's precursor text. In addition to Eastwood's *Invictus*, Steven Spielberg's *Schindler's List* (1993), as an adaptation of Thomas Keneally's documentary novel *Schindler's Ark*, is one such example; another is Simon Curtis' film *My Week with Marilyn* (2011), an adaptation of Colin Clark's memoirs, visually quoting numerous promotional stills and photos of Marilyn Monroe. In contrast, the scholars who focus on the matter within the adaptation studies field express a far more comprehensive stance toward what should be regarded as non-fiction adaptations, their originals included. In response to some of these scholars, I maintain that too broad an understanding makes it impossible to distinguish a feature film adaptation of a non-fiction account from any other feature film based on a researched script.

'Why not treat historical films as adaptations?' Dudley Andrew asks, drawing parallels between what he describes as the historians' debt owed to the traces of the past and the 'onus felt by the film-maker to respect some text from the cultural storehouse.'[29] This onus or responsibility regarding the text was the basis for Andrew's study comparing a film's account of a historical topic and other interpretations of the events or personages.[30] To Andrew, a historical fiction film could be the result either of an adaptation from an authoritative historical rendering or of a more indefinite archive of topics set up for the film, as was the case for Jean Renoir's *La Marseillaise* (1938).[31] However, the latter constitutes a methodological problem because the film in question will not be an adaptation of a pre-existing historical narrative, but of several historical records forged into an audio-visual discourse presenting a story of the past. There will be no way of separating such an adaptation from a film based on a researched script, and as a result every historical film, feature or documentary, could be seen as adaptation, as Andrew suggested. Therefore, Andrew's reflections on non-fiction adaptations – in my opinion, at least – will not contribute to any expansion of the field of adaptation studies, but instead will illustrate the consequences of too broad an understanding of what constitutes an original or a source text. As the category 'adaptation' loses its explanatory power as an identifying label, it becomes a concept of mere theoretical interest.

The same objection can be raised to Thomas Leitch's reflections on so-called 'based-on-a-true-story' films as adaptations.[32] In the last chapter of his book, *Film Adaptations and Its Discontents* (2007), Leitch discusses what he calls the 'precursor text' of a based-on-a-true-story film. In this type of film, he found the peculiar case of adaptations without any manifest source text. In his words, the description 'based on a true story' is 'always strategic or generic rather than historical or existential', always used at the film-makers' pleasure, and applied only when it is to the film's advantage.[33] This implies that to characterize a film as 'based on a true story' is an act reserved for the film-maker or production company. However, Leitch himself applies the label as an analytical category throughout his text, for example, when he discusses *Schindler's List*. By doing so, the very label and Leitch's use of it calls for theoretical scrutiny, especially regarding the basis of his argument. In particular, one reflection that summarizes Leitch's rather intricate discussion – and one often quoted – is that to label a film as based on a true story 'imputes that its source is a narrative that is constituted only through the act of invoking it.'[34] This is a rather intriguing way of thinking about the process of adaptation and its reception, but what does it actually imply? First, the implication is that such a film does not have an original that is being adapted, which is not necessarily the case, which many of Leitch's examples demonstrate. Even if the original is not always as clearly pronounced as in the case of *Schindler's List*, a based-on-a-true-story film at least would have to rely on some sort of source, if not a literary one, to be regarded as having a reference to a true story at all. Leitch ends his chapter and discussion with the claim, '[f]ilms based on true stories authenticate themselves by appealing to precursor texts that are nonexistent.'[35] To me, this statement is either saying that these films are not adaptations or is a way of avoiding the question of fidelity in the case of non-fiction adaptations.

A final encounter with *Invictus* exemplifies this, although the film does not profess to be based on a true story. On the contrary, according to the production notes, Clint Eastwood's *Invictus* tells 'an inspiring true story'.[36] However, in comparison to its main textual source, *Invictus* seems to be telling an inspiring story a bit *too good* to be true. No doubt, the originals most easily traced in the film have been transposed into a version of the story that does not express fidelity to any of them in the strictest sense. As a discourse representing the past, the film's historical accuracy can easily be questioned. Following Leitch's argument, the film should best be considered as 'based on a true story' because of the way it waivers from its originals, and presumably, the historical past as well. The highly condensed and emotionally laden narrative the film invokes is the result of an adaptation process in which a wide range of originals have been subject to a creative transformation into one unified version of the historical event. However, not being true to the originals in the traditional sense docs not exclude the film from being true to the very idea spurring the historical events that the sources refer to.

Some historians draw a distinction between an 'historical truth' and an 'emotional truth' when considering whether a historical fiction film accurately reflects the past.[37] However, as an alternative to an 'emotional truth', *Invictus* may communicate a 'conceptual truth' or a 'fidelity to the spirit'. *Invictus* expresses a version of the story Mandela once imagined as a foundation of community among the citizens of South Africa. In his book *Film Nation: Hollywood Looks at U.S. History*, Robert Burgoyne utilizes Benedict Anderson's term social 'unisonance' for the nation to discuss film as a means to find common ground for national identity.[38] Mandela's imaginings, which the Rugby World Cup made possible, was one such 'unisonance' made into a story. John Carlin presented the story of this idea in his chosen form and way of telling. With *Invictus*, Clint Eastwood culturally adapted the idea into an expression articulated by Hollywood, with the help of a set of pre-existing representations related to the event that contributed to the audio-visual version of the story. *Invictus* can be regarded as being based on a true story, but its precursor texts are far from non-existent, and the narrative that resulted from invoking these texts – under the influence of a poetic licence – is nothing but the film's very representation of the past.

Leitch's intention in his essay was not, I take it, to summon the question of fidelity. On the contrary, his text makes the case for a more equal status between various manifestations of a historical past, moving beyond a way of thinking about adaptation in which Spielberg's *Schindler's List* and Eastwood's *Invictus* are assessed based on how truthfully they have captures Keneally's and Carlin's books. However, Leitch neglects the question of what constitutes the range of originals in a non-fiction adaptation and the way in which a based-on-a-true-story film always will be a representation referring to an actual past; thus, he throws the baby out with the bathwater and ends up discussing a label, saying very little of relevance to adaptation studies.

Inherent in studies of specific cases such as *Invictus*, as well as more theoretical reflections on adaptation of non-fiction originals, lie questions of what should be considered an adaptation and on what basis to approach the concept of adaptation. Conceptual awareness is necessary to handle the double references of the non-fiction adaptation (the historical past and its already existing representations) while at the same time answering the questions being generated. In turn, such awareness will contribute to yet other insights relevant for the field of adaptation studies.

Concluding remarks

An adaptation of non-fiction sources must be studied as an intertextual and multi-referential universe.[39] At the same time, I maintain that to be regarded as an adaptation, there has to be a main original that provides a story to be adapted, and that this original is somehow announced or traceable by the discourses surrounding the film. *Invictus* is an adaption of Carlin's book *Playing the Enemy*, but it would never have become the version of the story it has without numerous other originals included as elements of the adaptation process. *Invictus* is a based-on-a-true-story film rather than an accurate account because of the poetic licence taken. The film's various uses of authentic audio-visual sources and its quoting of the picture of Mandela and Pienaar cause the story to reflect the actual past and the events taking place in the steady stream of history; yet the implementation of Henley's poem seems to have the opposite effect, enclosing the narrative around the events depicted, making the story complete in itself.

The complex character of a historical fiction film regarded as adaptation can be revealed only through a study of its cluster of originals. Like any other discourse representing historical events and matters, it can never do better than pursue the past. However, being an adaptation, a historical fiction film stands out as a representational discourse because of the way the play between originals and their transposed versions are foregrounded in the reception of the film – not with historical scrutiny in mind, but with an awareness and appreciation of the changed appearance of the originals – refracted.

Notes

1   This essay evolved in large part during a research stay at Centre for Film Studies, University of St. Andrews. I warmly thank the scholars of the centre for their stimulating and inspiring conversations, in particular Professor Robert Burgoyne.

2   John Carlin, *Playing The Enemy: Nelson Mandela and the Game That Made a Nation* (London: Atlantic Books, 2008). Morgan Freeman bought the film rights for Carlin's work on the basis of a book proposal circulating in Hollywood as early as 2006, two years prior to the publication of the book. After the release of the film *Invictus*, John Carlin's book was renamed *Invictus: Nelson Mandela and the Game That Made a Nation,* and was released as a tie-in edition with an image of the film poster as cover illustration.

3   For an overview of the typical traits of the historical fiction film genre, see Robert Brent Toplin, *Reel History: In Defense of Hollywood* (Lawrence: University of Kansas Press, 2002). What I call 'historical fiction film', drawing a distinction between fictional films and documentaries, is what Robert Brent Toplin calls 'cinematic history', and Robert Burgoyne names 'Hollywood historical film'.

4   Christine Geraghty, review, *Screen* 51:2 (2010) 168–73.

5   Christine Geraghty, *Now a Major Motion Picture: Film Adaptations of Literature and Drama* (Lanham, Toronto and Plymouth: Rowman & Littlefield Publishers, 2007), 4. Geraghty uses the term 'recall' with reference to Christine Grant, 'Recognizing *Billy Budd* in *Beau Travail*: Epistemology and Hermeneutics of an Auteurist "Free" Adaptation' *Screen* 43: 1 (2002), 57–73.

6   Thomas Leitch, 'Adaptation Studies at a Crossroad,' *Adaptation* 1:1 (2008), 67.

7   Linda Hutcheon, *A Theory of Adaptation* (New York: Routledge, 2006), 170.

8   Robert Burgoyne, *The Hollywood Historical Film* (Oxford: Blackwell Publishing, 2008), 148.

9   The film project's working title was 'The Human Factor' in the second draft of the screenplay, dated 22 May 2007.

10 International Rugby Board (2008), *The Story of Rugby World Cup 1995* (South Africa: Lace DVD).

11 Geraghty (2007), 167.

12 Geraghty (2007), 168. However, most visual source material never will be thought of as adapted or alluded to, unless a particularly cultural memory of them already exists or these sources are otherwise identified in reviews and articles about the film.

13 Natalie Zemon Davis, 'Any Resemblance to Persons Living or Dead: Film and the Challenge of Authenticity', Marnie Hughes-Warrington (ed), *The History on Film Reader* (New York and London: Routledge, 2009), 18.

14 Geraghty (2007), 5.

15 *The Daily Mail*, 'First pictures of Morgan Freeman playing Nelson Mandela in new film *Invictus*,' 4 April, 2009. http://www.dailymail. co.uk/tvshowbiz/article-1211274/First-look-Morgan-Freeman-playing-Nelson-Mandela-new-film-Invictus.html#ixzz1VMaQeqgT (accessed 8 April 2011).

16 Chris Irvine, 'Matt Damon touted to play ex-South Africa captain Francois Pienaar in World Cup movie,' *The Telegraph*, 6 September 2008. http://www.telegraph.co.uk/sport/rugbyunion/international/southafrica/2302793/Matt-Damon-touted-to-play-ex-South-Africa-captain-Francois-Pienaar-in-World-Cup-movie.html (accessed 8 April 2011).

17 Jean-Louis Comolli, 'Historical Fiction: A Body Too Much,' *The History on Film Reader*, op.cit., 65–74.

18 Ibid., 69.

19 Ibid., 72.

20 Hutcheon (2006), 4.

21 Ibid., 10.

22 Ibid.

23 Ibid., 170

23 David T. Johnson, 'Playground of Unlimited Potential: Adaptation, Documentary, and Dogtown and Z-boys,' *Adaptation* 2:1 (2009), 1–16.

25 Ibid., 2.

26 Ibid., 8–9.

27 Julie Sanders, *Adaptation and Appropriation* (New York and London: Routledge, 2006), 4.

28 *The Daily Mail*, 'First pictures of Morgan Freeman playing Nelson Mandela in new film *Invictus*,' 4 April 2009. http://www.dailymail.co.uk/tvshowbiz/article-1211274/First-look-Morgan-Freeman-playing-Nelson-Mandela-new-film-Invictus.html#ixzz1VMaQeqgT (accessed 8 April 2011).

29 Dudley Andrew, 'Adapting Cinema to History: A Revolution in the Making' Robert. Stam and Alessandra Raengo, (eds), *A Companion to Literature and Film* (Oxford: Boston Blackwell Publishing, 2004), 191.

30 Ibid., 191–2.

31 Ibid., 200.

32 Thomas Leitch, 'Based on a True Story', *Film Adaptations and Its Discontents* (Baltimore: The John Hopkins University Press, 2007), 280–304.

33 Ibid., 282.

34 Ibid., 290.

35 Ibid., 302

36 *Invictus* production notes, http://invictusmovie.warnerbros.com/dvd/assets/images/about/notes/invictus-notes.pdf (accessed 8 April 2011).

37 Frank Thompson, 'Getting It Right: The Alamo on Film,' James M. Welsh and Peter Lev (eds), *The Literature/Film Reader: Issues of Adaptation*, (Lanham, Toronto and Plymouth: The Scarecrow Press, 2007), 304.

38 Benedict Anderson, *Imagined Communities: Reflections on the Origin and Spread of Nationalism* (London: Verso, 1991), 45, and

Robert Burgoyne, *Film Nation. Hollywood Looks at U.S. History* (London: Minnesota University Press, 2010), 88.

39 For a telling example of this, see Jørgen Bruhn and Anne Gjelsvik,'Jan Troell's Fleeting Still Moments', *Journal of Scandinavian Cinema* 2:1 (2012), 55–72.

12

What novels can tell that movies can't show

Anne Gjelsvik

Violence is one of the cinematic things you can do with film. It's almost like Edison and the Lumière brothers invented the camera for filming violence. The most cinematic directors, they're taking cinema and exciting you, I really do think about it like that. Quentin Tarantino [1]

In his classic article 'What Novels Can Do That Films Can't (and Vice Versa)' (1980), Seymour Chatman starts his investigation of adaptation from literature to film with the following observation: 'In the course of studying and teaching film, I have been struck by the sorts of changes *typically* introduced by screen adaptation'.[2] This article has a similar point of departure, as it is inspired by the way many recent films based on novels have seemed to make certain type of changes to their source material, changes that struck me as peculiar.

This specific 'sort of change' first got my attention in relation to the adaptation of Swedish writer Johan Ajvide Lindqvist's novel *Let the Right One In* (2004) into an excellent film of the same name by director Thomas Alfredson (2008).[3] Whereas reading the novel was a shocking experience because of its explicit depictions

of violence, and in particular its provocative depictions of paedo-
philia, the movie left me in a different kind of shock: Where were
all the scenes that had frightened, challenged and provoked me in
the cold and terrifying novel? Most of them were gone.

I then started to notice several stories that were provocative
in novel form, but that when transformed into film seemed less
so. One example is John Hillcoat's adaptation (2009) of Cormac
McCarthy's *The Road* (2006). The most horrifying scene in the
novel, the one where cannibals barbecue their own newborn
baby, is not included in the movie. In the Norwegian movie *Fatso*
(Arild Frølich, 2008, based on Lars Ramslie's challenging novel
from 2004), both the protagonist's pornographic fantasies and the
rape of his roommate are omitted from the narrative. Why these
changes?

The aim of this article is to question if these changes can
illuminate the differences between the two media – literature
and cinema. I consider Chatman's article an illuminating point
of departure because it, by its title and conclusion, so clearly
states that each medium has it owns properties, 'limitations' and
'triumphs'.[4] According to Chatman, the close study of both the film
and novel version of the same narrative 'reveals with great clarity
the peculiar power of the two media. Once we grasp those peculiarities, the reasons for the differences, in form, content and impact
of the two versions strikingly emerge.'[5]

When investigating the changes made in the adaptation process,
one can use a lot of different angles or fields of investigation;
Chatman himself investigated description and point of view. Tom
Leitch, in *Adaptation and Its Discontents,* has offered a comprehensive overview of possible takes on adapting literature for
the screen, including: celebration, adjustments, revisions, decon-
structions or colonizations.[6] I will argue that within the broad
category of 'adjustments', there is a tendency for what I will term
'downplaying' of taboos and provocative content in mainstream
cinema, where challenging depictions of violence or sex are
modified to suit the conventions of cinema.[7]

In this article I will investigate the differences in what film and
literature can depict in terms of violence, sex or other transgressive
representations before it is considered to be 'too much', or in other
ways problematic, and what these differences can tell us about the
media in question. When I choose the representation of violence as

a tool for addressing new topics in adaptation studies, I do this for a set of intertwined reasons. My aim is to try to 'grasp the peculiar powers of the different media', by approaching them with the question: Is there in fact something, or some things, novels can tell that films can't show, because of the medium's 'particular power'? If so, are these differences 'typical', do they exhibit the essential characteristics of a group? Said in a different way, are these differences the result of medium specificity, or even essence?

Chatman wrote within a discourse, still inspired by a modernist Greenbergian idea, where medium specificity claims were still considered eligible, but during the 1980s this idea came under criticism. Within film theory, Noël Carroll was central in arguing against medium essentialism, which he claimed was a result of classical film theory's attempt to define the new medium of cinema by way of specificity claims.[8] Several theorists have considered cinema to be a hybrid or heterogeneous medium, without any significant component and impossible to reduce to a single essence, but rather 'open to a plethora of diverse and even incompatible styles and formal approaches', as D. N Rodowick formulates it.[9] Within recent theory, W. J. T Mitchell has been among the most influential, claiming that all media are in fact mixed media.[10]

In this article, however, I want to argue that the downsizing of the borders between media has been done to the extent that important differences seem to be forgotten. When arguing for a return to medium specificity research, I do however follow a new tendency within contemporary intermedial studies.[11] Jan Baetens argues that recent perspectives have brought new visions on what specificity means, which is 'no longer an eternal essence, but a permanently shifting effort to "link" signs, supports and contents'.[12] Following Baetens, this article will argue for a contextualized medium specificity that may come to the fore by comparisons between novel and film versions, first and foremost by contextualizing how we experience different media. I will argue that we tend to react differently towards different art forms due to a combination of medium characteristics and conventions. Accordingly, we need to investigate the links between media, particular cases and their audiences.

There is no going back to claims about eternal medium essence, but looking into the different media's different impacts is still worthwhile. In relation to violence, it is commonly argued that violence in audiovisual media has a strong impact on its viewers, and I will return to this claim later in the article. For now, I will claim that adaptation theorists should take into consideration the phenomenological experience in relation to adaptations. The emotional difference between (to put it bluntly) reading and watching controversial representations calls for a phenomenological approach to the question of medium specificity. I will use violent representations as my case study to illustrate this.

Too hard to watch

Chatman suggested that the chosen method should be close readings of both the novel and the film in question, and I have chosen Michael Winterbottom's 2010 adaptation of Jim Thompson's *The Killer Inside Me* (1952) as my principal example.[13] I chose this movie because it stirred up quite a bit of controversy at the time of its release due to its depictions of violence. The violent content was considered to be 'too much'. My case study first and foremost sheds light on the question of violent representations, but I will argue that some of the aspects are transferable to other controversial and affective issues, such as sexual depictions, of which there also are some challenging examples in Winterbottom's movie.

Jim Thompson (1906–72) wrote mostly crime novels, several of them adapted to film. *The Killer Inside Me* is, together with *Pop.1280 (1964)*, considered to be his best novel. Writing within a pulp noir tradition, Thompson has been given status as a master of his genre, particularly because of his use of unreliable first-person narration. He also wrote some notable screenplays: *The Killing* and *Paths of Glory*, both directed by Stanley Kubrick. However, according to Peter Standfield, Thompson's status as a writer who bridges the gap between pop and high-brow literature was only gained after his death. The critical discourse during the 1980s was in part a result of the film industry's interest in his work, and has been described by Richard Corliss as a renovation project turning him into the 'overrated underrated writer'.[14]

Michael Winterbottom is among the most productive, provocative and acclaimed contemporary directors in Europe today.[15] Coming from television, he moved on to explore both fiction and documentary in cinema and is known for testing all kinds of boundaries in film-making: between genres, fiction and truth, literature and film, or the limits of representation of sex and violence. As a neo-noir made by a European art director, based on an American pulp novel, the movie perfectly fits James Naremore's famous description of film noir as a genre occupying 'a liminal space somewhere between Europe and America, between high modernism and "blood melodrama," and between low-budget crime movies and art cinema'.[16] In short, this adaptation is a meeting between the mainstream popular culture represented by crime fiction and thrillers and provocative art cinema.

Winterbottom's movie became infamous after the screening at the important independent Sundance Film Festival 2010, where a journalist opened the press conference with an attack on both the director and the festival: 'I don't understand how Sundance could book this movie', she said. 'How dare you? How dare Sundance?'[17]

The reviews and the ways in which the movie was received at the festival, and after, were divided, but the perspective was set with this incident, and the violence became a central topic in the discourse concerning the movie. Central elements in the criticism against the movie were that the movie was misogynistic and the fact that the most brutal acts of violence depicted were directed against women.[18] Michael Winterbottom defended his movie and the violence with the arguments that he was faithful to Thompson's pulp novel, that the violence was all there in the novel and that a first person story narrated by a crazy killer should be shocking.[19] Film critic Anne Thompson reflected on his arguments in her article, and followed the director on the central point, that Winterbottom had visualized the words Jim Thompson had written: 'But he may not realize how hard these scenes are to watch. It's the tactile, intimate aspect that is so disturbing, as beating these women is an extension of Ford's love for them'.[20]

In my discussion of the adaptation, I will take as my starting point the assumption that these scenes are hard to watch, but also investigate if these scenes are in fact represented 'faithfully', and try to illuminate whether or not they are harder to watch than to read.[21]

The novel is the first person narrative of Lou Ford, who behind his façade as a deputy sheriff hides a 'sickness', a deranged mind and dangerous behaviour that will lead him into killing. The narrative is presented chronologically and starts with the deputy getting an assignment from the sheriff to check on a 'Hustlin lady', with the name of Joyce Lakeland; he is asked to handle it 'as gentle and pleasant as you can be'.[22] Events prior to Ford's violent sexual relationship with Joyce are told through dialogue or as flash-back memories, elaborating on his background: how he used to live with his adopted brother and his father, a doctor and widower practicing a S/M relationship with his young housekeeper Helene. The relationship with his father is suggested as the reason for Lou Ford's disturbed mind, while the accidental (?) death of his brother explains his antipathy against the city capitalist, Chester Conway. In sum, these events and his encounter with Joyce trigger the killer inside him.

Both the dialogue and the first-person narration are carefully transferred from the novel to the movie. The dialogue in the movie follows that in the book quite closely, both in terms of content, amount and tone (with some cuts due to time constraints), whereas Lou Ford's voice-over in the movie is used to a somewhat lesser degree than the first-person narration in the novel. Both novel and movie do, however, stick closely to Ford's version of the narrative, what he knows is what we know, and we know what he feels and thinks. In the movie, the protagonist is within the picture frame in almost every shot, and his emotional responses to the situations are depicted through an extended use of close-ups of his (Casey Affleck's) face. In addition, on a few subtle occasions, the actor looks directly into the camera, smiling the way you smile to a secret ally, almost turning the viewer into an accomplice. The film thus combines the classical genre cinema's 'invisible' style with a more reflective mode, changing thus between an indulging viewing position and a distant one more common in modernist and European art cinema.

I will argue that Winterbottom's colourful film noir style captures the dichotomy between the narrator's concealed self-presentation and his calculated cruelty in a visually disturbing way. The contrast between the close to perfect, often pastel coloured, surface and the dark inner world creates a disturbing feeling that lingers almost throughout the movie. (An illustrative example is the ending of the movie where the tragic outcome for Lou and Joyce is painted in a pink and dusky picture of the smoke from the mortal fire). Casey Affleck's cute face and childish, high-pitched voice contribute to an ambivalent engagement with the psychopath. Ford has a gentle appearance, but both novel and film soon challenge their audience's sympathy with the protagonist.[23]

Overall, the movie doesn't contain more violence than any ordinary crime or action movie from Hollywood. But there are two particularly violent and challenging scenes in the movie, both of which show Ford giving a deadly beating to a woman with whom he is having a long-term sexual relationship. There are also scenes depicting violent sex, two different shootings, and two deaths occurring off-screen – one where Ford kills an innocent young man, one a suicide that is a result of his other acts. All these events take place in the novel as well, but, as I will argue, they are not as disturbing in writing.

The scene that is by far hardest to watch takes place approximately 23 minutes into the film.[24] At this point in the narrative, Ford has made a set-up for his enemy Conway and his son Elmer, as well as Joyce (Jessica Alba). Joyce thinks that the two of them will elope with the money they get from blackmailing Elmer, money Chester Conway pays her in order to prevent his son's relationship with a prostitute from becoming public. Ford, however, has planned to kill both Joyce and Elmer and make it look like a lover's quarrel with a deadly ending.

In the novel this event plays out as follows:

She still didn't get it. She laughed, frowning a little at the same time. 'But Lou – that doesn't make sense. How can I be dead when –'.

'Easy,' I said and I gave her a slap. And still she didn't get it.

She put a hand to her face and rubbed it slowly. 'Y- you'd better not do that, now, Lou. I've got to travel and – '. 'You're not going anywhere, baby,' I said, and I hit her again.

And at last she got it.

She jumped up and I jumped with her. I whirled her around and gave her quick one-two, and she shot backwards across the room and bounced and slumped against the wall. She staggered to her feet, weaving, mumbling, and half-fell toward me. I let her have it again.

I backed her against the wall, slugging, and it was like pounding a pumpkin. Hard, then everything giving away at once. She slumped down, her knees bent under her, her head hanging limp; and then slowly, an inch at the time, she pushed herself up again.

She couldn't see; I don't know how she could. I don't know how she could stand or go on breathing. But she brought her head up, wobbling, and she raised her arms, raised them and spread them and held them out. And then she staggered toward me, just as a car pulled into the yard.

'Guhguh-guhby...kiss guguh-guh—

I brought an uppercut up from the floor. There was a sharp *cr-aack!* And her whole body shot upward, and came down in a heap. And that time it stayed down.

I wiped my gloves on her body; it was her blood and it belonged there. I took the gun from the dresser, turned off the light and closed the door.[25]

In the following passage, Elmer Conway arrives and Lou Ford shoots him and arranges the scene so it looks as Joyce shot him before she died from the injuries from Elmer's beating. As it turns out in the end, Joyce, who was taken to hospital in a coma, survived. At this point in the narrative, however, Lou Ford does not know this and neither does the reader or viewer. In the following I will treat this scene as a murder scene, then, because that is in fact what the first time reader or viewer experiences it as.

In the film, this scene, from the first time Ford slaps Joyce in the face until she stays down apparently killed, lasts for almost three minutes, which I will imagine is longer than the passage takes to read, and it certainly feels longer.

The scene takes place in Joyce´s feminine, pink bedroom, the wallpaper covered in flowers and mirrors on every wall. The biggest change between novel and film is that, while the beating takes place immediately after the couple has had sex in both narratives, this part is briefly depicted in the novel, whereas in the film the sex is explicit. In the movie, the sex scene shows an unusual mixture of rough and tender sex, with elements of bondage as well as gentle caresses and kisses. Some dialogue is added in the film; while beating the woman, Leo continuously says that he is sorry and that he loves her. When it comes to the depiction of the violence, the film follows the course of events in the description above. However, whereas the amount of punches is not concretized in the novel, but rather indicated by way of descriptions such as slugging – a phrase like 'let her have it' may indicate either one or more hits – the movie shows us every punch. In the film the first strokes mirror the way Lou slaps Joyce during sex[26], the next three are extremely forceful punches in her face, making her nose bleed. He then hits her in the stomach so hard that her body flies across the room and crashes against the wall. The subsequent punches are mostly shown from behind her, showing more of Ford than of Joyce, focusing on the physical strain he is going through (his heavy breathing and perspiration) in order to actually beat her to death.

Chatman argued that a comparison between a novel and film would give the result that the 'reasons for the differences, in form, content and impact of the two versions strikingly emerge.'[27] So why is it more disturbing to watch Lou beat Joyce 'to death' than to read about it? Is this related to specific powers of cinema?

The violent impact of this particular scene could be summarized as follows: By way of cinematic techniques, editing, sound and extensive use of close-ups, the violence is rendered as repetitive, forceful, physical, intimate and close.[28] Some of the camera positions place the viewers in the victim's position, almost making us feel as if we ourselves are getting hit. Finally, the bodily damages, in particular those on the woman's face, are shown in detail and close-ups. Accordingly, the cinematic violence can be described as close, detailed, concrete and embodied.

The intimacy and closeness of the scene is amplified by the closeness in the two lovers' relationship, with the intimate sex scene contextualizing the violent event. The scene not only shows the extremely brutal beating of a lover, it is made crueller by the fact that she is a young beautiful woman. This sets it apart from more ordinary thriller scenes depicting fights between, for instance, criminal men. The fact that the victims were women played an important role in the critical debate, and as a critic said: that the women were played 'by Kate Hudson and Jessica Alba only compounded the horror that seemed to ricochet around the auditorium'.[29]

The critical discourse around the film was supplemented with the impact of Winterbottom being a provocative British art director now working within American popular culture, or even pulp culture. The differences in the ways in which violently or sexually explicit works are received are in part the result of cinematic conventions or what we can call 'contextualized medium specificity'. For instance, in terms of violence in cinema, there are great differences between how violence used for artistic or educational reasons (say, for instance, *Saving Private Ryan*) and more entertaining violence (say, for instance, *Pulp Fiction*) are received.

Following this, I would like to stress that, in a discussion of medium specific differences between novel and film, it is pivotal to distinguish between *a particular scene, a particular movie* and *movies as such*. Bearing such distinctions in mind, I will however try to sort out what is a result of medium specificity and what should be considered dependent on the context. The specific scene in the film in question is hard to watch because of a combination of immediacy, concreteness and closeness. This is a result of audio-visual representations of violence, editing and movements. The question is to what degree these elements and these characteristics are typical of the medium.

Violence against the eye

The claim that cinematic violence is hard to watch is by no means something that can be limited to the case in question. Violence in cinema is generally understood to have strong effects. This is one of the reasons for the strict regulation of the distribution and exhibition of film, including censorship. After 1907, movies were censored in the United States, and many other countries that do not practice censorship of written media, through the cutting out of problematic scenes or banning of movies due to their content. Age limits are common, also in countries that no longer practice censorship. These ratings are based on the same idea as censorship: the audience's need for protection against strong impressions, in particular sex and violence. In 1996, the Norwegian government even launched a campaign against violence in audio-visual media. Their worries were related to media, but only those that could be categorised as audio-visual (not newspapers, for instance), and there were no special measures taken against violence in literature, a medium which traditionally has been protected against such interventions because they have been deemed violations against freedom of speech.[30] What can account for these differences in the regulations of cinema and novels? Can this be explained by the particular powers of cinema?

First, cinema is commonly understood as the art of the visual and of vision. This presumption has had several theoretical ramifications, and it has also been criticized from different theoretical angles. However, cinema is still, especially in public debate, considered to have a peculiar power as a witness and with an immediate closeness to the real, due to being based on photography (or more precisely cinematography). Seymour Chatman can serve as a representative for this tradition:

> So in its essential visual mode, film does not describe at all but merely presents; or better, it depicts, in the original etymological sense of that word: renders in pictorial form. I don't think that this is mere purism or a die-hard adherence to silent films. Film attracts that component of our perceptual apparatus which we tend to favour over the other senses. Seeing, after all, is believing.[31]

When watching violent representations in a movie, we usually do not take them to be the depictions of factual incidents, but as fictitious, fantasy, and – in relation to violence – always a result of cinematic effects. Violence in fiction is rarely depicted 'the way it is', but is rather made into something spectacular, or an attempt to create suspense rather than accuracy. I will however argue that the emotional response to visual violence, even when related to cinematic fiction, is related to the fact that we 'see it with our own eyes'. When we watch violence in fiction film, we do of course know that the violence is not real, and that Jessica Alba is not actually harmed, but we tend to become what I will call 'intoxicated by the indexical illusion', that is to say that when we see it, it is harder to accept that this is only imagery.[32] As the debate around *The Killer Inside Me* showed, such violent imagery is hard to see as pure fiction.

This was also the case with *Irreversible* (Caspar Noe 2002), an illustrative case, famous for its gut wrenchingly realistic violence. One of the reasons why Noe's movie became notorious for its extreme violence was the opening scene, where a man kills another man by smashing his face in with a fire extinguisher. The scene is seemingly non-edited, so the viewer has to watch the repeated and heavy beating towards the man's face in semi close-ups without any pauses. And more importantly, with the feeling that this is actual, live and present, and that we as viewers are witnesses. As shown above, the brutal scene in *The Killer Inside Me*, although more edited, achieves some of the same effect by way of closeness, sound and the time and rhythm of the beating.

This leads me to the second of what traditionally has been accounted for as cinema's peculiar powers, the idea that the medium is immediate, which again has been used to claim that cinema is easy to understand, and yet hard for the spectator to distance herself from. An example of this is to be found in the debate around the age limit for *The Lord of the Rings* trilogy in Norway. Here, a representative for The Ombudsman for Children argued against allowing 11-year-old children to see the films with the following argument: 'I read Tolkien with great pleasure as a little boy. There is a great difference between reading and creating your own images, and to sit and be flooded with the effects on the screen.'[33]

This view is common in the public debate, but has also had its ambassadors within academic circles. Most influential is perhaps Marshall McLuhan's distinction between hot and cold media, where cinema is considered to be hot and literature cold. A medium is hot when it enhances one single sense with high definition, and accordingly requires a less active response from the viewer.[34] Although widely criticized, this notion tends to reappear every now and then. Linda Hutcheon, for instance, when addressing how audiences respond to adaptations, briefly touches upon what she terms both modes of engagement and degrees of immersion: 'The act of reading a print text immerses us through imagination in another world, seeing a play or film immerses us visually and aurally, and interacting with a story in a videogame or a theme park adds a physical, enacted dimension.'[35] In *Camera Lucida*, Roland Barthes claims that: 'The Photograph is violent: not because it shows violent things, but because on each occasion it fills the sight by force, and because in it nothing can be refused or transformed'.[36] In his usual way, Barthes captures what he sees as the essence of photography in a few words; and in this case he also captures what I have heard repeated as the main argument when violence in movies is discussed: Violence in the movies is problematic because it is violence against the eye, against perception, something that is forced upon you and that you can't protect yourself from or transform into something else, like metaphor, so that you can distance yourself from it.[37]

I see this summarized position as highly problematic, and the notion that cinema should be all perception, not to say all vision, has also been heavily criticized, by, among others, researchers within adaptation studies such as Thomas Leitch and Robert Stam. In his article 'Twelve Fallacies in Adaption Theories', Leitch voices strong criticism of these kinds of media ontologists.[38] Leitch criticizes those who claim that 'moviegoers watch films only for their kinesthetic images, not for their conceptual implications.'[39] In order to do away with the fallacy that 'literary texts are verbal, films visual' he simply points out the obvious point that film is an audio-visual medium. And, as my example showed, sound is extremely important in the experience of violent film scenes.

Robert Stam contests (among other prejudices against cinema) both the 'myth of facility', that movies are so easy to understand, and the 'embodiedness' of the visual image.[40]

Although I fully share Stam and Leitch's wish to emphasize the importance of watching movies for their conceptual implications, I will however argue that when it comes to depictions of sex and violence, cinema has a particularly strong effect on its viewer precisely because of its 'embodiedness'. In the next section I want to pursue this idea a bit further.

Moving Pictures

As Vivian Sobchack foregrounds by quoting Heidegger: 'The essence of technology is nothing technological'.[41] And she continues by arguing that medium specificity never 'functions in a neutral context for neutral effects. Rather, it is always historically informed by its materiality but also by its political, economic, and social context, and thus always both constitutes and express cultural values'.[42] This notion is comparable with what I see as contextualised medium specificity. Nevertheless, Sobchack concludes that it is impossible to reflect upon texts and medium technology without considering how we engage with them in a sensorial way, that is to say, with our own bodies.

Following a similar line of thought, Tom Gunning claims that there is an increasing need to offer thick descriptions of how media work, that is, phenomenological approaches that avoid defining media logically before examining the experience of their power.[43] While stressing that all media work 'in concert and in contest rather than isolation', Gunning argues that the formal properties of different media do convey aesthetic values in non-neutral ways. Accordingly, Gunning encourages scholars to probe for the power of cinema and to once again put its affinities and differentiations from other media on our research agenda. While Gunning also sees cinema's relation to photography as central in terms of 'what really moves me...' he stresses the importance of cinematic motion.' We do not just *see* motion and we are not simply affected emotionally by its role within a plot; we *feel* it in our guts or throughout our bodies.'[44] Accordingly, Gunning foregrounds how the experience of motion based sequences affect viewers physiologically and emotionally.

The philosopher Berys Gaut also highlights motion in his discussion of cinema as an art form by stating: 'cinema is the medium of the moving image'.[45] His starting point is etymological: cinema is related to kinematics, the study of things that move. In his discussion of historical approaches to medium specificity he distinguishes between what he calls a globalizing tendency (theories seeking to explain general characteristics of art in general) and a localizing tendency (theories that apply to particular art forms).[46] Advocating a medium-specificity claim himself, Gaut in particular uses film philosopher Noël Carroll, famous for his 'Forget the Medium!' postulate, as his rhetorical opponent.[47]

Gaut distinguishes between medium uniqueness (which he claims that Carroll employs) and distinctness which he himself uses as an analytical framework.[48] This way, Gaut can distinguish between medium specificity and medium essence, and develop a theory that investigates both the features that cinema share with other art forms and the features that separates cinema from them.[49] Consequently Gaut argues that: 'there is no reason to assume that a feature of a medium in order to be genuinely explanatory must be unique to it'.[50]

Following this framework, Gaut investigates several instances of what he calls 'medium-involving explanations' for how cinema works and is received, the emotional impact of cinema being one.[51] This is particularly relevant for my argument here. Among Gaut's arguments for a medium distinctive impact on the viewer's emotional response are the following: Cinema can generate a more immediate and visceral response than can novels, cinema has, for instance, the ability to startle the viewer due to sensory input (novels do not). Photographs tend to have a greater emotional impact than paintings, because photographs seem transparent and evidential. Different cinematic devices (editing, movement, music) can be used to control the timing of the flow emotions precisely.

The strong impact of the scene in *The Killer Inside Me* was in part created by the visual imagery of the victim's distorted face, in part the use of close-ups, in part the rhythm of the editing, in part the sounds of the beating. All of these are distinct properties of cinema, but used in a distinctive way in this particular context. Violence in cinema doesn't have to be detailed and concrete, but when it is, it is also close and embodied, and makes the viewer feel it with her body.

In this particular scene, the impressions from the violent moving images are strong, because of the movements, sound and the photographic image, or what we could call 'the relative distinctiveness' of the medium.[52] In addition to that, the reactions towards this particular film were particularly strong due to the context: a festival film that did not meet the audience's expectations of art cinema as it turned out to be a somewhat kitschy violent genre film. Conventions and expectations do play a part in the effects of a movie or a novel, and should be a part of a discussion about medium specificity. Taking into account the role of bodily feelings and cognitive emotions when describing the effects of a movie, or like in my case violence, could be said to represent a paradigmatic turn in film studies.[53] In order to gain a better understanding of what motion pictures are, we need (as Rodowick, Sobchack, Gunning and Gaut argue) to take into consideration perceptual and emotional descriptions.

I argue that the differences in how we feel when we read something and when we see something cannot be ignored, and should be used as an analytical tool when analysing the artworks in question, they should also be used for theoretical perspective in the studies of media transformations, such as the adaptation of novels into films. Having done research on violent fiction for a long period of time, I will argue that one conclusion is absolute:

the representation of violence creates strong emotions. In order to understand the impact of these representations and the difference between, for instance, written and audio-visual representations of violence, we have to take their emotional impact into account. Adaptation studies might illuminate the role of emotions in art; emotions in art might illuminate adaptation studies.

Notes

1   Quentin, Tarantino, 'I call the shots here', *Sunday Times* 4 March 2007. http://entertainment.timesonline.co.uk/tol/arts_and_ entertainment/film/article1454042.ece (accessed 25 May 2011).

2   My italics. Seymour Chatman,'What Novel Can Do That Films Can't (and Vice Versa)', *Critical Inquiry*, Vol. 8, 1980, 122–3.

3   See also Jørgen Bruhn, Anne Gjelsvik and Henriette Thune, 'Windows to Parallel Worlds in *Let The Right One In*', in *Word and Image*, 2011:1, on different aspects of this adaptation. The movie has later been remade into an American version *Let Me In* (Matt Reeves 2010). The movie is based on the original screenplay, it follows the movie's plot more than the novel's, and is also clearly inspired by Alfredson's version both in visual and auditive style. The American version is somewhat more horrifying and explicit in violent details, but the main differences between the novel and film is to be found in both versions.

4   Chatman, 140. Also Chatman argues that 'narrative itself is a deep structure quite independent of its medium', 121. This assumption is of course not a given fact, but a discussion beyond the scope of this article.

5   Chatman, 123.

6   Thomas Leitch, *Film Adaptation and Its Discontents: From* Gone with the Wind *to* The Passion of the Christ (Baltimore: Johns Hopkins University Press 2007), 93–127. See Linda Hutcheon, *A Theory of Adaptation* (New York and London: Routledge, 2006) for different categories.

7   See my article 'Downplaying Taboos in Contemporary Cinema' in Sarah Paulson and Anders Malvik (eds), *Across Media* (forthcoming). Here I provide some more examples and more detailed analysis of this tendency. An important exception to this tendency is to be found within European art cinema, in particular

French cinema. One example here is the extremely controversial adaptation of Virgine Despentes' *Baise Moi*. See Wencke Mühleisen, '*Baise-moi* and feminism's Filmic Intercourse with the Aesthetics of Pornography' in Rikke Schubart and Anne Gjelsvik (eds), *Femme Fatalities: Representations of Strong Women in Media* (Gothenburg: Nordicom, 2004).

8   Noël Carroll, *Theorizing the Moving Image* (Cambridge: Cambridge University Press, 1996).

9   D. N. Rodowick, The *Virtual Life of Film* (Cambridge: Harvard University Press, 2007).

10 W. J. T. Mitchell, *What Do Pictures Want? The Lives and Loves of Images* (Chicago: The University of Chicago Press, 2005), 215. Or as stated in *Aesthetics of film*, Jacques Aumont et al, (eds) (Austin: University of Texas Press, 1992). 'The cinema, however, is not only heterogeneous in terms of its material, but also heterogeneous because of the co-presence within a film of elements specific to the cinema alongside elements that are not at all specific to the cinema', 158.

11 Jan Baetens, 'Conceptional Limitations of Our Reflection on Photography: The Question of 'Interdisciplinarity'', in James Elkins (ed.), *Photography Theory* (New York and London: Routledge, 2011).

12 Ibid., 55.

13 The novel is adapted once before in Burt Kennedy's version from 1976. According to Peter Stanfield this movie sunk without a trace; *Maximum Movies, Pulp Fictions: Film Culture and the Worlds of Samuel Fuller, Mickey Spillane, and Jim Thompson* (New Brunswick: Rutgers University Press, 2011), 152.

14 Stanfield, 153.

15 See Deborah Allison's profile of Winterbottom in *Senses of Cinema*: http://archive.sensesofcinema.com/contents/directors/05/winterbottom.html (accessed 20 May 2012).

16 James Naremore, *More than Night Film Noir in Its Contexts* (Berkeley: California University Press, 1998), 220.

17 See for instance Anne Thompson's festival report: http://blogs.indiewire.com/thompsononhollywood/1,539/-470/-444/sundance_winterbottom_defends_the_killer_inside_me/ (accessed 3 January 2013).

18 For a selection of reviews and comments which focus on this, see for instance such different reviews as: http://www.guardian.co.uk/

film/filmblog/2010/jan/26/the-killer-inside-me-sundance, http://ibyen.
dk/film/anmeldelser/article1008011.ece, http://www.empireonline.
com/empireblogs/words-from-the-wise/post/p756 (all accessed 9
December 2011). The rating on Rotten Tomatoes is characteristic,
as the responses are almost divided on the middle, with 41 per
cent negative and 44 per cent positive feedback. http://www.
rottentomatoes.com/m/the_killer_inside_me/

19 http://www.guardian.co.uk/film/filmblog/2010/jan/26/the-killer-
    inside-me-sundance (accessed 3 January 2013).

20 Thompson (2010).

21 On the question of fidelity within adaptation studies, see
    for instance Thomas Leitch, 'Twelve Fallacies in Adaptation
    Theories', *Criticism*, Spring 2003, and Deborah Cartmell and
    Imelda Wheelhan, *Screen Adaptation. Impure cinema* (New York:
    Palgrave Macmillan, 2010).

22 Jim Thompson, *The Killer Inside Me* (1952) (2006, 5), this line of
    dialogue is also in the movie.

23 On sympathy with characters in film, see Murray Smith, *Engaging
    Characters. Fiction, Emotion and Cinema* (Oxford: Claredon Press,
    1995), and for work on empathy see Margrethe Bruun Vaage,
    'What Kind of Fiction Film Elicits What Kind of Empathy" *Midwest
    Studies in Philosophy*, vol. 34, (2010), 158–79.

24 Thompson 41–3.

25 Thompson 42–3.

26 Due to the violent nature of their sexual relationship, Joyce (as
    indicated in the quotation cited) takes his slapping as an indication
    of sexual foreplay.

27 Chatman 123.

28 In my dissertation, *Fiksjonsvoldens etiske betydninger (Fictional
    violence and ethical judgements*, 2004), I have investigated how
    Norwegian reviewers react on violence in cinema, and how their
    response differs depending on the representations' form and content.
    One of the central findings in study is that close ups and explicit
    details triggered the strongest emotional reactions.

29 Damon Wise, 'Sundance 2010: The Killer Inside Me causes outrage!'
    http://www.empireonline.com/empireblogs/words-from-the-wise/post/
    p756 (accessed 3 January 2013).

30 *Regjeringens handlingsplan mot vold i bildemediene*, 1996.

31 Chatman, 121–40. See also for instance Virginia Woolf's similar
    statement 'Photographs are not an argument: they are simply a

crude statement of fact addressed to the eye', quoted in Susan
Sontag, *Regarding the Pain of Others* (New York: Farrar, Strauss
and Giroux, 2003), 26.

32   For the sake of clarity I downplay the role of difference between
analogue and digital pictures here. See Berys Gaut, *A Philosophy of
Cinematic Art* (Cambridge: Cambridge University Press, 2010) for
a good discussion on medium specificity and the difference between
photographic cinema and digital cinema in this respect.

33   Knut Haanes, in a radio interview in 2002.

34   Marshall McLuhan, *Understanding Media: The Extension of Man*
(New York: McGraw Hill, 1964), 22.

35   Linda Hutcheon, *A Theory of Adaptation* (New York: Routledge,
2006), 133. Hutcheon also mentions that each medium and each
mode of engagements also brings with it each own critical tradition,
134. However her claim that video gamers, in order to enjoy
gaming have to forget that they are gaming is a simplification,
135–7.

36   And he continues 'that we can sometimes call it mild does not
contradict its violence: many say sugar is mild, but to me sugar is
violent, and I call it so'. Roland Barthes, *Camera Lucida* (London:
Vintage 2000), 91.

37   In *'Metaphor of the Eye'* Roland Barthes also points towards
an interesting difference in how we interpret different kinds of
artworks. He describes the subversive in Georges Bataille's work as
something that should not be read in its literal sense (or as novel
describing something that could had happened), but that Bataille's
History of the Eye should be understood as a poem, and accordingly
be read metaphorically 'since poetic technique consists, in his case,
of undoing the usual contiguities of objects'.

38   Thomas Leitch, 'Twelve Fallacies in Contemporary Adaptation
Theory', *Criticism* 45:2 (2003).

39   Ibid., 156

40   Robert Stam, *Literature and Film, A Guide to the Theory and
Practice of Film Adaptation* (Malden: Blackwell, 2005).

41   Vivian Sobchack, 'The Scene of the Screen, Envisioning, Cinematic
and Electronic "Presence"' in *Materialities of Communication*, (eds)
Hans Ulrich Gumbrecht and K. Ludwig Pfeiffer (Stanford: Stanford
University Press, 1994, 83–106, 84.

42   Ibid.

43   Tom Gunning, 'Moving Away From the Index', in Marc Furstenau,

The Film Theory Reader. Debates and Arguments (London and New York: Routledge, 2009), 260

44 Ibid., 261.

45 Gaut, 1.

46 Ibid., 282.

47 Noël Carroll, 'Forget the Medium!' in *Engaging the Moving Image* (New Haven: Yale University Press, 2003). Carroll argued against medium specificity as early as 1984, 'Medium Specificity Arguments and the Self-Consciously Invented Arts: Film, Video, and Photography', *Millennium Film Journal* nos. 14/15. Reprinted in *Theorizing the Moving Image* (Cambridge, Cambridge University Press, 1996). See also W. J. T Mitchell, 'There Is No Visual Media', *Journal of Visual Culture* 4:2 (2005), 257–66

48 Gaut, 290–2. Gaut bases his position on an argumentation for a more developed and precise definition of medium, where he argues that a) a medium can consist of different media, a phenomena he terms nesting, and b) we need to distinguish between 'the *material,* the stuff of art and the *medium*'. See Elleström in this volume for a more elaborated medium theory.

49 Gaut, 6, 290.

50 Gaut, 292.

51 Gaut, 299.

52 Rodowick, 39. Here, the full context is 'the relative distinctiveness of various mobbing-image media'.

53 From phenomenology Vivian Sobchack, The *Adress of the Eye* (Princeton: University of Princeton Press, 1992), *Carnal Thoughts* (Berkeley: Univeristy of California Press, 2004) to cognitive film theory, for instance Torben Grodal, Carl Plantinga, and Murray Smith.

13

Literature through radio: Distance and silence in *The War of the Worlds*, 1938/1898

Jonas Ingvarsson

The moment of translation is the moment of creativity (and discovery).

MARSHALL MCLUHAN, THE BOOK OF PROBES, 2003

Discursive fidelity

On 30 October, 1938, CBS Radio broadcast Orson Welles' *The War of the Worlds* as a Halloween episode of the Mercury Theatre on the Air. The play was staged as a sequence of interrupted live broadcasts, and the resulting panic among listeners who confused fact with fiction made the event a landmark in the history of media.

However, this essay does not discuss the Halloween panic; instead, I take this famous broadcast as the starting point for a reading of the source novel, H. G. Wells' *The War of the Worlds* from 1898. We might call this approach an 'adaptation analysis in reverse', in which Orson Welles' play of 1938 (counterfactually) works as the primary text. Even if H. G. Wells' purpose in 1898 could not have been (in all likelihood) to produce an adaptation of Orson Welles' production, the radio play nevertheless exerts an intertextual influence on the novel as we 'read literature through radio.'[1] Since the play is a staging of a media situation to a great extent, this adaptation analysis focuses on the role of media in both works.[2] However, in accordance with theorists such as Jørgen Bruhn and Thomas Leitch, this study does not primarily deal with the *essences* of the respective media – the fact that a radio play and a novel differ because they have different technological and semiotic set-ups.[3] Rather, the *representation* of communication technologies in the different versions and its media historical *significance* is the focus. By reading literature through radio, it becomes clear that both works relate to, and are structured around contemporary communication technologies. The geographic and temporal differences between novel and radio play are indeed quite obvious, but it is exactly these discrepancies that establish what may be the most conspicuous relationship between Welles and Wells, and between 1938 and 1898. From the media historical angle established in this article, the mimetic infidelity turns out to be a discursive fidelity.

From interpretation to simultaneity: Remediation and media archaeology

One of Marshall McLuhan's better-known assertions is that 'the "content" of any medium is always another medium.'[4] According to Christine Geraghty, a common device in adaptations is to represent different forms of mediations (the simplest examples are scenes with typewriters in films that are based on novels). For filmgoers who are not familiar with the original novel, Geraghty claims, this device can act as a marker that the film is after all an adaptation.[5] In light of McLuhan, Jay David Bolter and David Grusin suggest that the term *remediation* be used to describe the condition in which every medium throughout history reuses one or more other media.[6] According to Bolter and Grusin, there are primarily two ways that a medium remediates other media:

immediacy and *hypermediacy*. Immediacy is the epitome of the realistic novel and the aesthetic illusion, that is, the 'disappearance' of mediation in the artistic experience as in an exciting detective story, a captivating movie, or a virtual reality environment. Hypermediacy occurs when mediation comes to the foreground, for example, in different kinds of metadevices: when the narrator in a novel suddenly addresses the reader; when the pages of *Tristram Shandy* display a radical typography; when the picture and sound in a movie by Godard are not at all coherent; or at the normal Web site for any news bureau where text, film, pictures, sound, and different screens are mixed together. Hypermediacy need not be deliberate, but simply may be an effect of mediation's requirements: Live broadcasts are often hypermediated as we are continually reminded that there is a broadcast underway. Neither are certain media hypermediated while others are immediate, as each medium can exhibit both of these conditions.

Discussing Wells and Welles in terms of remediation can shed light on the media dictated logic that controls the different representations. When both works staged the conditions of communication, they simultaneously expressed what Friedrich Kittler might call the *discourse networks 1938/1898*; that is, media not only communicate messages, they inform and structure the production of power and meaning in historically given moments.[7] Moreover, if focus lies on remediation as well as on the particular publication years of the novel and radio play, the study of adaptation becomes a *media archaeological* survey. Within media archaeology, simultaneties are equally important as correlations. Inspired by Michel Foucault (particularly his *L'Archéologie Du Savoir*, 1969), the media archaeologist focuses on the position of media and cultural artifacts in their own times, as well as on the conditions for the production of statements. One central concern is why particular texts or statements occur at given historical moments. By applying this perspective, literary texts (or other statements) are juxtaposed to a number of other statements, such as newspapers, nonfiction, radio, movies, TV, and other media.[8] In the introduction to the anthology *Media Archaeology: Approaches, Applications, and Implications* (2011), the editors state:

> Media archaeology rummages textual, visual, and auditory archives as well as collections of artifacts, emphasizing both the

discursive and the material manifestations of culture. Its explorations move fluidly between disciplines, although it does not have a permanent home within any of them.[9]

Accordingly, media archaeologists such as Wolfgang Ernst, Hans Ulrich Gumbrecht and Erkki Huhtamo – just like Foucault – attempt to avoid cemented epoch and genre labels; they emphasize marginalized phenomena; and, with the materiality of media as a starting point, they demonstrate that an understanding of accepted perceptions and concepts can be historically situated. Hans Ulrich Gumbrecht terms this a 'theory of the present,' in which 'present' could be understood in the double meaning of 'being present' and the 'present situation'.[10] One way of dealing with this presence is to perform a study with *one year* as an analytic period.[11] By framing the object of study in a way that is not dependent on genres or epochs, new connections and relations are observable. Thus, in this essay, special attention is paid to the production year of the respective works, although by no means will there be room for a more thorough cultural historical inventory of the years 1938 and 1898.

Similar to Robert Stam's Bakhtinian-inspired intertextual adaptation analysis, media archaeology can be seen as a movement away from the creative subject, away from the hermeneutic understanding of (the relation between) individual works, towards the (media) historical requirements for the work's appearance and the uncovering of new relationships.[12] Below, we will see how remediations in both versions of *The War of the Worlds* provide the conditions for the portrayal of distance and silence. Thus, the concept of remediation and the perspective of media archaeology will provide adaptation analysis with a shift in focus from content to form, from narrative to settings, from interpretation to simultaneity.

1938. Staging radio

'I realized I could use practically nothing but the author's idea of a Martian invasion and his description of their appearance and their machines.'

These words are from Howard Koch, the radio play's original scriptwriter, who in his book *The Panic Broadcast* (1970) laconically comments on the relationship between the novel, set in turn-of-the-century Surrey, England, and the radio version in which the first cylinder lands in Grover's Mill, New Jersey in 1938.[13] Whether one should doubt Koch's claim and presume that Welles made substantial additions, or believe that the correspondences are simply coincidences, the dramatic effect in *both* works was possible through remediations of contemporary communication technologies: live broadcast and reporter presence, microphone sounds and interruptions (the *simultaneity* in Orson Welles' version) seem to correspond with the printer's ink and the paperboys, the heliographs, the cessation of telegrams and the breakdown of the train lines (the *slowness* in H. G. Wells' original). The relationship between simultaneity and slowness thus forms the outline of a 40-year media history.

At an early stage, Orson Welles' radio dramatization accentuates the role of mediation. With a device so typical of Welles, the director immediately creates uncertainty regarding the epistemological status of the radio broadcast. After Mercury Theatre of the Air's signature, the announcer introduces Welles: 'Ladies and gentlemen, the director of the Mercury Theatre and star of these broadcasts, Orson Welles.' Then, these words from the 'director and star' follows

> We know now that in the early years of the twentieth century this world was being watched closely by intelligences greater than man's and yet as mortal as his own. We know now that as human beings busied themselves about their various concerns they were scrutinized and studied, perhaps almost as narrowly as a man with a microscope might scrutinize the transient creatures that swarm and multiply in a drop of water.
> (WoW, 0.37–1.08; Koch, 33f.)[14]

Orson Welles' introduction is almost identical with the opening lines of the novel. Thus, in the first sentences of the radio play and the novel, the fate of the invading extraterrestrials' are (proleptically, as Genette would say) introduced: It is precisely those small creeping things in a drop of water – bacteria, viruses – that in the end will rescue humankind from the Martian's threatening domination. From this perspective, the bombastic title – *The War of the Worlds* – seems to be particularly ironic.

However, more important, the director's introduction to the radio play erases the boundary between media event and fiction. Welles, the announced – and authentic – director and star, is *simultaneously* an intradiegetic narrator (Orson Welles) and, eventually, an actor in the play. The narrator soon informs the audience of the present conditions of mediation:

> In the thirty-[ninth] year of the twentieth century came the great disillusionment.[15] It was near the end of October. Business was better. The war [scare] was over. More men were back at work. Sales were picking up. On this particular evening, October 30th, the Crossley service estimated that thirty-two million people were listening in on radios.
> (WoW, 1.52–2.19; Koch, 36, addition in brackets mine)

The 'thirty-two million' radio listeners are then carefully led into Welles' nightmare via a weather forecast from Nova Scotia to (the fictional) Hotel Park Plaza in New York, where Ramón Raquello's orchestra entertains a live audience as well as the radio listeners.

1898. Distance and communication: trains, telegraphs and newspapers

The opening lines of H. G. Wells' *The War of the Worlds* (1898) are classic, and one understands why Orson Welles chose to keep them almost completely intact. The only – and necessary – difference is the historical setting, which in the novel is 'the last years of the nineteenth century' (Wells, I:1).[16] At the conclusion of the same chapter, the theme that Orson Welles draws our attention to in 1938 is introduced: distance and communication. The anonymous narrator's friend, the astronomer Ogilvy, has observed that something has happened on Mars – what, is uncertain, perhaps an erupting volcano. The narrator thinks it strange that life continues tranquilly while at the same time, projectiles speedily approach our planet:

It seems to me now almost incredibly wonderful that, with that swift fate hanging over us, men could go about their petty concerns as they did. I remember how jubilant Markham was at securing a new photograph of the planet for the illustrated paper he edited in those days. People in these latter times scarcely realise the abundance and enterprise of our nineteenth-century papers.

(Wells, I:1)

In a time when most illustrations in newspapers and magazines were drawn, it is quite easy to understand journalist Markham's delight in the published photograph.[17] The narrator's thoughts regarding how laborious newspaper production once was carries a tone of forbearance; however, starting from Chapter 14 of the book, where Markham's brother's account from London begins, the same slow newspaper production is a central theme. Thus, both radio play and novel early on give an account of communication conditions in the respective works.

Wells' novel continues:

One night (the first missile then could scarcely have been 10,000,000 miles away), I went for a walk with my wife. It was starlight and I explained the Signs of the Zodiac to her, and pointed out Mars, a bright dot of light creeping zenithward, towards which so many telescopes were pointed. It was a warm night. Coming home, a party of excursionists from Chertsey or Isleworth passed us singing and playing music. There were lights in the upper windows of the houses as the people went to bed. From the railway station in the distance came the sound of shunting trains, ringing and rumbling, softened almost into melody by the distance. My wife pointed out to me the brightness of the red, green, and yellow signal lights hanging in a framework against the sky. It seemed so safe and tranquil.

(Wells, I:1)

Distance and communication: The first missile is approaching and is 'scarcely' 10 million miles from Earth's surface. The light from the stars contrasts with the lights in people's houses and the safe and tranquil lights from the railway's red, green, and yellow signal lights. The train lines, and their close association with the distribution of the telegraph network, will be of great importance in the latter London passages of the novel, and therefore, the almost lyrical observation regarding the signal lights becomes an ironic portent. For it is the *absence* of train service that eventually illustrates the novel's implicit thesis, a thesis accentuated with careful geographic information about roads and crossroads, commons and bridges, places quite likely only a few hundred meters, or perhaps a few kilometers apart, and which describe the protagonist's slow movement across the landscape: It is farther from Woking to London than from Mars to Earth.

The *slow* newspaper production of 1898, Woking, and England mirrors the *simultaneous* presence of different spaces and sounds in 1938: The Weather Bureau and Park Plaza, and the announcer who breaks in and reports on the peculiar light phenomenon before returning the listener to Ramón Raquello's orchestra (performing Star Dust!). Musical entertainment on the radio was common in the 1930s, and the orchestral feature thus expresses the radio play's realism. However, the use of music also directs attention to H. G. Wells' novel: In the above quotation (Wells I:1), the narrator hears songs and music from a group of people on their way home from an outing, and yes, even the sound from the train's rattling and jingling is described in melodious terms. That which for Orson Welles is a normal radio evening's pleasant trot between announcer, weather, and entertainment is for H. G. Wells a calm observation of the songs of people, the music of machines, and the tranquil light from traffic signals at Woking train station.[18]

1938 and 1898. Remediations

'The media archaeological ear', writes Wolfgang Ernst, 'listens to radio in an extreme way: listening to the noise of the transmitting system itself.'[19] To a great extent, Orson Welles' production remediates itself: The content of the radio play is simply – radio. In a short essay on Orson Welles' *The War of the Worlds*, Friedrich Kittler effectively describes this effect:

> Nobody listens to radio. What loudspeakers or headsets provide for their users is always just radio programming. Only in

emergencies, when broadcasts are interrupted, announcer voices are stifled, or stations drift away from their proper frequencies are there any moments at all for hearing what radio listening could be.[20]

One can moderate Kittler's description somewhat; it is hardly 'only in emergencies' that radio's hypermediating logic becomes obvious to listeners, but rather in most live broadcasts in general. However, Kittler's main point is that in Orson Welles' play, fiction's communicative collapse caused the public to listen to *radio* instead of to a radio program. Harry M. Geduld describes four formal devices that Welles uses to create this effect:

1   Marshalling the entire spectrum of news broadcasting styles of the 1930s. Among these were the voices of a forecaster giving a weather report, familiar-sounding announcers interrupting regular programming to issue statements and flash bulletins; [and] a mobile radio unit providing a field report [...].

2   Using program interruptions, fades, and various sound glitches supposedly caused by atmospheric or on-location conditions.

3   Making direct allusions to the microphone [...].

4   Indiscriminately referring to real and imaginary places, thereby deliberately blurring the distinction between fact and fiction.[21]

By using these devices to skillfully imitate hypermediacy (Bolter and Grusin), Welles managed to show the radio medium's presence as well as its *vulnerability*, in a manner that caused the play to be perceived as real; the fiction was mistaken for the medium. Hypermediacy created immediacy.[22]

One of the most suggestive elements in the radio play is certainly the dramatic set-up with news reporters who are making radio. Harry M. Geduld calls attention to the fact that this device shows great similarities with the dramatized episodes that made up the main feature of the popular news program 'The March of Time'. This show conveyed authentic news a few days after the fact, so that the events could be dramatized with victims and perpetrators as well as reporters and studio announcers, all portrayed by actors. Among those who staged these news events was – of course – Orson Welles, as well as several of those who would later be a part of his Mercury Theatre and *Citizen Kane* (whose introductory journal film not coincidentally is titled 'News on the March').

Therefore, the media discourse of the 1930s, even before Orson Welles' dramatization, exhibited particularly complex relationships between news, authenticity, and staging, a relationship that radio listeners frequently had to deal with. Both the radio play and the novel, despite all remediations, are primarily reminders of the *silence* created by the *absence* of communication, an absence that paradoxically makes the media present.

1938 and 1898. The dying of reporters

Absence – silence: The first news bulletins that interrupt Ramón Raquello's orchestra are not, strictly speaking, *mediating interruptions* or silence, but rather the opposite – proof that radio communications are working very much as they should. Instead, the first real interruption occurs in connection with the death of reporter Carl Phillips at Grover's Mill. He falls victim to the heat-rays, and the manuscript notes: ('*Crash of microphone ... then dead silence*'). The announcer concludes that 'there's some difficulty with our field transmission' (the whole sequence: WoW, 18.08–18.41; Koch, 51–52).

The H. G. Wells novel contains a direct and accordingly much slower counterpart to this tragic incident: In this case the unfortunate person is the journalist Henderson, whom after the cylinder lands, travels to Woking train station to send a telegraph to the news agency in London (Wells I:2). The news reaches the agency, but the newspaper sees it as a joke and sends a telegram in return to have the news confirmed. At this point, Henderson is already dead and the first, unconfirmed telegram passes unnoticed (Wells I:5, I:8). Again, the difference between radio and telegraph/newspaper is apparent: Phillips dies during a live broadcast, but the information lost by Henderson's death is not revealed in London until several days later. From the point of view of media history, it is indeed not *possible* for a big city in 1938 – New York – to have an information lag in the same manner as London in 1898.

The most dramatic break in the radio dramatization – and most alluring from a media aspect – is the combined sequence that ends Section 1, including the fighter planes frantically attacking the Martian tripods, and – three years before Pearl Harbor – ends in a kamikaze attack. The pilot's last sentence, accompanied by the sounds of a racing engine, is abruptly interrupted: 'We're diving on the first one. Now the engine's gone!' ... Deathly silence descends over the air. Five long seconds pass (an eternity on the air) before other communication takes over, a number of radio operators come on and then disappear, all contact is implacably broken down. Operator Four desperately asks, 'What's the matter? Where are you?' and the announcer returns:

ANNOUNCER
I'm speaking from the roof of the Broadcasting Building, New York City. The bells you hear are ringing to warn the people to evacuate the city as the Martians approach. [– – –] This may be the last broadcast. [– – –] This is the end now. Smoke comes out ... black smoke, drifting over the city. People in the streets see it now. They're running towards the East River ... thousands of them, dropping in like rats. Now the smoke's spreading faster. It's reached Times Square. People trying to run away from it, but it's no use. They're falling like flies. Now the smoke's crossing Sixth Avenue ... Fifth Avenue ... one hundred yards away ... it's fifty feet ...
(The whole sequence: WoW, 34.16–39.50; Koch, 64–67)

As the announcer dies during what he is convinced is 'the very last broadcast', his dropped microphone continues to send the sounds of sirens, boat horns, all in all a soundscape of evacuation, the noise of war. In the next cut, the command headquarters (Operator Four) tries in vain to contact the military forces. After a last troubled call – 'Isn't there anyone on the air? ... Isn't there anyone?' – another spooky silence follows, the silence of the air. The line is broken.[23]

1898. The streets of London (today's papers telling yesterday's news)

Reading *The War of the Worlds* through the *ears*, so to speak, of Orson Welles, makes absence present in Wells' novel as well. This is especially tangible in the longer sequence from London in which the narrator is not only *not* present (the narrator gives an account of his brother's testimony), but the description includes a striking absence of *information* as a result of several interruptions in the communications.

The evening papers' early edition report the news of the cylinder in Woking with rather large headlines, but the reports are still few and far between. Troop movements around the commons where the cylinder impacted and a few fires in some pine woods are reported. The same evening, an extra edition of *St. James Gazette* reports the interruption of telegraphic communication (Wells I:14), thought to have been caused by burning trees falling on the lines. Therefore, the brother finds no cause for alarm regarding the narrator's situation in Woking; however, he thinks he might like to see such creatures before they die (according to the reports, gravitational forces will prevent the Martians from moving from the pit in which they have fallen). Thus, he sends a telegram to the narrator that afternoon – a telegram that never arrives, of course.

Later the same night, at Waterloo Station, the brother discovers that no trains will be leaving for Woking. It is no coincidence that the telegraph and the trains stop working at the same time in Wells' novel: 'By 1848 about half of the country's railway tracks had telegraph wires running alongside them', as Tom Standage notes in *The Victorian Internet* (1998).[24] The narrator comments:

> I have read, in another account of these events, that on Sunday morning all London was electrified by the news from Woking. As a matter of fact, there was nothing to justify that very extravagant phrase. Plenty of Londoners did not hear of the Martians until the panic of Monday morning. Those who did took some time to realise all that the hastily worded telegrams in the Sunday papers conveyed. The majority of people in London do not read Sunday papers.
>
> (Wells, I:14)

Certainly most ironic here is that all of London would have been 'electrified' by the news from Woking while at the same time the line to Woking had in fact been affected by a power failure – the telegraph line is dead. The concluding laconic observation summarizes the narrator's skepticism: Most Londoners do not read the Sunday papers – another broken line of information.

In *Discourse Networks 1800/1900* (*Aufschreibesysteme 1800/1900*) Friedrich Kittler describes the discursive practices and logics characterizing the respective centuries and what imprints of these one can observe in written and printed texts. With an exposition that could have been about the loss of communication in *The War of the Worlds*, Kittler describes the media's increasing abstraction of human speech and language through mechanization of the daily press as well as electronic media such as the telegraph and movies:

> The Discourse Network of 1900 could not build on the three functions of production, distribution, and consumption. Discursive practises are so historically variable that even elementary and apparently universal concepts are lacking in certain systems [...]. In 1900, no authority of production determines the inarticulate beginning of articulation. An inhuman noise is the Other of all signs and written works.[25]

The new media in 1900 brought with them a 'noise' that had not been encountered previously: The renouncement of speech and language for new storage and distribution media such as the telegraph, phonograph, and film created a presence of something that was previously not there or not registered. (Technological and occult media are indeed very similar). This inhuman noise that is the 'Other' of all signs and written works takes on an almost parodic clarity in Wells' novel. Accordingly, one can replace 1900 with *The War of the Worlds* in the above quotation. When the production of signs – the telegraph, the heliograph, the newspaper – and the written word become silent, the tripods take on the role of the 'Other' in relation to the presence and absence of signs and written works. For each inaccuracy presented in *The War of the Worlds*, the 'inhuman noise' becomes increasingly apparent. In the novel's diegesis, the circumstances for maintaining a model of communication based on production, distribution, and consumption are missing, since every link in the chain of communications breaks down in different ways. The authorities in Wells' novel comprise the government and the media, and both completely lose control over country, law and order, as well as the production of power and meaning.

When the novel shifts focus from the narrator in the countryside to the report of his brother's experiences in London, communications become incorrect, incomplete, or interrupted. In this manner, the distance between Woking and London is amplified: When the telegraph lines are broken, the temporal distance becomes equivalent to the geographical distance, and since no one from Woking has yet reached London, the reports are unreliable. Therefore, the first really ominous (and more correct) news logically reaches London with the first stream of refugees from Surrey:

> It was the dawn of the great panic. London, which had gone to bed on Sunday night oblivious and inert, was awakened, in the small hours of Monday morning, to a vivid sense of danger.
>
> (Wells, I:14)

By reading literature through radio, we can observe how Orson Welles, somehow, prefigures this:

> The monster is now in control of the middle section of New Jersey and has effectively cut the state through its center. Communication lines are down from Pennsylvania to the Atlantic Ocean. Railroad tracks are torn and service from New York to Philadelphia discontinued except routing some of the trains through Allentown and Phoenixville. Highways to the north, south, and west are clogged with frantic human traffic. Police and army reserves are unable to control the mad flight. By morning the fugitives will have swelled Philadelphia, Camden, and Trenton, it is estimated, to twice their normal population.
>
> (WoW, 26.17–26:46; Koch 57–58)

In Orson Welles' depiction of communicative disruption, the stream of refugees becomes a mediated fact during the live broadcast, emphasizing the speed and simultaneity of radio in 1938 in contrast to the slowness and distance of newspapers in 1898. Thus, Mercury Theatre of the Air's adaptation, exactly by being so different from its source, actually produces a historical statement about its own time and its predecessor's as well.

2013. Media archaeology and adaptation studies

Robert Stam frequently uses Gérard Genette's terminology from *Palimpsestes: La Literature au Second Degré* (1982), in which Genette labels all relationships between different texts as transtextuality and then divided transtextuality into five subcategories.[26] According to Stam, the subcategories of hypotext and hypertext are particularly useful in an adaptation context (Genette describes the hypotext as a necessary continuation that hypertexts can vary, comment on, change, parody, and so on):[27]

> Filmic adaptations, in this sense, are hypertexts spun from pre-existing hypotexts which have been transformed by operations of selection, amplification, concretization, and actualization.[28]

Therefore, it would probably be impossible in this case for the radio play to make up a hypotext to the novel; nevertheless, this essay argues that in an adaptation analytical context, that is exactly what occurs in the relationship between *The War of the Worlds* 1938 and 1898. The reading of the novel is deeply dependent on the radio play's hypermediated immediacy. As a media archaeological object, the novel would not stand out in the same way if the radio play had not preceded the reading. Moreover, by reading in reverse – literature through radio – and applying a media archaeological perspective, adaptation analysis achieves a more complex level of the fidelity discourse.

The uses of remediation and media archaeology in this study of adaptation shed light on two aspects of particular interest: 1) the description of media's influence on the shaping of distance, time, and silence in both works, and 2) how the works are presented historically as perfect statements for their respective surrounding media networks. Obviously, the media described in *The War of the Worlds* 1898 and 1938 have a crucial significance for the forming of geographical and temporal distance and for the silence that occurs when communications stop functioning. Of course, a media archaeological approach, or using the year as a method for selection, could be and has been tested on individual works. (Several of Orson Welles' productions invite such scrutiny, with *Citizen Kane* as the most flamboyant example). However, what interests us here is the privileged relationship of adaptation: Which factors must be fulfilled in order to conduct a media archaeological study of adaptation? In this text, a relationship is established between the respective works and the periods in which they were produced, using the media historical markers found in staging (novel, radio) as well as content (newspaper and telegraph, and radio). No doubt similar relationships between the two works can be traced whether reading in reverse or not. However, how would one proceed if the adaptation were of a historical novel, for example? Everything is certainly dependent on how the novel stages its story and how a movie (or other medium) in turn chooses to stage the novel. Even if the technological conditions of the times are rarely introduced as explicitly as in Orson Welles' radio play and (as it turns out) in H. G. Wells' novel, one can surmise that in one way or another, every aesthetic object mirrors the media situation of its times. And vice versa, if one discovers media-specific elements in an adaptation of a work – for example, the use of *special effects* or metalevels in a film – these may open up new perspectives in the original.[29]

Another productive approach is to apply a media-semiotic perspective on the different works and on the media they address. Media-semiotics, in Lars Elleström's version, for example, pinpoints the different modalities every medium puts in play, and in the case of Wells/Welles, observations definitely convey such a fine-gauged apparatus.[30] Applying a media historical perspective to the semiotic toolbox calls for further exploration, not least in adaptation studies: What modalities are emphasized, and critically received, in different media in different historical moments?

Even if the works analysed here certainly address media history, and even if every adaptation in some sense brings to the fore the media's role, an archaeological examination does not need to focus on media aspects only. Nevertheless, one important conclusion must be that using the year as an analytical method can contribute to (in Linda Hutcheon's words) *oscillating* readings, but this oscillation takes place not only between the works as such, but also between the works and their historical environments. Thus, the method becomes a way to bring some order in the plethora of intertextual references at the same time that the adapted works become historically situated.[31] The aim must be to describe *something more* than adaptation alone.

2013. How I stopped worrying and learned to embrace fidelity

A futile battle is fought by the soldiers in Woking and in Grover's Mill, in London and in New York. Different productions depict this struggle by remediating different technologies, through producing different distances and different relationships between time and space. These media historical time-space-relationships (what Bakhtin might call the *chronotopes*) establish a difference between the works.[32] The mere 50 kilometers between Woking and London is still desperately far for all but the Martian's tripods. The distance between Grover's Mill and New York is more than double that between Woking and London, and yet it seems significantly shorter as the listener is not only cast between the different arenas, but also is an attending witness to what is happening, something that in no way stems the tripods' rampaging. The destruction is just as complete in Wells as in Welles. All the queen's horses, trains, and soldiers are not enough. All the president's men, airplanes, and bombs are not enough. Newspapers, telegraphs, and heliographs make no difference. The radio makes no difference. Only the very tiniest of all creatures on our planet – virus and bacteria – can withstand the attack from space and defeat the Martians and their Red Weed.

The communication media do not achieve any kind of decisive change in the fictional worlds of these two works. On the other hand, Orson Welles and Howard Koch's adaptation stages a distance of 40 years in media history with knife-sharp precision. In such a reading, the works do not act as significant objects but as *nodes* that connect to a series of occurrences in their historical periods. These nodes adapt themselves to our times as well: Since media is portrayed as being vulnerable, both works stage the fragility of the communication systems as a *paranoia* more persistent and more pervasive in its consequences than the more obvious paranoia concerning an alien invasion. Thus, Wells and Welles indicate that there may be more severe threats to our contemporary society than aliens (of any kind).

Finally, this essay demonstrates that it makes perfect sense to discuss Orson Welles and Howard Koch in terms of how they truthfully and with utter correctness adapted the source novel's staging of media. To make their own version as contemporary as the novel was in its time, another true translation, they simply *had* to make a radio broadcast.

In the end, alas, it's all about fidelity.

Notes

1   Jørgen Bruhn also follows this line of thought when in another part of the present book, he writes that 'both texts [are] secondary to each other.' Robert Stam and Thomas Leitch, who both draw from the works of Gérard Genette and Mikhail Bakhtin, emphasize that all works are already a part of a number of intertextual networks and in one way or another can be considered as adaptations. See, Bruhn's chapter in the present volume, Robert Stam and Alessandra Raengo (eds), *Literature and Film: A Guide to the Theory and Practice of Film Adaptation*, (eds) (Malden: Blackwell, 2004), especially p. 165, and Thomas Leitch, *Film Adaptation and Its Discontents* (Baltimore: The Johns Hopkins University Press, 2001), especially Chapter 5, 'Between Adaptation and Allusion', 93–126.

2   Quotes from radio broadcasts are noted as time (minutes and seconds, for example, WoW 11.20–11.51) together with the page number from the version published in scriptwriter Howard Koch's book *The Panic Broadcast: Portrait of an Event, With an Introductory Interview With Arthur Clarke and the Complete Text of the Radio Play "Invasion From Mars"* (New York: Avon Books, 1971, 1970), 31–80. This manuscript does not exactly follow the radio version, but the omissions and differences are very small and not of crucial importance for the argument here. Therefore, I have generally not corrected Koch's manuscript. See note 15 below.

3   Bruhn in this volume, and Thomas Leitch, 'Twelve Fallacies in Contemporary Adaptation Theory', in *Criticism* 45:2 (2003), 150–3 and entirety.

4 McLuhan's proclamation quoted from *Understanding Media: The Extensions of Man* (New York: McGraw-Hill, 1964), 8.

5 See especially Christine Geraghty, 'Foregrounding the Media: *Atonement* (2007) as an Adaptation', in *Adaptation* 2009:2: 91–109. The article can be seen as a reply to Linda Hutcheon's assumption that an adaptation acts as such only if the audience is familiar enough with the original that the film experience can be said to 'oscillate' between the original and the adaptation. See Linda Hutcheon, *A Theory of Adaptation* (Abingdon/Oxon: Routledge, 2006), 120–1. Also see Geraghty, *Now a Major Motion Picture: Film Adaptations of Literature and Drama* (Lanham: Rowman & Littlefield Publishers, 2008).

6 Jay David Bolter and Richard Grusin, *Remediation: Understanding New Media* (Cambridge, MA: MIT Press, 1999).

7 Friedrich A. Kittler, *Discourse Networks 1800/1900*, Michael Metteer and Chris Cullens, trans. (Stanford: Stanford University Press, 1991).

8 As mentioned, media archaeology is associated with Michel Foucault, in particular his *L'Archéologie du Savoir* (Paris: Gallimard, 1969); see also *The Archaeology of Knowledge*, A. M. Sheridan Smith, trans. (London and New York: Routledge, 2002). However, media archaeology also has its roots in Walter Benjamin's Arcades Project, among others. To the contemporary list of media archaeologists, we can name theoreticians such as Siegfried Zielinski, Friedrich Kittler, Hans Ulrich Gumbrecht, Wolfgang Ernst, and Erkki Huhtamo, all very different among themselves. For an introduction to the field of media archaeology, see the anthology *Media Archaeology: Approaches, Applications, and Implications*, Erkki Huhtamo and Jussi Parikka, (eds) (Berkeley: University of California Press, 2011), especially the editors' 'Introduction: An Archaeology of Media Archaeology', 1–21.

9 Huhtamo and Parikka, 3. See also, in the same volume, Wolfgang Ernst, 'Media Archaeography', 241: 'Both classical archaeologists and media archaeologists are fascinated by the hardware of culture, its artifacts – from ancient marbles up to electromechanical engineering products'.

10 On the notion of 'presence' and media archaeology, see especially Vivian Sobchack, 'Afterword: Media Archaeology and Re-presencing the Past', in Huhtamo/Parikka, *Media Archaeology*. In the same volume, Wolfgang Ernst ('Media Archaeography') and Erkki Huhtamo ('Dismantling the Fairy Engine: Media Archaeology as Topos Study') discuss aspects of 'presence.' See also Hans Ulrich

Gumbrecht, *In 1926: Living at the Edge of Time* (Cambridge, MA: Harvard University Press, 1997), and *Production of Presence: What Meaning Cannot Convey* (Stanford, CA: Stanford University Press, 2004).

11 This is, of course, what Gumbrecht does in *In 1926: Living at the Edge of Time*. See also Michael North, 'Virtual Histories: The Year as Literary Period', *Modern Language Quarterly* 62:4 (2001).

12 For example, Stam writes in *Literature through film: realism, magic, and the art of adaptation* (Malden: Blackwell 2005): 'What interests me, in this sense, is the historicity of forms themselves [...]', 18.

13 Koch, 13. There is relative consensus for the view that Koch laid the groundwork of the manuscript and that Welles put in the finishing touches; however, on various occasions Welles sought to take a larger part of the credit. See Simon Callow, *Orson Welles: The Road to Xanadu* (London: Vintage, 1995), 398, 490; Paul Heyer, *The Medium and the Magician: Orson Welles and the Radio Years, 1934–1952* (Oxford: Rowman & Littlefield Publishers Inc., 2005), 107–11; and Harry M. Geduld, 'Welles or Wells – A Matter of Adaptation', *Perspectives on Orson Welles,* (ed.) Morris Beja (New York: G. K. Hall & Co., 1995), 265–7.

14 This opening passage strikingly resembles the H. C. Andersen fairytale 'Vanddråben' (1848). See Jean Hersholt's translation, "The Drop of Water," http://www.andersen.sdu.dk/vaerk/hersholt/TheDropOfWater.html (accessed 3 January 2012). I am indebted to Jørgen Bruhn for this suggestion.

15 The Koch manuscript in *The Panic Broadcast* contains the incorrect reference, 'thirty-eighth, when it should have been the 'thirty-ninth,' a number that has caused some confusion, strangely enough. The thirty-ninth year of the nineteenth century is of course 1938.

16 I follow the praxis developed within Wells research (due to the large number of editions of *The War of the Worlds*, including digital formats), in which instead of providing exact page references, I refer to Book I and II using roman numerals, and chapter numbers using Arabic numerals.

17 W. Joseph Campbell shows how the year 1897 (Wells' novel is from 1898) can be seen in many ways as a pivotal year within (primarily American) journalism, and additionally, how the year marked a breakthrough for the reproduction of photographs using halftones in American newspapers. See W. Joseph Campbell, '1897: American Journalism's Exceptional Year', in *Journalism History* 29: 4 (2004),

here quoted from http://academic2.american.edu/~wjc/exceptyear1. htm#top (accessed 3 January 2012).

18   These pedantic similarities should be seen as a typical example of the analytical effects that arise when one reads 'literature through radio,' as well as an argument for continuing to credit the relationship between the works of adaptation with a privileged status, not because of what they explain, but for what they *generate*.

19   Wolfgang Ernst, op.cit., 250.

20   Friedrich Kittler, 'The Last Radio Broadcast', *Re-Inventing Radio: Aspects of Radio as Art*, Heidi Grundmann, *et al.*, (eds) (Frankfurt am Main: Revolver, 2008), 17–25.

21   Geduld, 269, See also Heyer, 86.

22   There are several reasons why the effect was so much stronger in the radio version, but the most significant is certainly that the radio medium (especially when compared with the novel) was still very young in 1938, and its full potential was just being realized. On the increasing uses of radio in the 1930s, see William C. Ackerman, 'The Dimensions of American Broadcasting', *The Public Opinion Quarterly* 9:1 (1945), 1–18; and 'U.S. Radio: Record of a Decade', *The Public Opinion Quarterly* 12:3 (1948), 440–54. On Herbert Morrison's famous report from the Hindenburg disaster and *The War of the Worlds*, see Callow, 400, and Heyer, 86. See also Koch, 155.

23   The play's first part ends here, after which an abrupt announcement from CBS reminds listeners that the broadcast is a radio play, which will resume after a short break. However, this commercial break (and announcement) was not triggered by the 'panic': Part 1 and 2 in the radio play are equivalent to the division between the novel's Book 1 and Book 2.

24   Tom Standage, *The Victorian Internet: The Remarkable Story of the Telegraph and the Nineteenth Century's Online Pioneers* (London: Phoenix Paperback, 2003, 1998), 60.

25   Kittler, *Discourse Networks*, 186,

26   Gérard Genette, *Palimpsestes: La Literature au Second Degré* (Paris: Seuil, 1982), 7–14, and entirety.

27   Genette's text was written in 1982, and therefore, 'hypertext' should not (at least not without consideration) be confused with today's prevalent usage of the term in which one alludes to nonlinear texts (often digital) that are realized via hyperlinks that connect the text with other texts.

28   Stam, 5.

29 Christine Geraghty's analyses (for example, in *Now a Major Motion Picture*) are an important contribution to the investigation of the adaptation as a remediation, not only of the original but also of other media (that may or may not come from the original).

30 Elleström suggests four modalities that he arguesare active in all media: material modality, sensorial modality, spatiotemporal modality, and semiotic modality. See Lars Elleström, 'The Modalities of Media: A Model for Understanding Intermedial Relations', *Media Borders, Multimodality and Intermediality*, Elleström, (ed.) (Basingstoke: Palgrave Macmillan, 2010).

31 For better or worse, adaptation analysis does the same to media archaeology: By taking two priviliged texts as points of departure, the often desired 'arbitraryness' of the archaeological survey is restrained. See North, 415.

32 Michail Bakhtin, 'Forms of Time and Chronotope in the Novel', in *The Dialogic Imagination: Four Essays*, Michael Holquist, (ed.) (Austin: University of Texas Press, 1981), 84–258.

INDEX